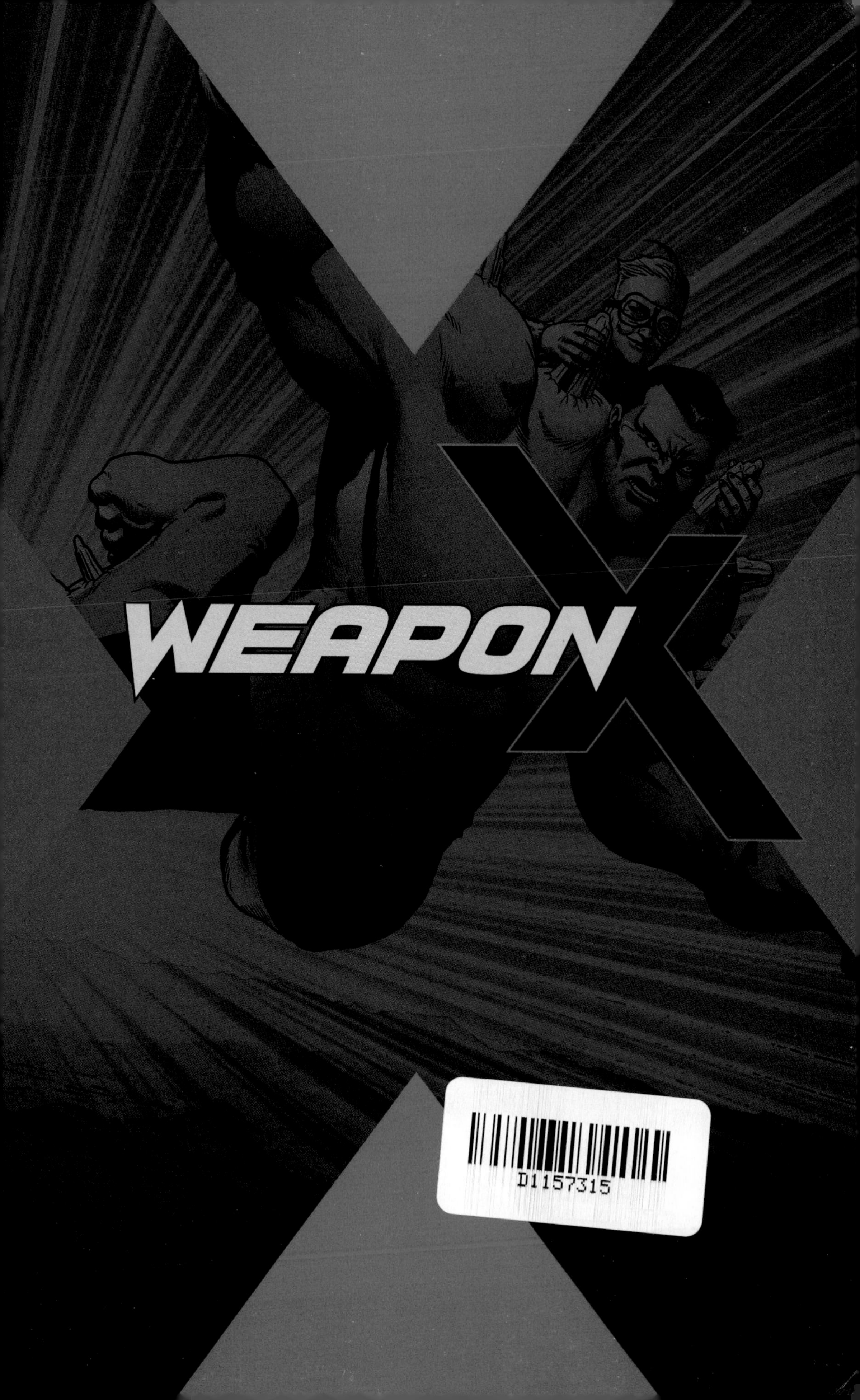
WEAPON X

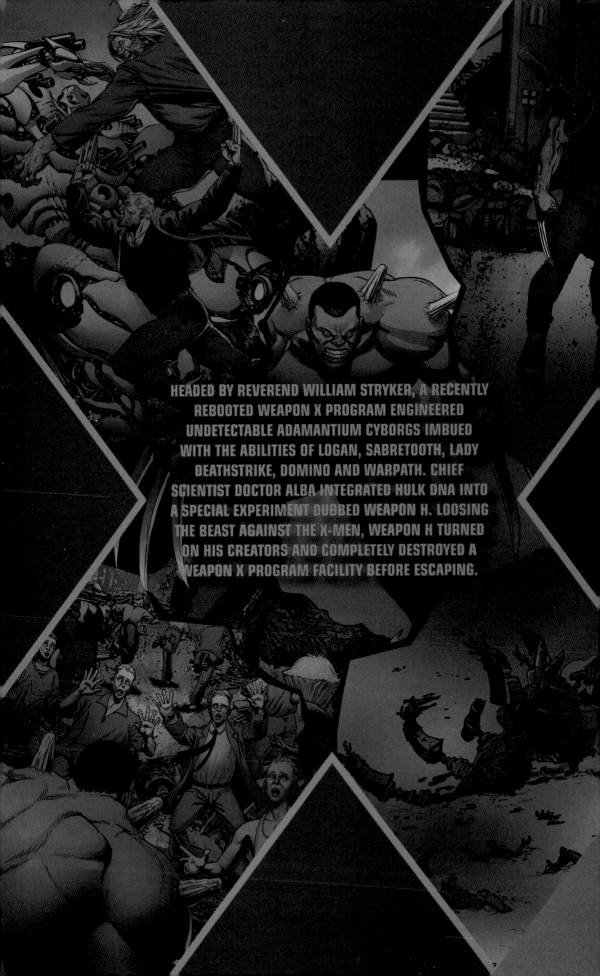

HEADED BY REVEREND WILLIAM STRYKER, A RECENTLY REBOOTED WEAPON X PROGRAM ENGINEERED UNDETECTABLE ADAMANTIUM CYBORGS IMBUED WITH THE ABILITIES OF LOGAN, SABRETOOTH, LADY DEATHSTRIKE, DOMINO AND WARPATH. CHIEF SCIENTIST DOCTOR ALBA INTEGRATED HULK DNA INTO A SPECIAL EXPERIMENT DUBBED WEAPON H. LOOSING THE BEAST AGAINST THE X-MEN, WEAPON H TURNED ON HIS CREATORS AND COMPLETELY DESTROYED A WEAPON X PROGRAM FACILITY BEFORE ESCAPING.

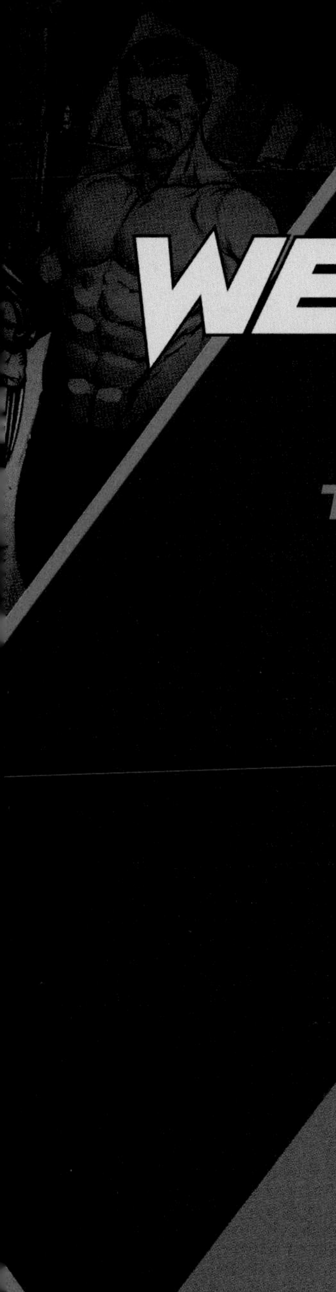

WEAPON X

THE HUNT FOR WEAPON H

Writers/**GREG PAK** &
FRED VAN LENTE

Artists/**MARC BORSTEL** &
IBRAIM ROBERSON

Colorist/**FRANK D'ARMATA**

Letterer/**VC's JOE CARAMAGNA**

Cover Art/**SKAN** (#7-9), **STONEHOUSE** (#10)
& **DAVID NAKAYAMA** (#11)

Assistant Editor/**CHRIS ROBINSON**
Editor/**DARREN SHAN**
X-Men Group Editor/**MARK PANICCIA**

Collection Editor/**JENNIFER GRÜNWALD** • Assistant Editor/**CAITLIN O'CONNELL**
Associate Managing Editor/**KATERI WOODY** • Editor, Special Projects/**MARK D. BEAZLEY**
VP Production & Special Projects/**JEFF YOUNGQUIST** • SVP Print, Sales & Marketing/**DAVID GABRIEL**
Book Designer/**JAY BOWEN**

Editor in Chief/**C.B. CEBULSKI** • Chief Creative Officer/**JOE QUESADA**
President/**DAN BUCKLEY** • Executive Producer/**ALAN FINE**

WEAPON X VOL. 2: THE HUNT FOR WEAPON H. Contains material originally published in magazine form as WEAPON X #7-11. First printing 2018. ISBN 978-1-302-90735-8. Published by MARVEL WORLDWIDE, INC., a subsidiary of MARVEL ENTERTAINMENT, LLC. OFFICE OF PUBLICATION: 135 West 50th Street, New York, NY 10020. Copyright © 2018 MARVEL No similarity between any of the names, characters, persons, and/or institutions in this magazine with those of any living or dead person or institution is intended, and any such similarity which may exist is purely coincidental. **Printed in the U.S.A.** DAN BUCKLEY, President, Marvel Entertainment; JOE QUESADA, Chief Creative Officer; TOM BREVOORT, SVP of Publishing; DAVID BOGART, SVP of Business Affairs & Operations, Publishing & Partnership; DAVID GABRIEL, SVP of Sales & Marketing, Publishing; JEFF YOUNGQUIST, VP of Production & Special Projects; DAN CARR, Executive Director of Publishing Technology; ALEX MORALES, Director of Publishing Operations; SUSAN CRESPI, Production Manager; STAN LEE, Chairman Emeritus. For information regarding advertising in Marvel Comics or on Marvel.com, please contact Vit DeBellis, Custom Solutions & Integrated Advertising Manager, at vdebellis@marvel.com. For Marvel subscription inquiries, please call 888-511-5480. **Manufactured between 12/29/2017 and 1/30/2018 by LSC COMMUNICATIONS INC., KENDALLVILLE, IN, USA.**

10 9 8 7 6 5 4 3 2 1

7

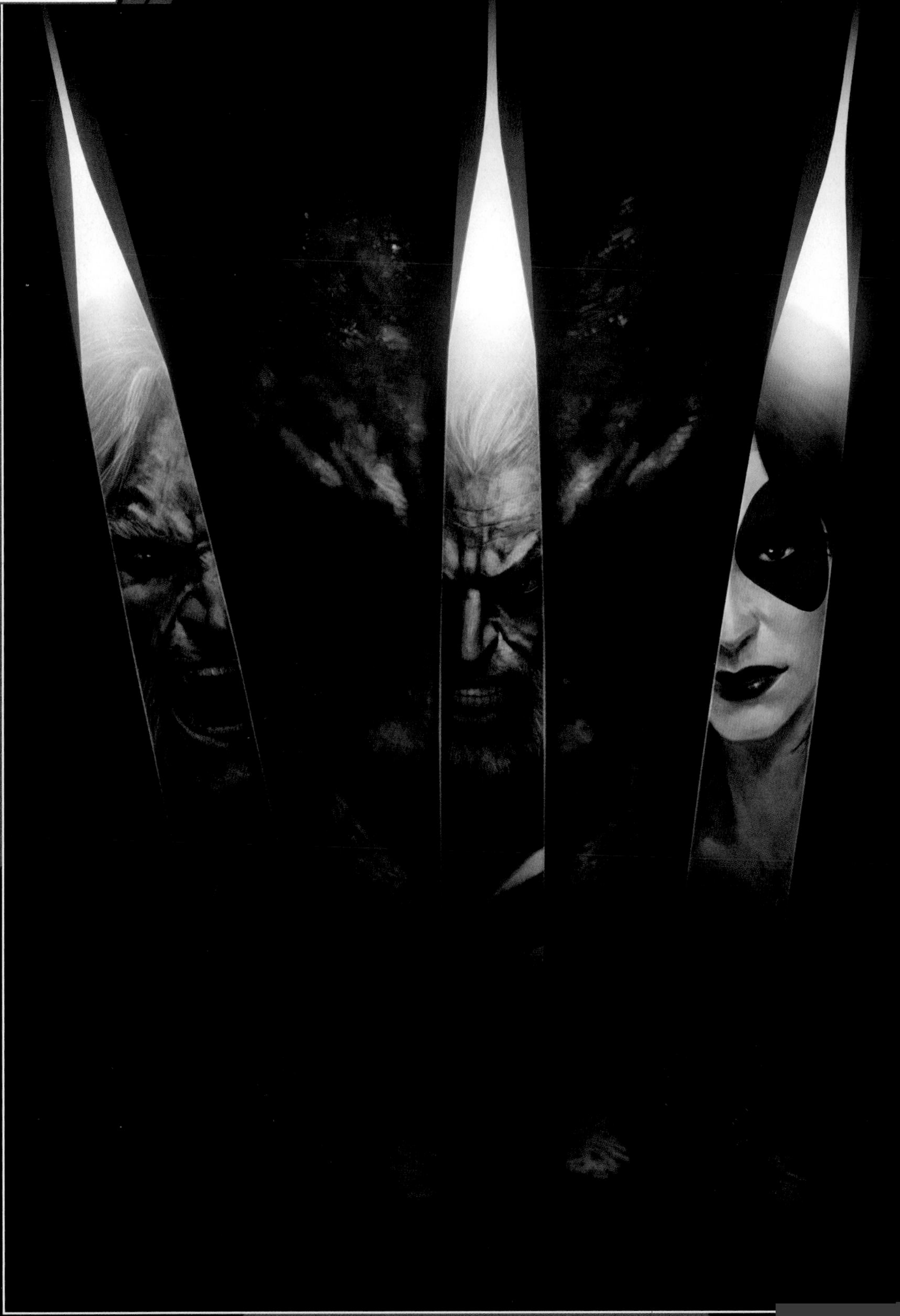

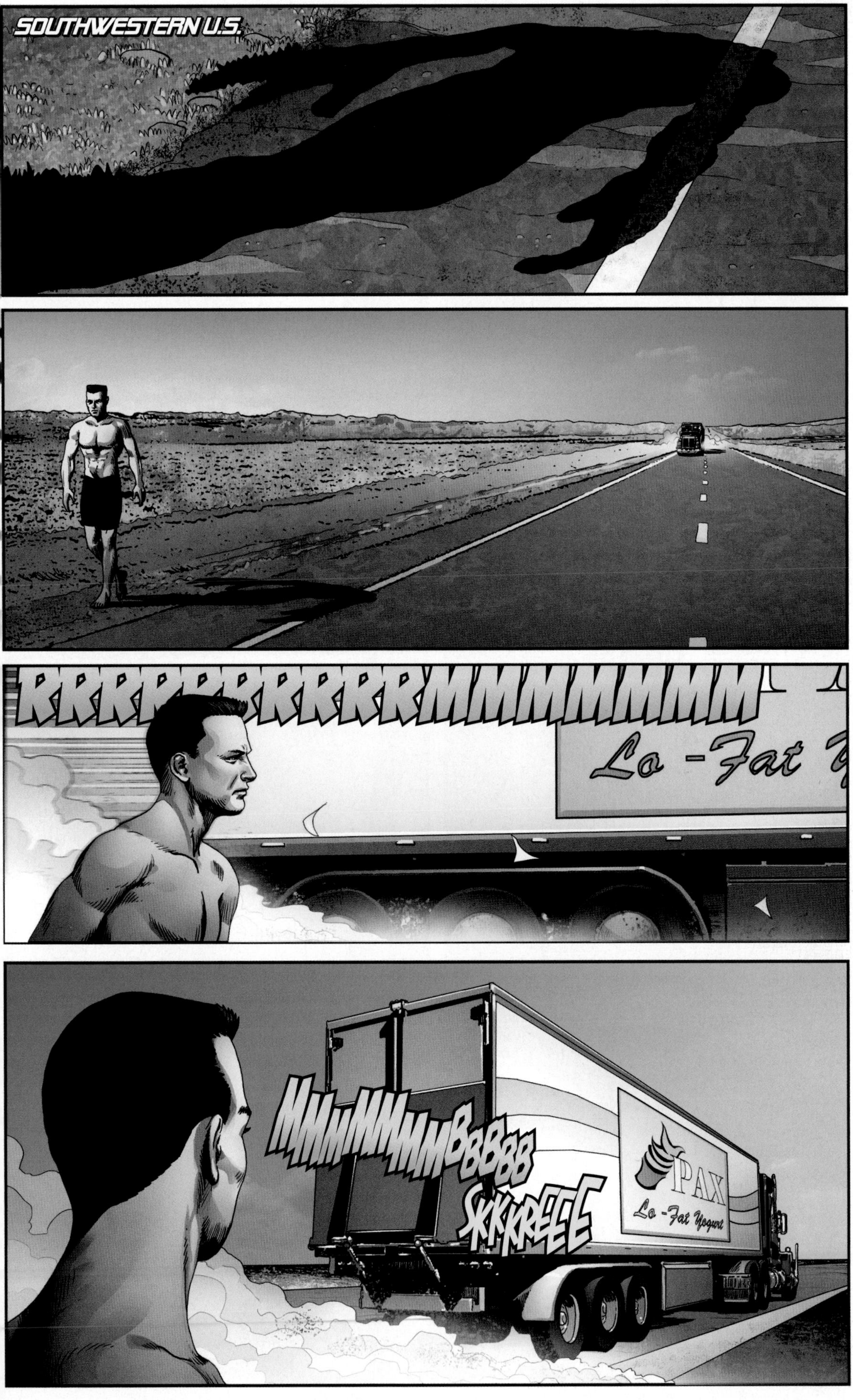
SOUTHWESTERN U.S.
RRRRRRRRRRRRMMMMMMMMMM
Lo -Fat
MMMMMMMMMBBBB
SKKKREEEE
PAX
Lo -Fat Yogurt

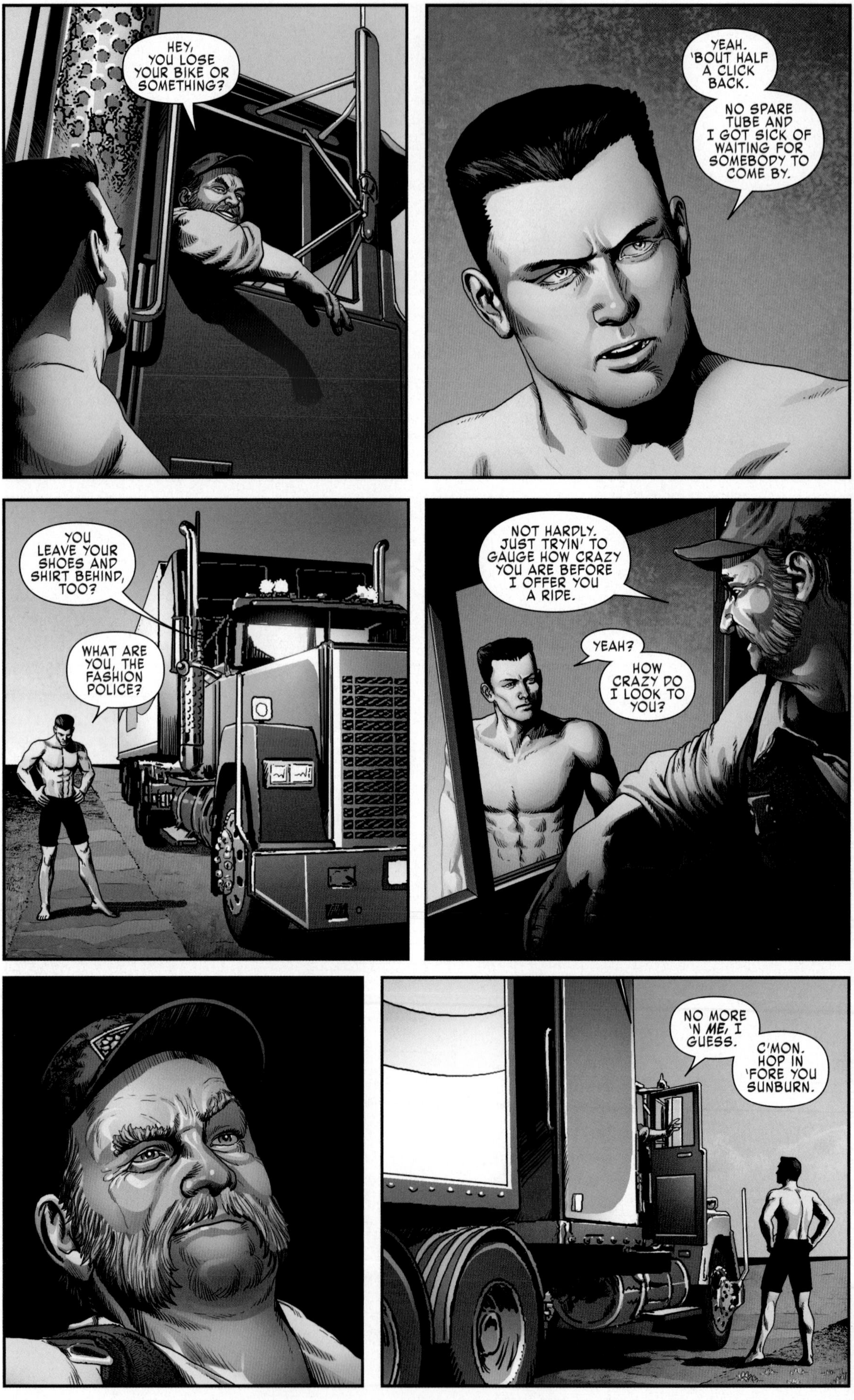
HEY, YOU LOSE YOUR BIKE OR SOMETHING?
YEAH. 'BOUT HALF A CLICK BACK.
NO SPARE TUBE AND I GOT SICK OF WAITING FOR SOMEBODY TO COME BY.
YOU LEAVE YOUR SHOES AND SHIRT BEHIND, TOO?
WHAT ARE YOU, THE FASHION POLICE?
NOT HARDLY. JUST TRYIN' TO GAUGE HOW CRAZY YOU ARE BEFORE I OFFER YOU A RIDE.
YEAH?
HOW CRAZY DO I LOOK TO YOU?
NO MORE 'N ME, I GUESS.
C'MON. HOP IN 'FORE YOU SUNBURN.

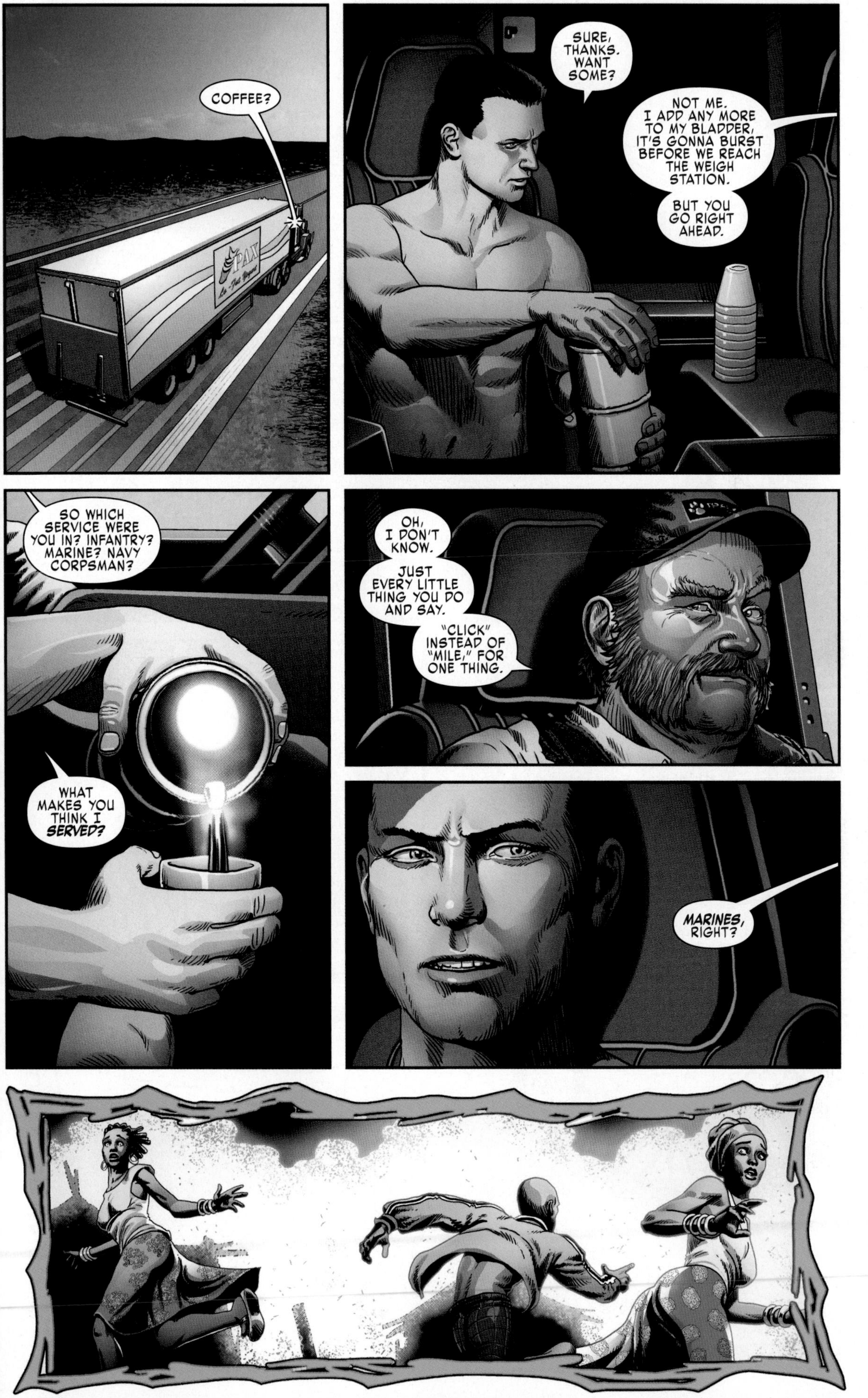
COFFEE?
SURE, THANKS. WANT SOME?
NOT ME. I ADD ANY MORE TO MY BLADDER, IT'S GONNA BURST BEFORE WE REACH THE WEIGH STATION.
BUT YOU GO RIGHT AHEAD.
SO WHICH SERVICE WERE YOU IN? INFANTRY? MARINE? NAVY CORPSMAN?
WHAT MAKES YOU THINK I *SERVED?*
OH, I DON'T KNOW.
JUST EVERY LITTLE THING YOU DO AND SAY.
"CLICK" INSTEAD OF "MILE," FOR ONE THING.
MARINES, RIGHT?

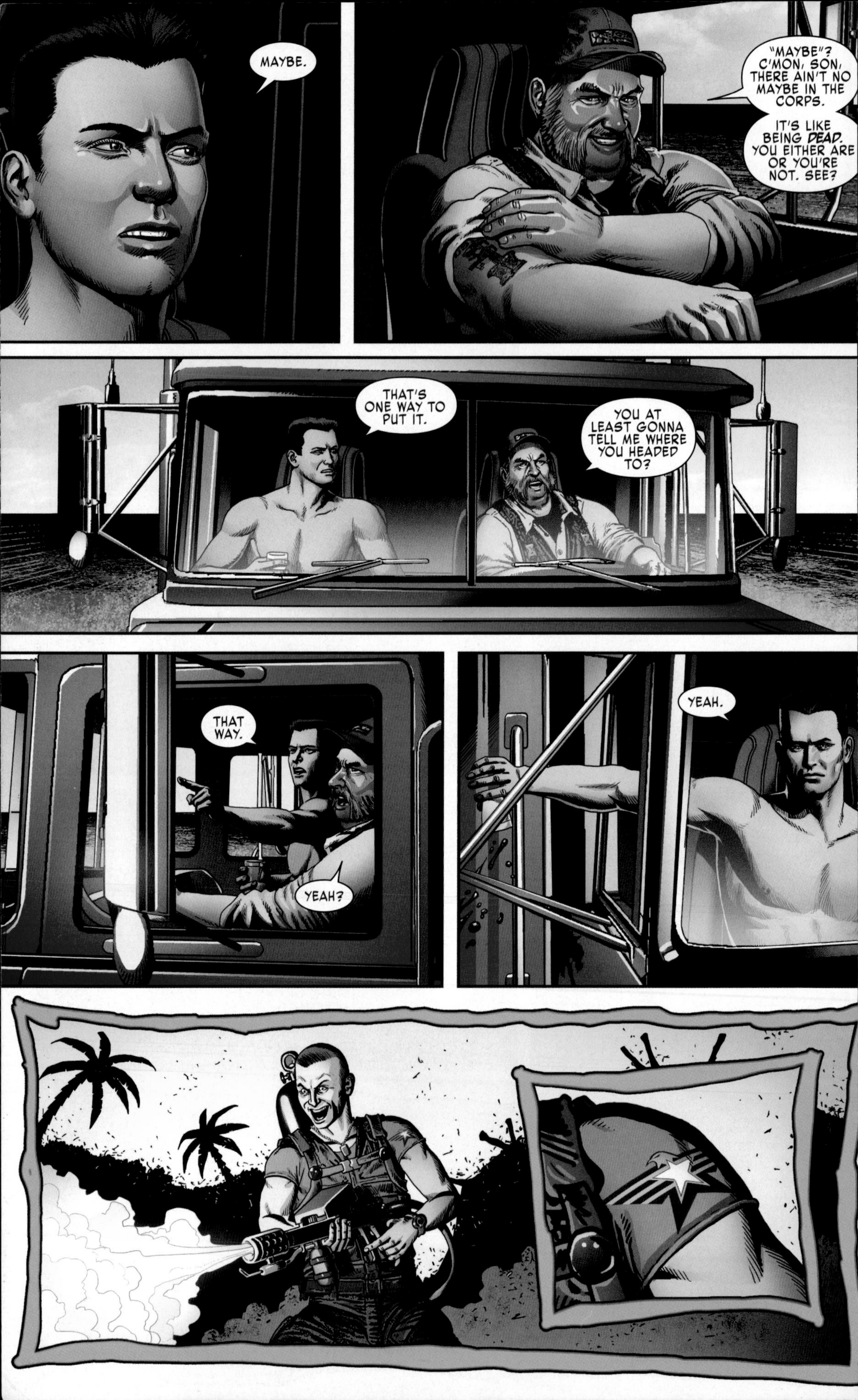
MAYBE.
"MAYBE"? C'MON, SON, THERE AIN'T NO MAYBE IN THE CORPS.
IT'S LIKE BEING DEAD. YOU EITHER ARE OR YOU'RE NOT. SEE?
THAT'S ONE WAY TO PUT IT.
YOU AT LEAST GONNA TELL ME WHERE YOU HEADED TO?
THAT WAY.
YEAH?
YEAH.

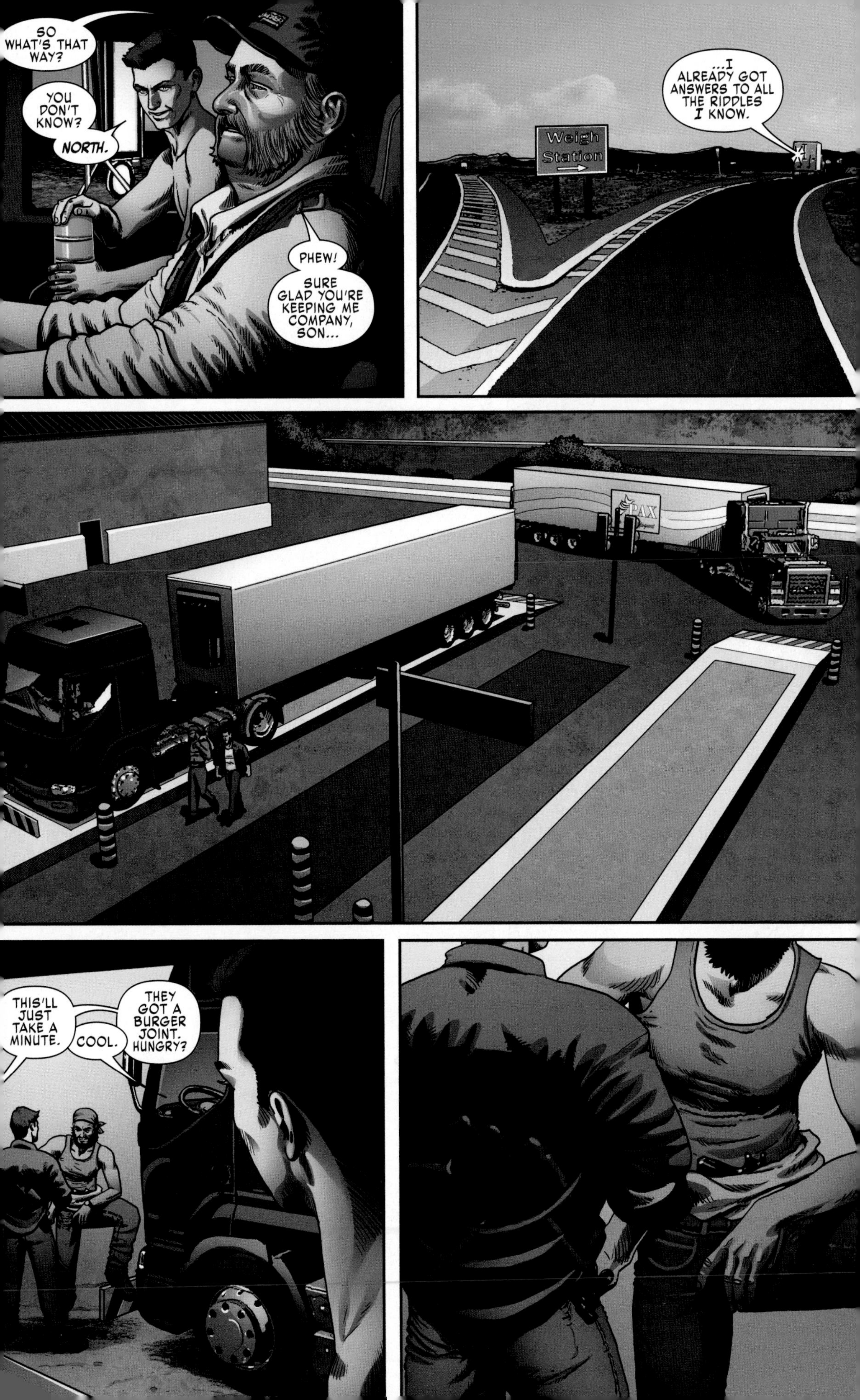
SO WHAT'S THAT WAY?
YOU DON'T KNOW? NORTH.
PHEW! SURE GLAD YOU'RE KEEPING ME COMPANY, SON...
...I ALREADY GOT ANSWERS TO ALL THE RIDDLES I KNOW.
Weigh Station
PAX
THIS'LL JUST TAKE A MINUTE.
THEY GOT A BURGER JOINT. HUNGRY?
COOL.

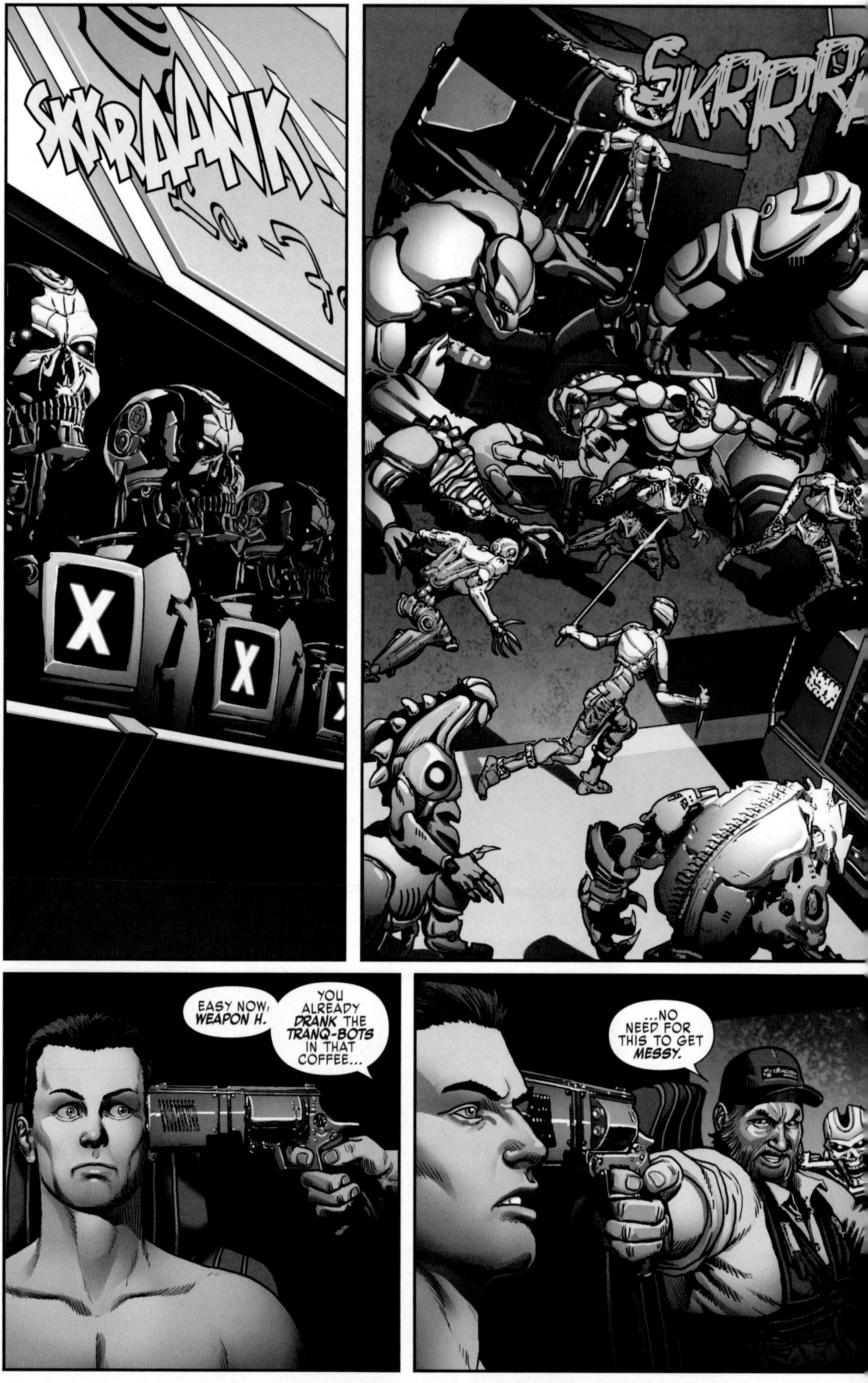
SKKRAANK
SKRRRR
EASY NOW, WEAPON H.
YOU ALREADY DRANK THE TRANQ-BOTS IN THAT COFFEE...
...NO NEED FOR THIS TO GET MESSY.

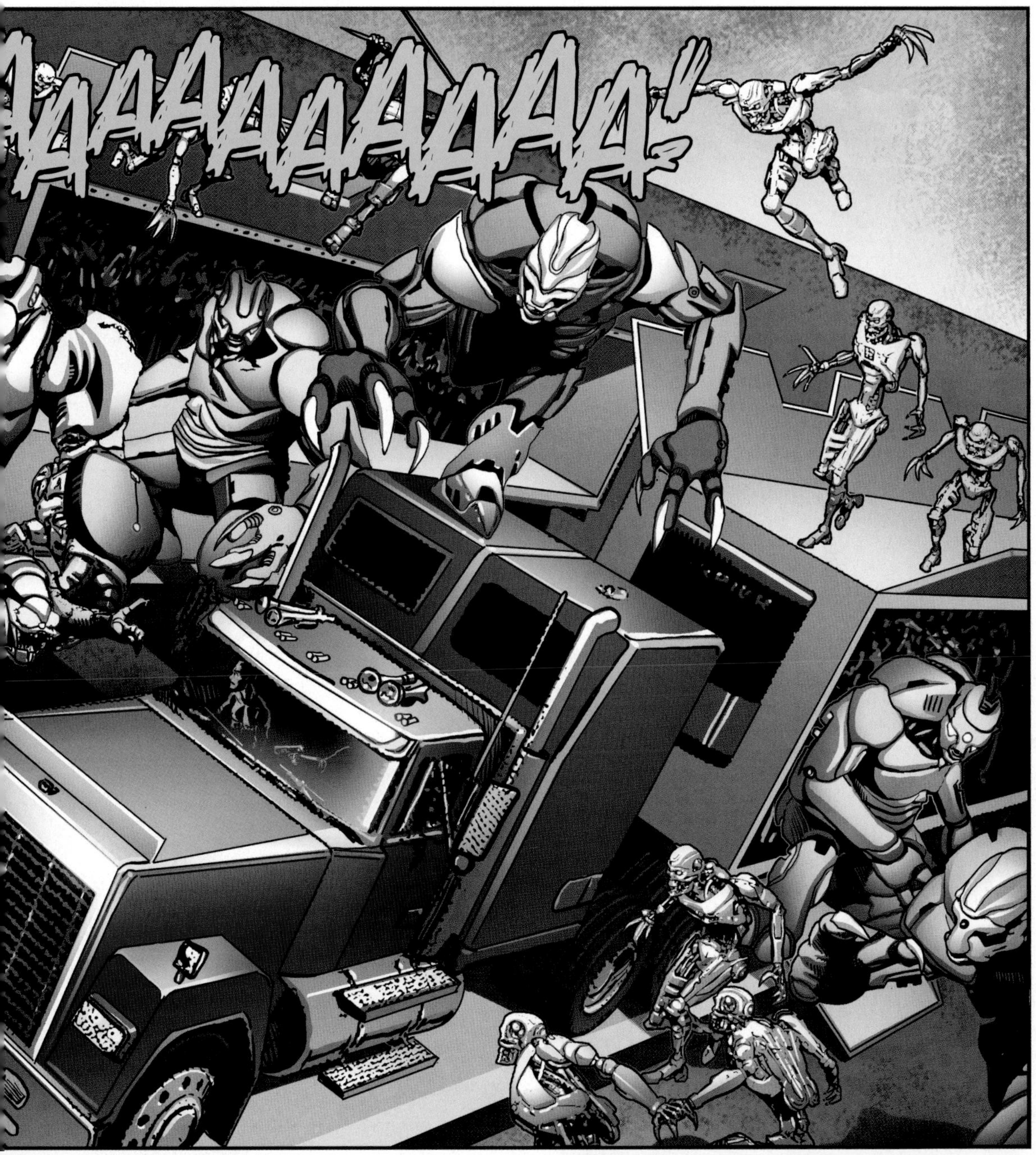
AAAAAAAAAAA!

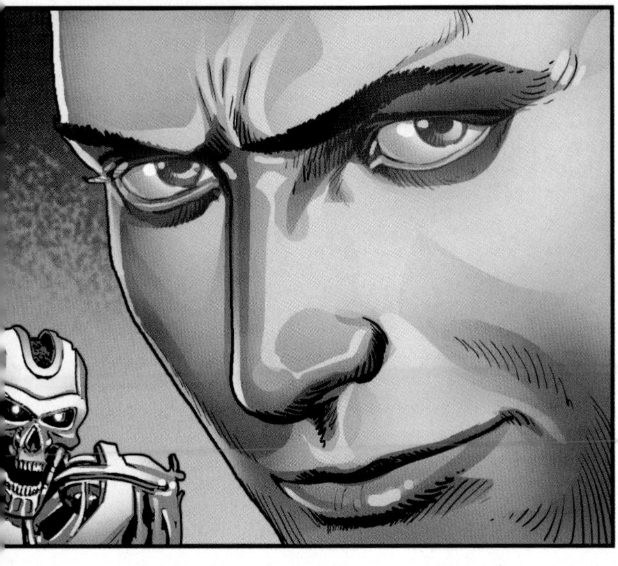

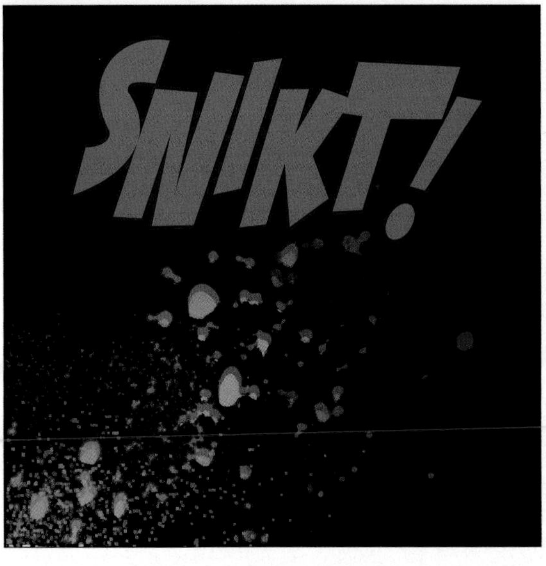
SNIKT!

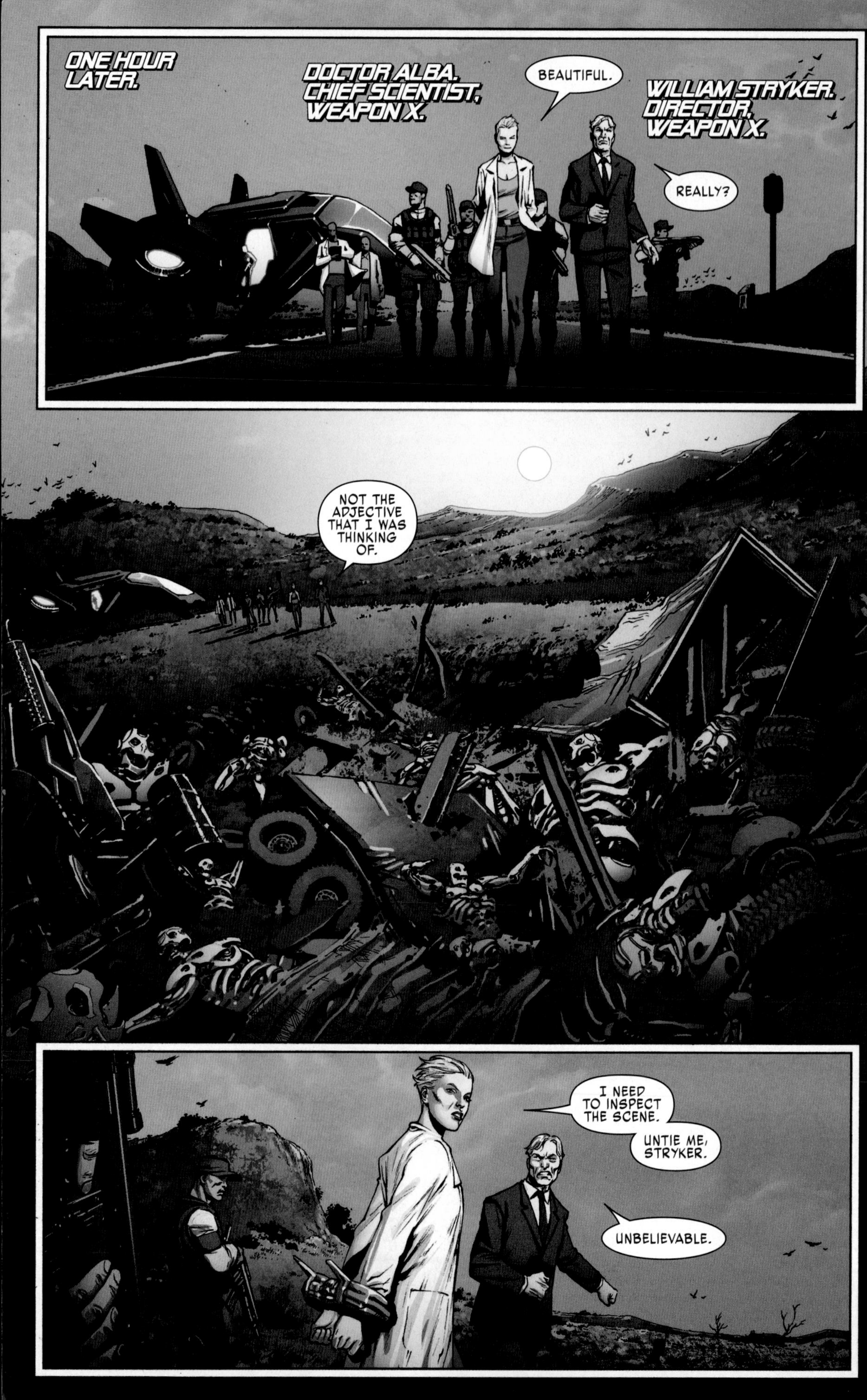
ONE HOUR LATER.
DOCTOR ALBA. CHIEF SCIENTIST, WEAPON X.
BEAUTIFUL.
WILLIAM STRYKER. DIRECTOR, WEAPON X.
REALLY?
NOT THE ADJECTIVE THAT I WAS THINKING OF.
I NEED TO INSPECT THE SCENE.
UNTIE ME, STRYKER.
UNBELIEVABLE.

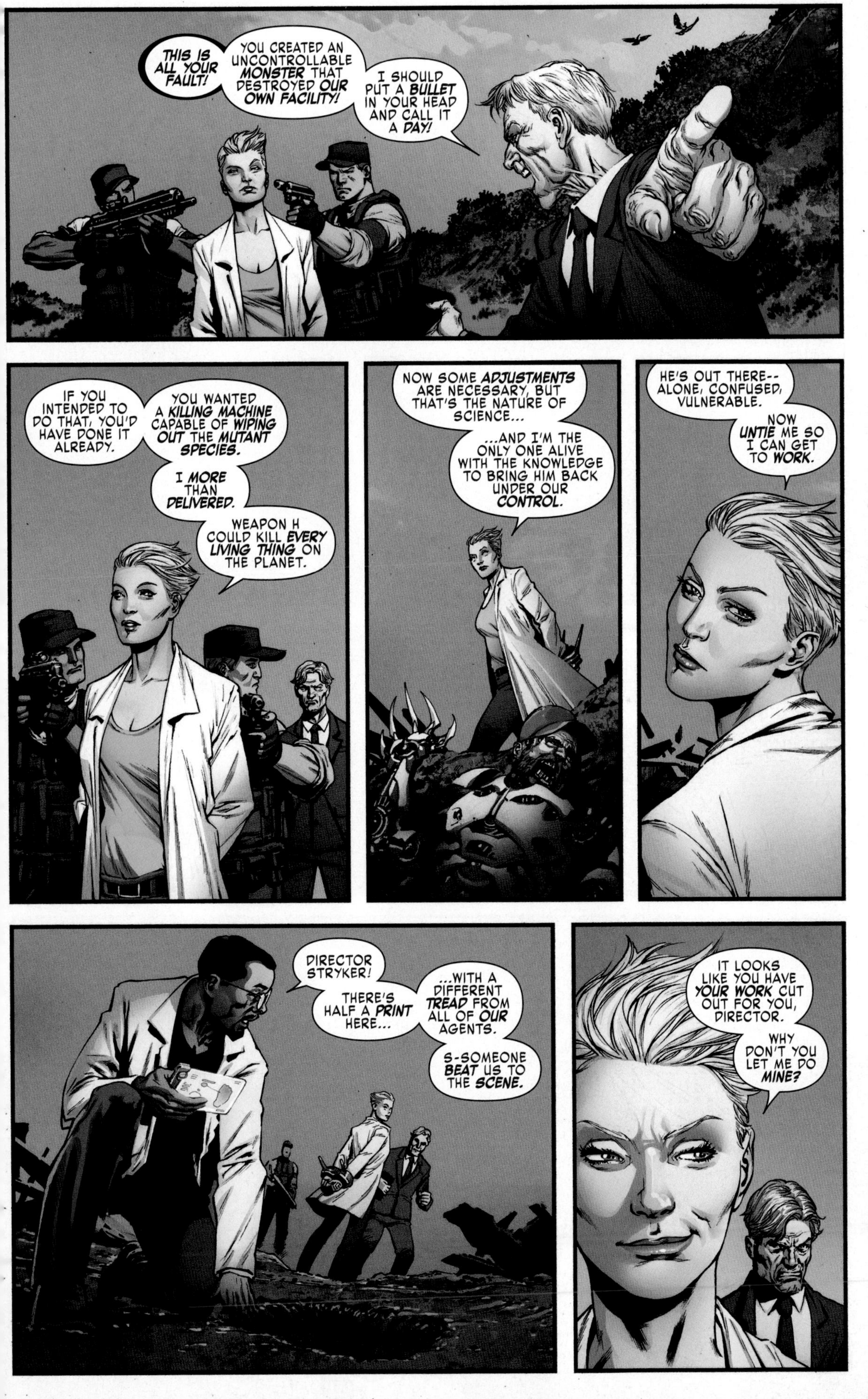
THIS IS ALL YOUR FAULT!
YOU CREATED AN UNCONTROLLABLE MONSTER THAT DESTROYED OUR OWN FACILITY!
I SHOULD PUT A BULLET IN YOUR HEAD AND CALL IT A DAY!
IF YOU INTENDED TO DO THAT, YOU'D HAVE DONE IT ALREADY.
YOU WANTED A KILLING MACHINE CAPABLE OF WIPING OUT THE MUTANT SPECIES.
I MORE THAN DELIVERED.
WEAPON H COULD KILL EVERY LIVING THING ON THE PLANET.
NOW SOME ADJUSTMENTS ARE NECESSARY, BUT THAT'S THE NATURE OF SCIENCE...
...AND I'M THE ONLY ONE ALIVE WITH THE KNOWLEDGE TO BRING HIM BACK UNDER OUR CONTROL.
HE'S OUT THERE-- ALONE, CONFUSED, VULNERABLE.
NOW UNTIE ME SO I CAN GET TO WORK.
DIRECTOR STRYKER!
THERE'S HALF A PRINT HERE...
...WITH A DIFFERENT TREAD FROM ALL OF OUR AGENTS.
S-SOMEONE BEAT US TO THE SCENE.
IT LOOKS LIKE YOU HAVE YOUR WORK CUT OUT FOR YOU, DIRECTOR.
WHY DON'T YOU LET ME DO MINE?

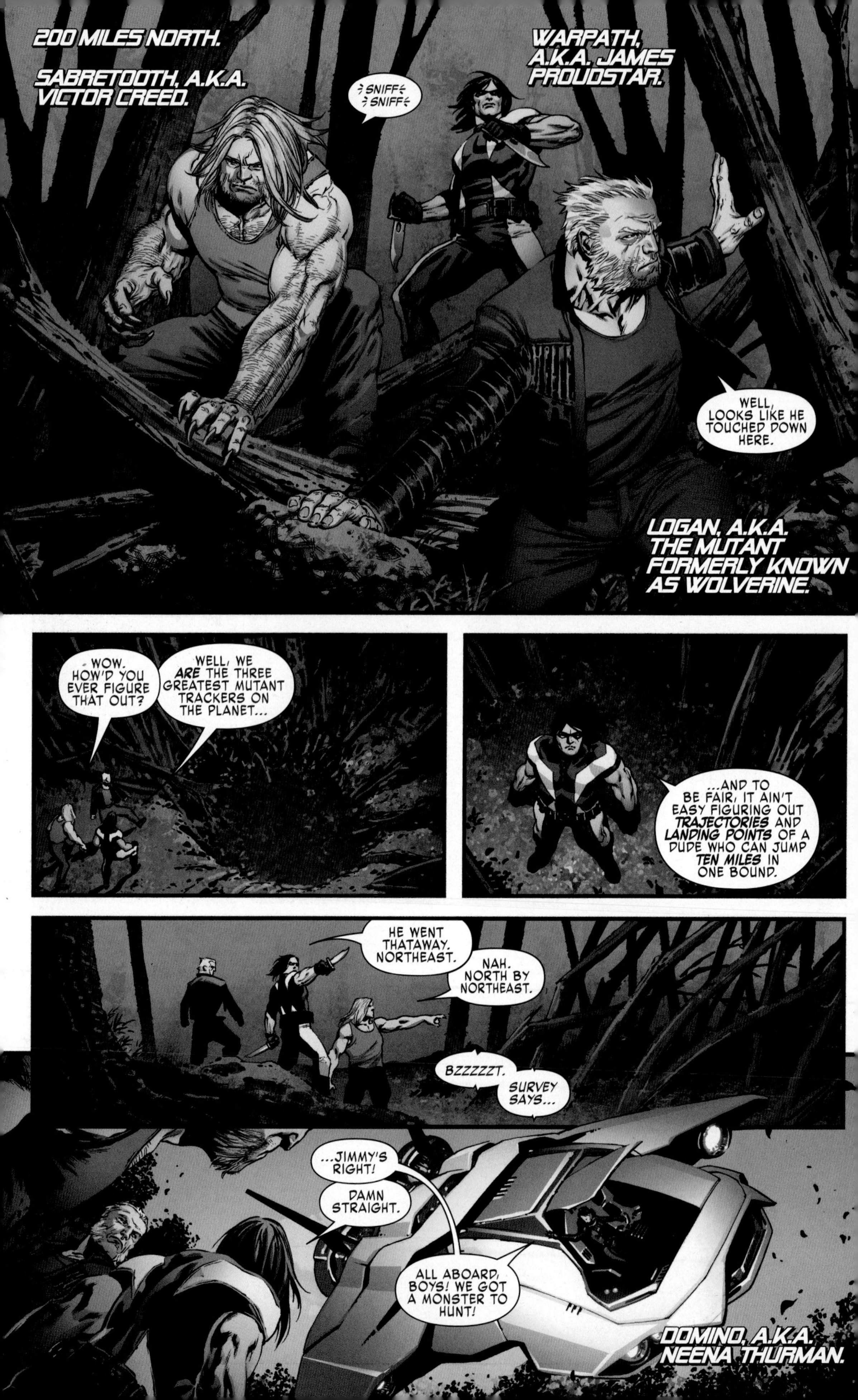
200 MILES NORTH.
SABRETOOTH, A.K.A. VICTOR CREED.
WARPATH, A.K.A. JAMES PROUDSTAR.
SNIFF SNIFF
WELL, LOOKS LIKE HE TOUCHED DOWN HERE.
LOGAN, A.K.A. THE MUTANT FORMERLY KNOWN AS WOLVERINE.
WOW. HOW'D YOU EVER FIGURE THAT OUT?
WELL, WE ARE THE THREE GREATEST MUTANT TRACKERS ON THE PLANET...
...AND TO BE FAIR, IT AIN'T EASY FIGURING OUT TRAJECTORIES AND LANDING POINTS OF A DUDE WHO CAN JUMP TEN MILES IN ONE BOUND.
HE WENT THATAWAY. NORTHEAST.
NAH. NORTH BY NORTHEAST.
BZZZZZT.
SURVEY SAYS...
...JIMMY'S RIGHT!
DAMN STRAIGHT.
ALL ABOARD, BOYS! WE GOT A MONSTER TO HUNT!
DOMINO, A.K.A. NEENA THURMAN.

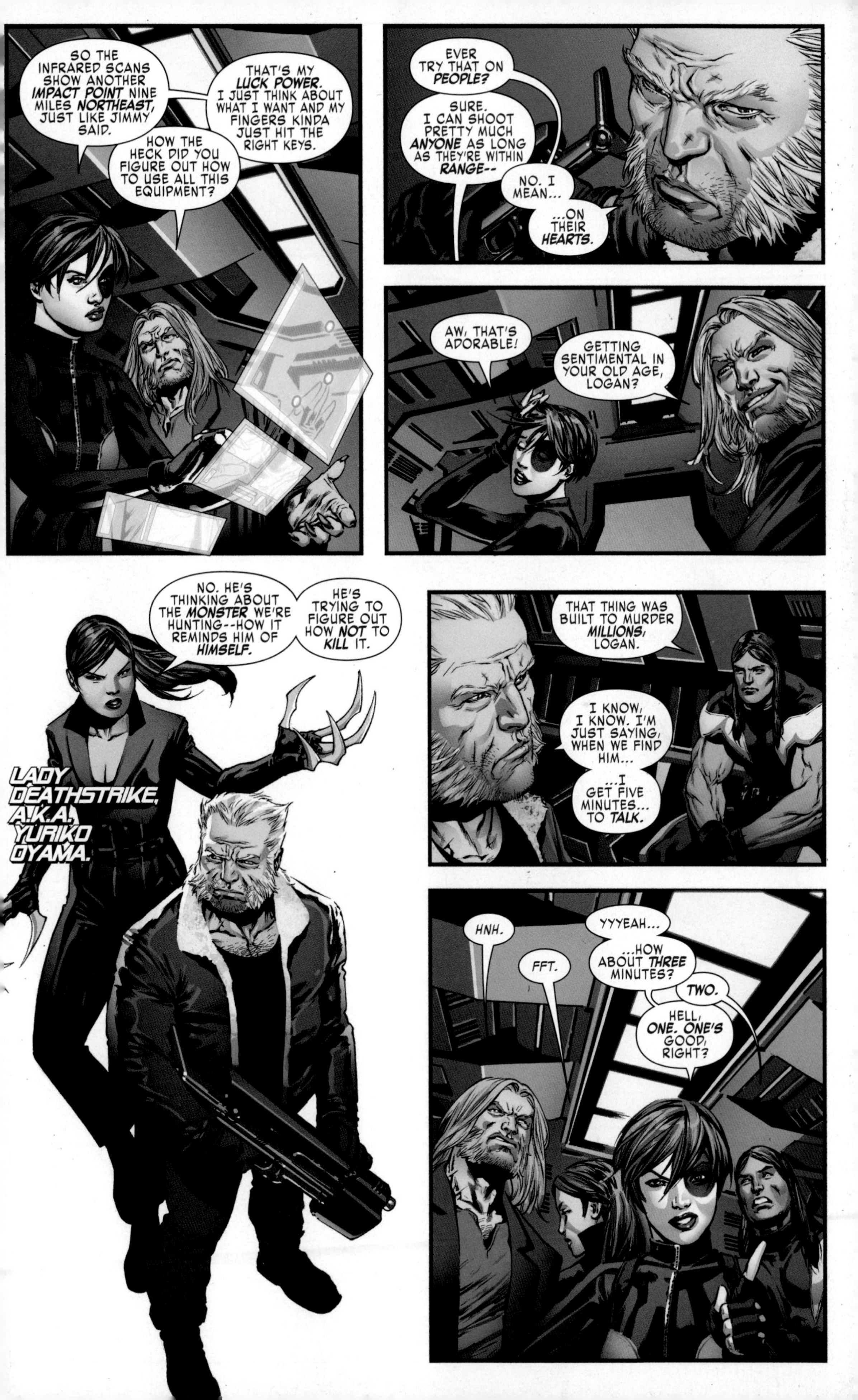
SO THE INFRARED SCANS SHOW ANOTHER IMPACT POINT NINE MILES NORTHEAST, JUST LIKE JIMMY SAID.
HOW THE HECK DID YOU FIGURE OUT HOW TO USE ALL THIS EQUIPMENT?
THAT'S MY LUCK POWER. I JUST THINK ABOUT WHAT I WANT AND MY FINGERS KINDA JUST HIT THE RIGHT KEYS.
EVER TRY THAT ON PEOPLE?
SURE. I CAN SHOOT PRETTY MUCH ANYONE AS LONG AS THEY'RE WITHIN RANGE--
NO. I MEAN...
...ON THEIR HEARTS.
AW, THAT'S ADORABLE!
GETTING SENTIMENTAL IN YOUR OLD AGE, LOGAN?
NO. HE'S THINKING ABOUT THE MONSTER WE'RE HUNTING--HOW IT REMINDS HIM OF HIMSELF.
HE'S TRYING TO FIGURE OUT HOW NOT TO KILL IT.
LADY DEATHSTRIKE, A.K.A. YURIKO OYAMA.
THAT THING WAS BUILT TO MURDER MILLIONS, LOGAN.
I KNOW, I KNOW. I'M JUST SAYING, WHEN WE FIND HIM...
...I GET FIVE MINUTES... TO TALK.
HNH.
FFT.
YYYEAH...
...HOW ABOUT THREE MINUTES?
TWO.
HELL, ONE. ONE'S GOOD, RIGHT?

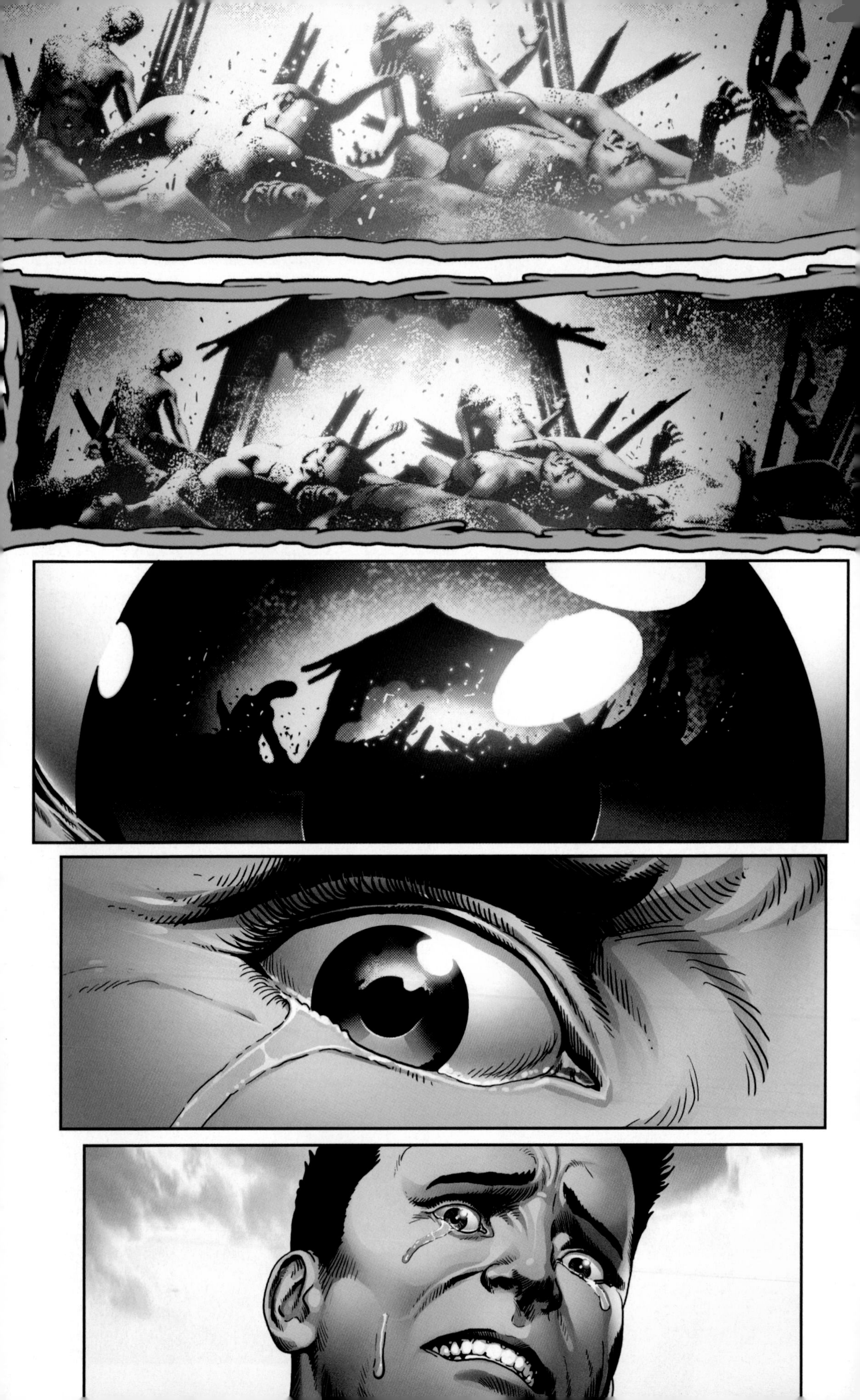

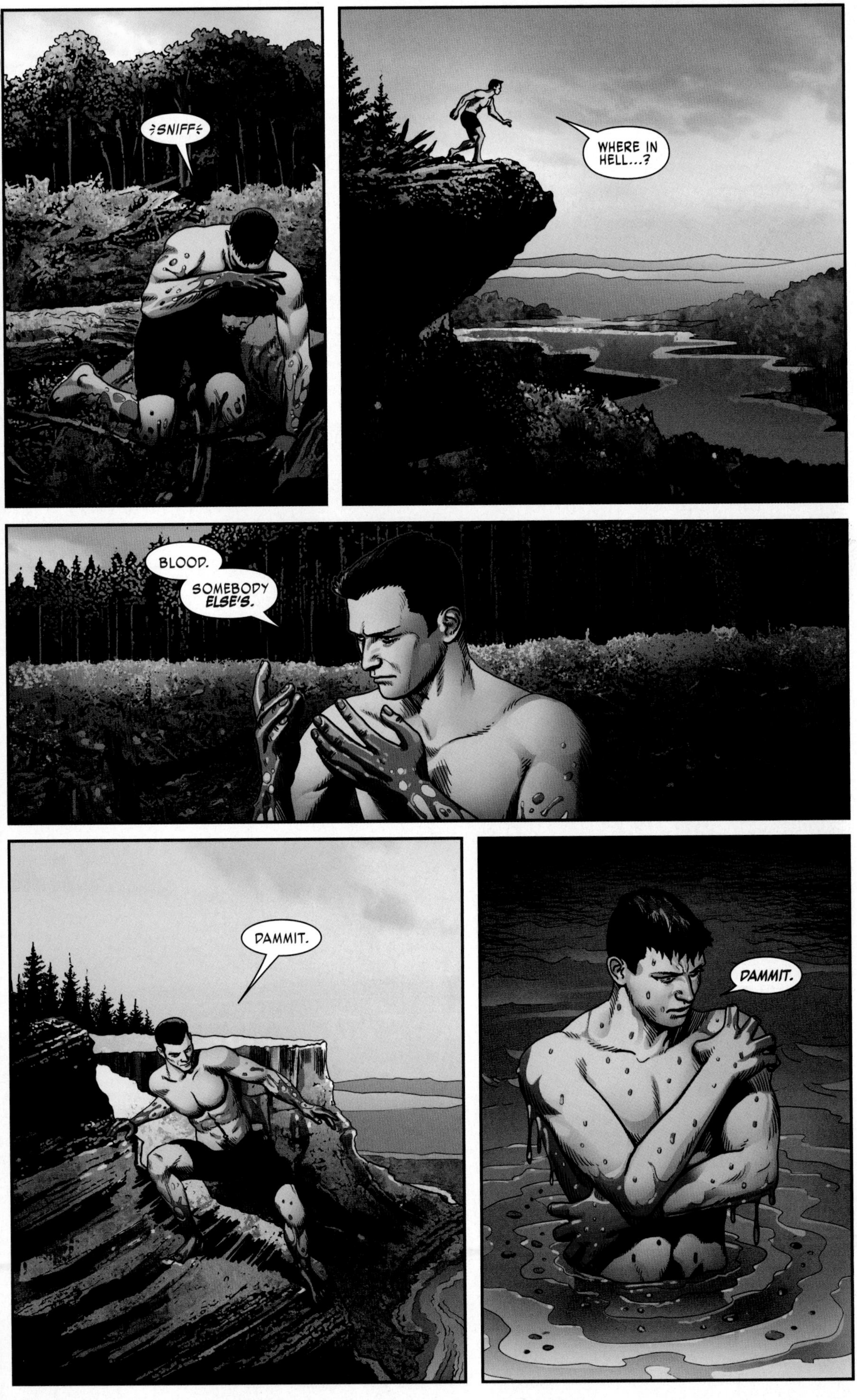
SNIFF
WHERE IN HELL...?
BLOOD.
SOMEBODY ELSE'S.
DAMMIT.
DAMMIT.

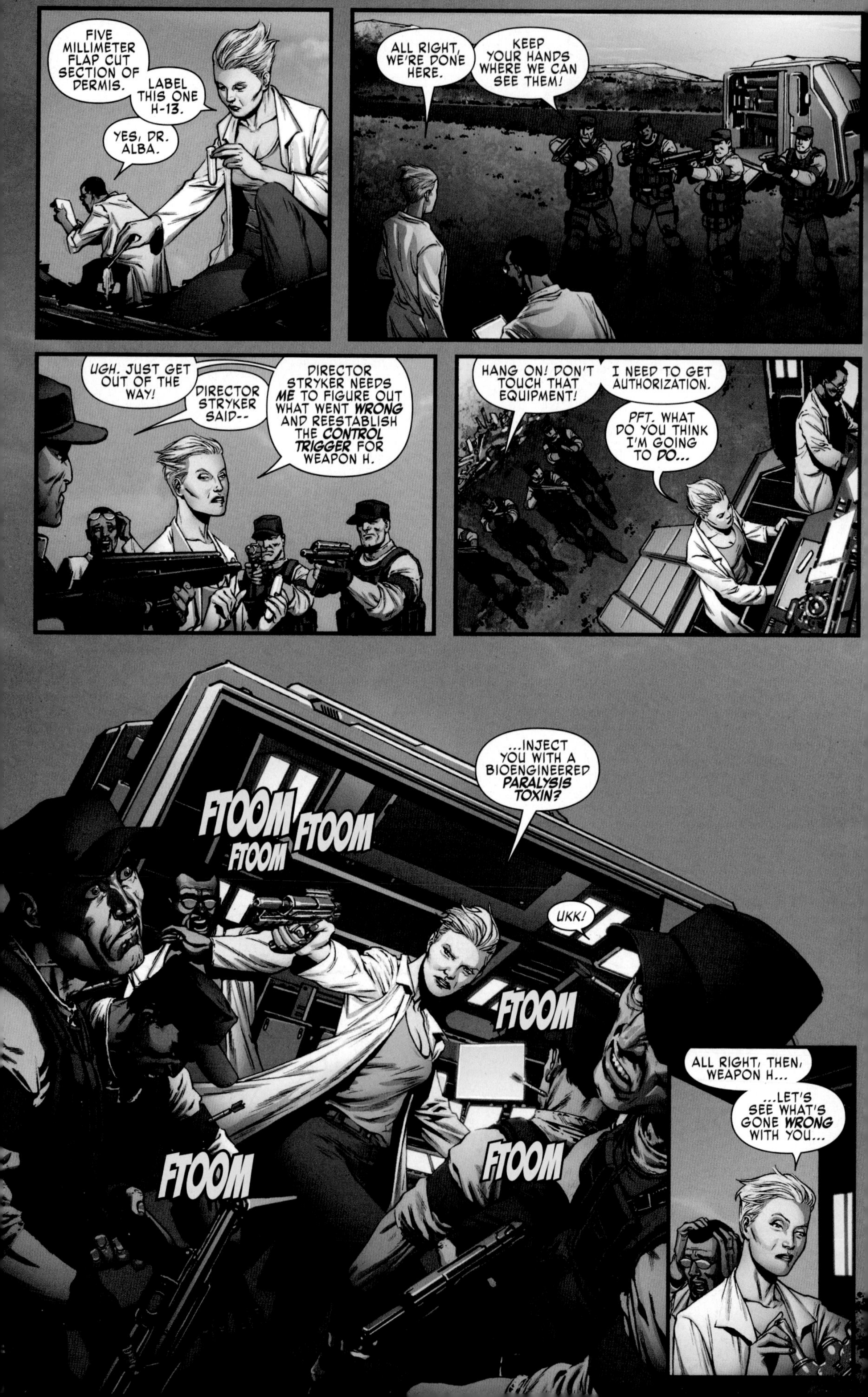
FIVE MILLIMETER FLAP CUT SECTION OF DERMIS.
LABEL THIS ONE H-13.
YES, DR. ALBA.
ALL RIGHT, WE'RE DONE HERE.
KEEP YOUR HANDS WHERE WE CAN SEE THEM!
UGH. JUST GET OUT OF THE WAY!
DIRECTOR STRYKER SAID--
DIRECTOR STRYKER NEEDS ME TO FIGURE OUT WHAT WENT WRONG AND REESTABLISH THE CONTROL TRIGGER FOR WEAPON H.
HANG ON! DON'T TOUCH THAT EQUIPMENT!
I NEED TO GET AUTHORIZATION.
PFT. WHAT DO YOU THINK I'M GOING TO DO...
...INJECT YOU WITH A BIOENGINEERED PARALYSIS TOXIN?
FTOOM
FTOOM
FTOOM
UKK!
FTOOM
FTOOM
FTOOM
ALL RIGHT, THEN, WEAPON H...
...LET'S SEE WHAT'S GONE WRONG WITH YOU...

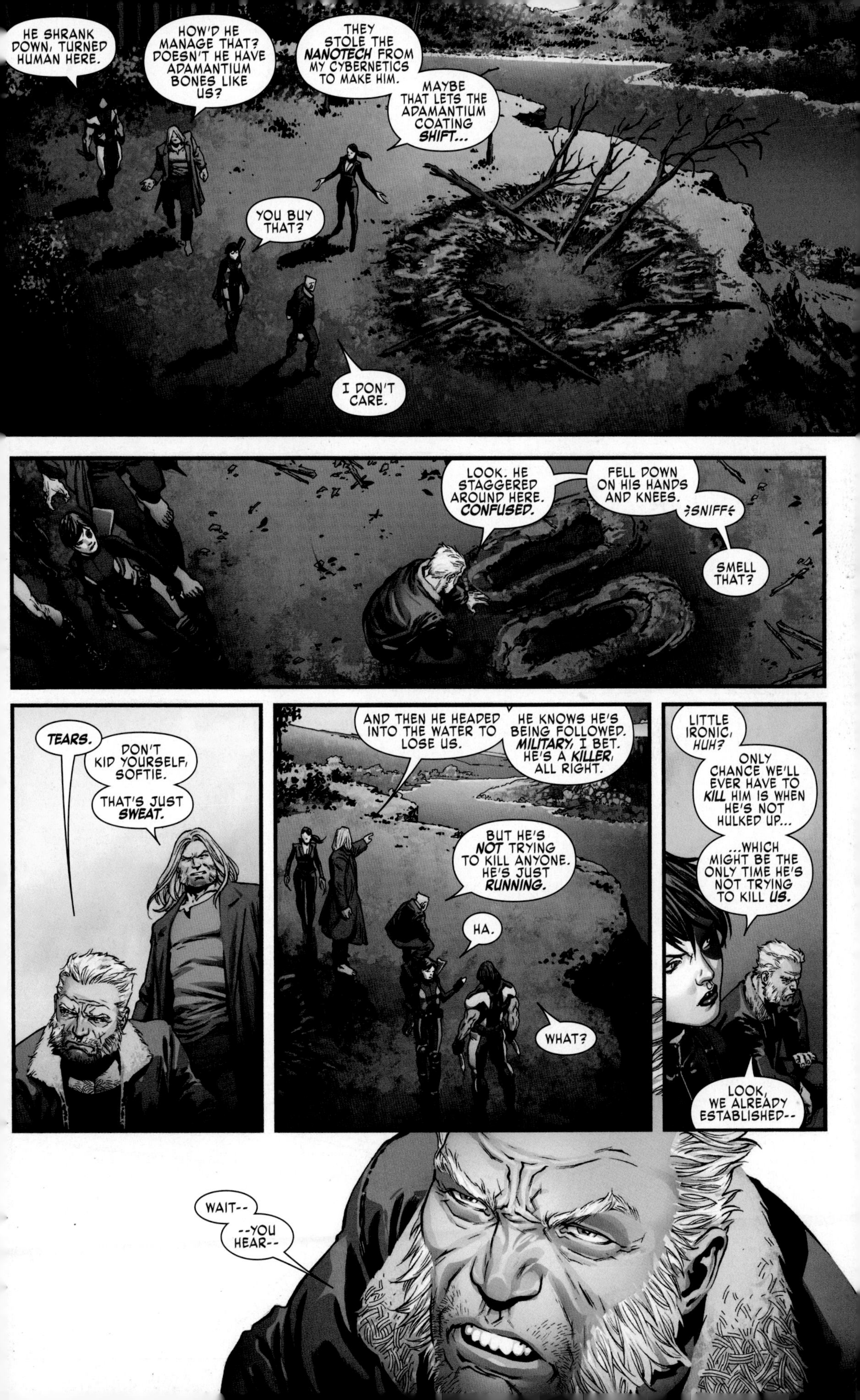
HE SHRANK DOWN, TURNED HUMAN HERE.
HOW'D HE MANAGE THAT? DOESN'T HE HAVE ADAMANTIUM BONES LIKE US?
THEY STOLE THE NANOTECH FROM MY CYBERNETICS TO MAKE HIM.
MAYBE THAT LETS THE ADAMANTIUM COATING SHIFT...
YOU BUY THAT?
I DON'T CARE.
LOOK. HE STAGGERED AROUND HERE. CONFUSED.
FELL DOWN ON HIS HANDS AND KNEES.
SNIFF
SMELL THAT?
TEARS.
DON'T KID YOURSELF, SOFTIE.
THAT'S JUST SWEAT.
AND THEN HE HEADED INTO THE WATER TO LOSE US.
HE KNOWS HE'S BEING FOLLOWED. MILITARY, I BET. HE'S A KILLER, ALL RIGHT.
BUT HE'S NOT TRYING TO KILL ANYONE. HE'S JUST RUNNING.
HA.
WHAT?
LITTLE IRONIC, HUH?
ONLY CHANCE WE'LL EVER HAVE TO KILL HIM IS WHEN HE'S NOT HULKED UP...
...WHICH MIGHT BE THE ONLY TIME HE'S NOT TRYING TO KILL US.
LOOK, WE ALREADY ESTABLISHED--
WAIT--
--YOU HEAR--

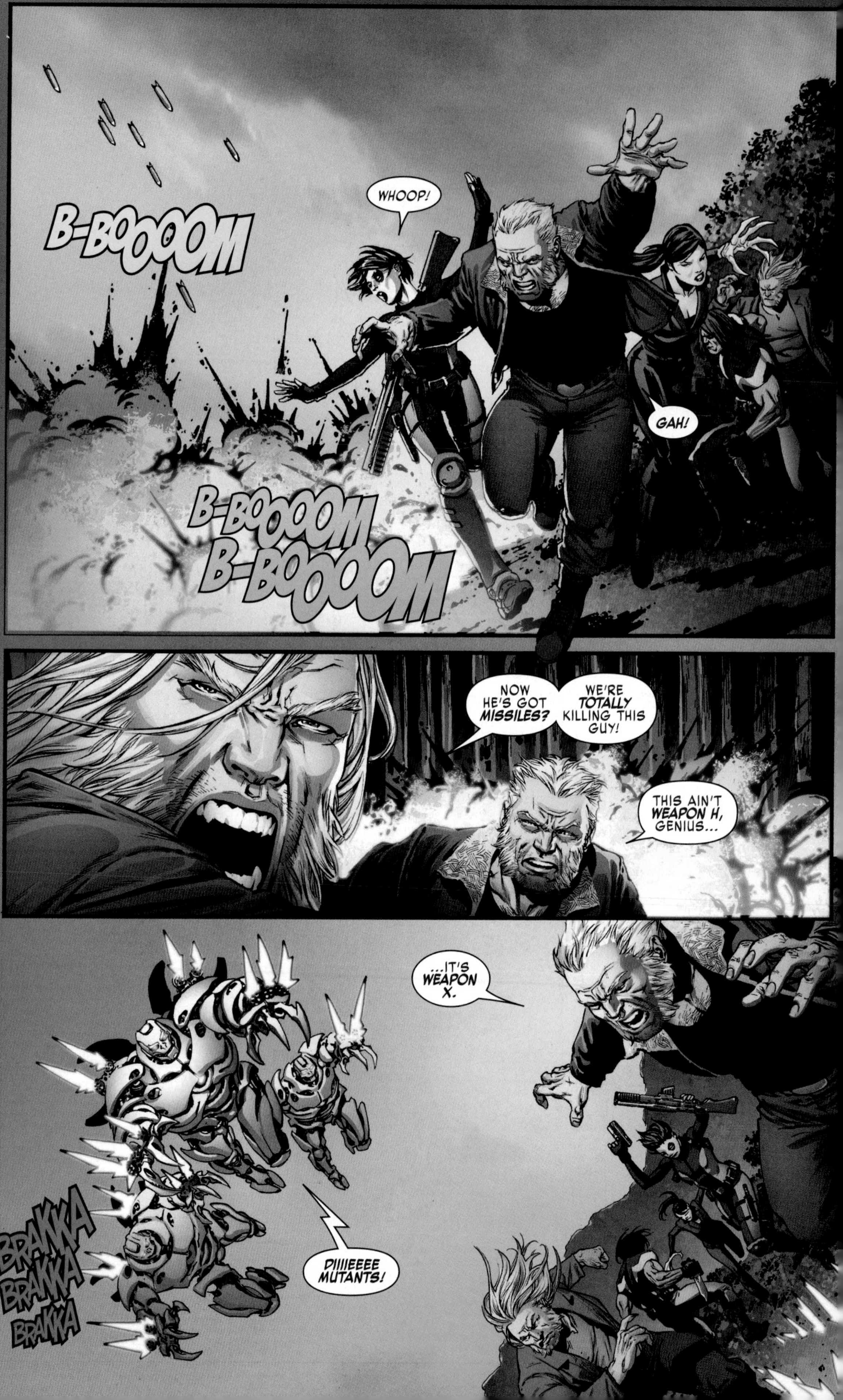
B-BOOOOM
WHOOP!
GAH!
B-BOOOOM
B-BOOOOM
NOW HE'S GOT MISSILES?
WE'RE TOTALLY KILLING THIS GUY!
THIS AIN'T WEAPON H, GENIUS...
...IT'S WEAPON X.
DIIIIEEEE MUTANTS!
BRAKKA
BRAKKA
BRAKKA

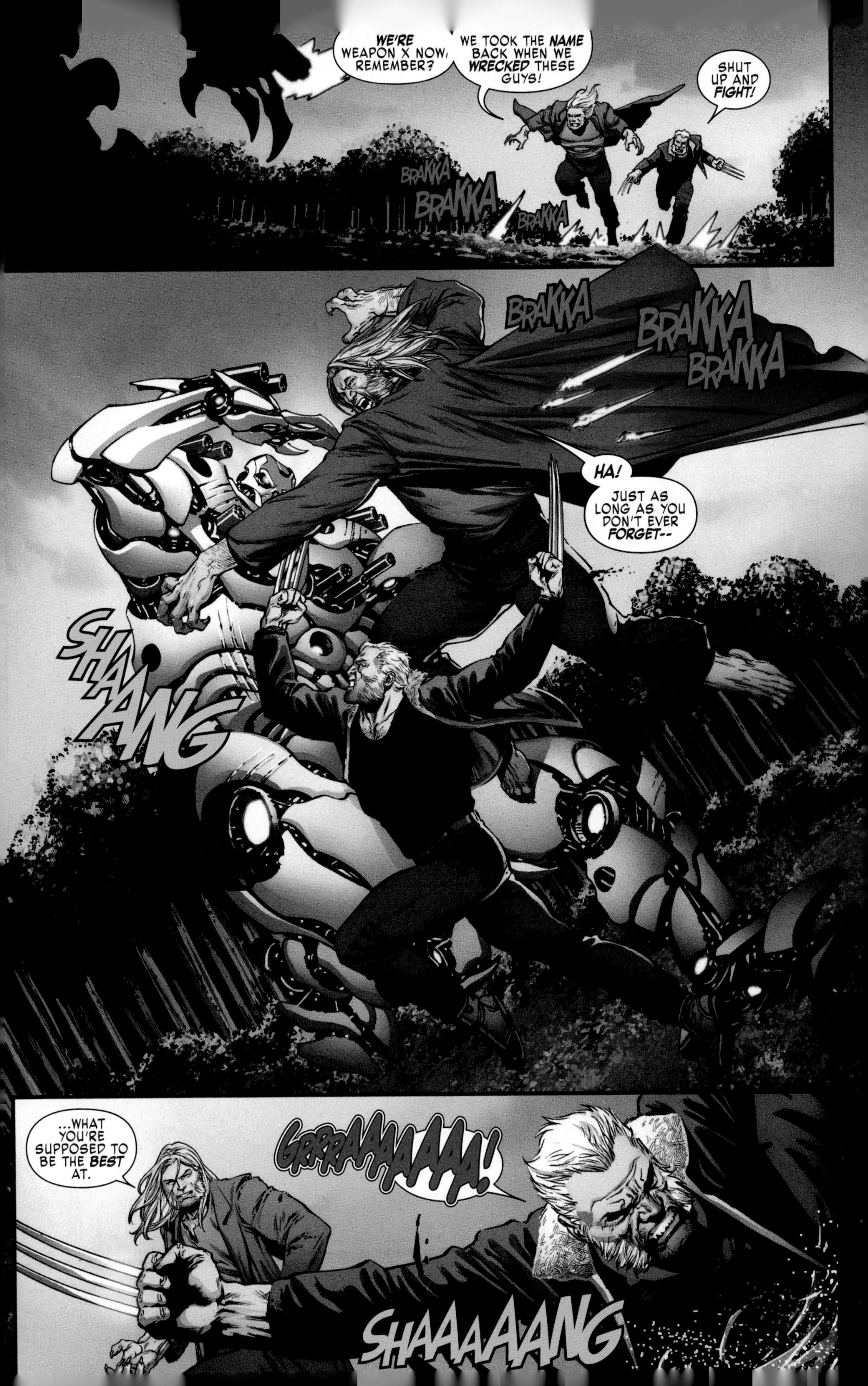

WE'RE WEAPON X NOW, REMEMBER?
WE TOOK THE NAME BACK WHEN WE WRECKED THESE GUYS!
SHUT UP AND FIGHT!
BRAKKA
BRAKKA
BRAKKA
BRAKKA
BRAKKA
BRAKKA
HA!
JUST AS LONG AS YOU DON'T EVER FORGET--
SHAAANG
...WHAT YOU'RE SUPPOSED TO BE THE BEST AT.
GRRRAAAAAAAA!
SHAAAAAANG

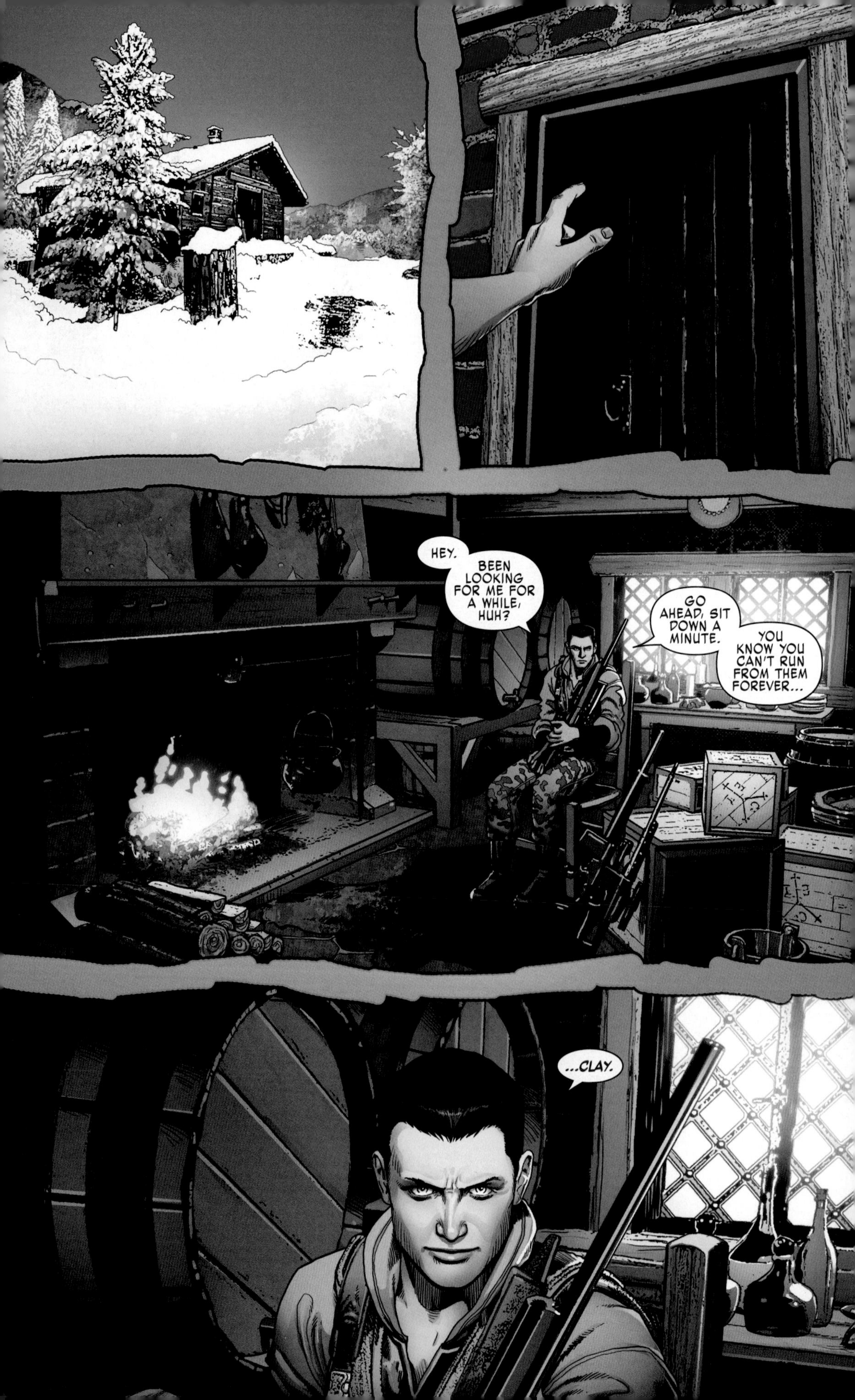
HEY.
BEEN LOOKING FOR ME FOR A WHILE, HUH?
GO AHEAD, SIT DOWN A MINUTE.
YOU KNOW YOU CAN'T RUN FROM THEM FOREVER...
...CLAY.

NNH!

"CLAY"...?

SNIFF
SNIFF

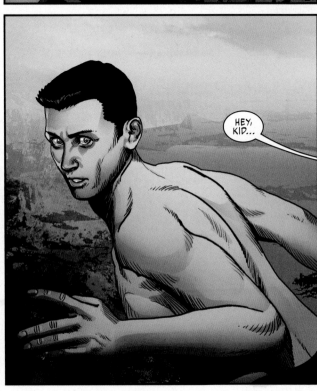

HEY, KID...

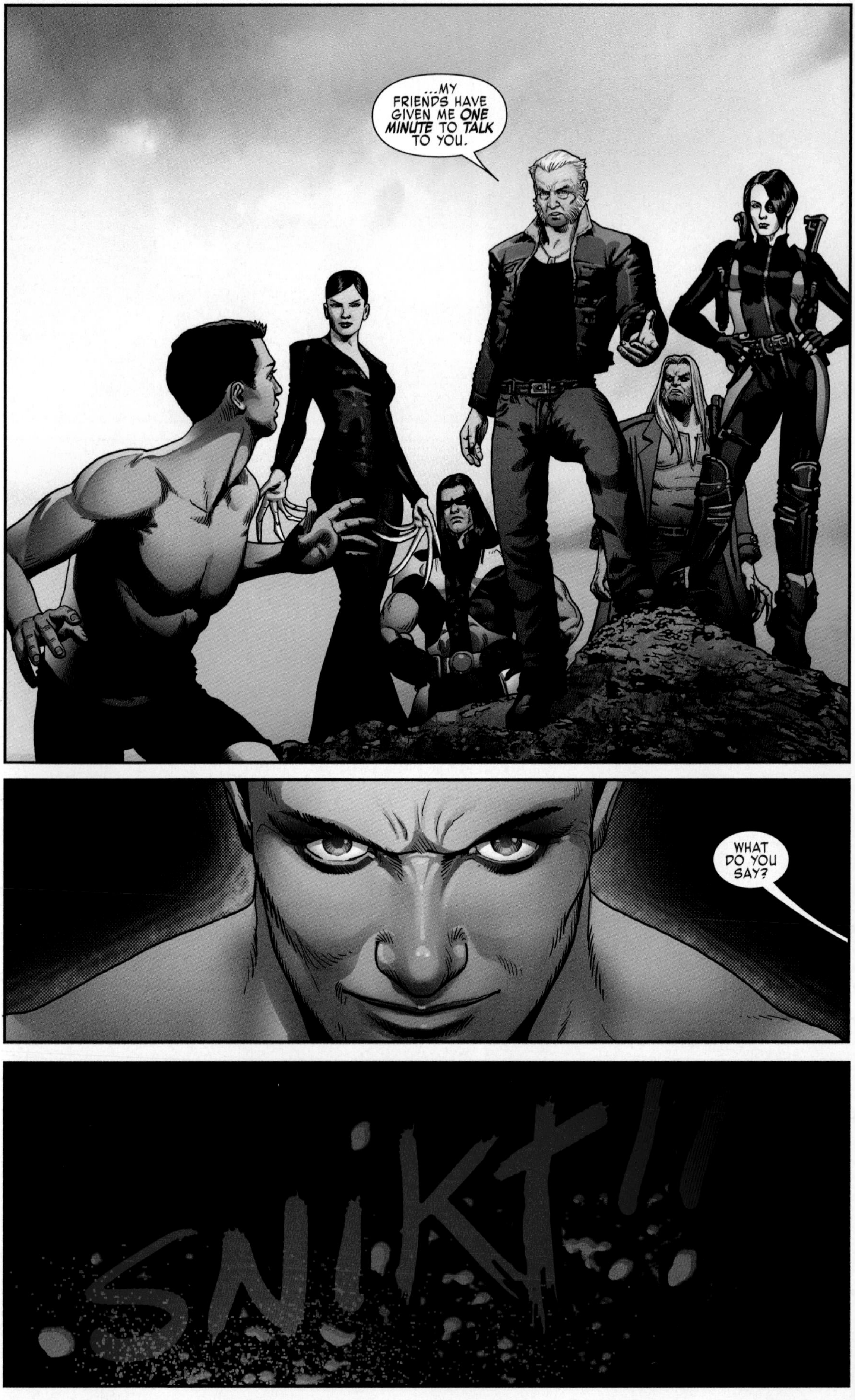
...MY FRIENDS HAVE GIVEN ME ONE MINUTE TO TALK TO YOU.
WHAT DO YOU SAY?
SNIKT!!

8

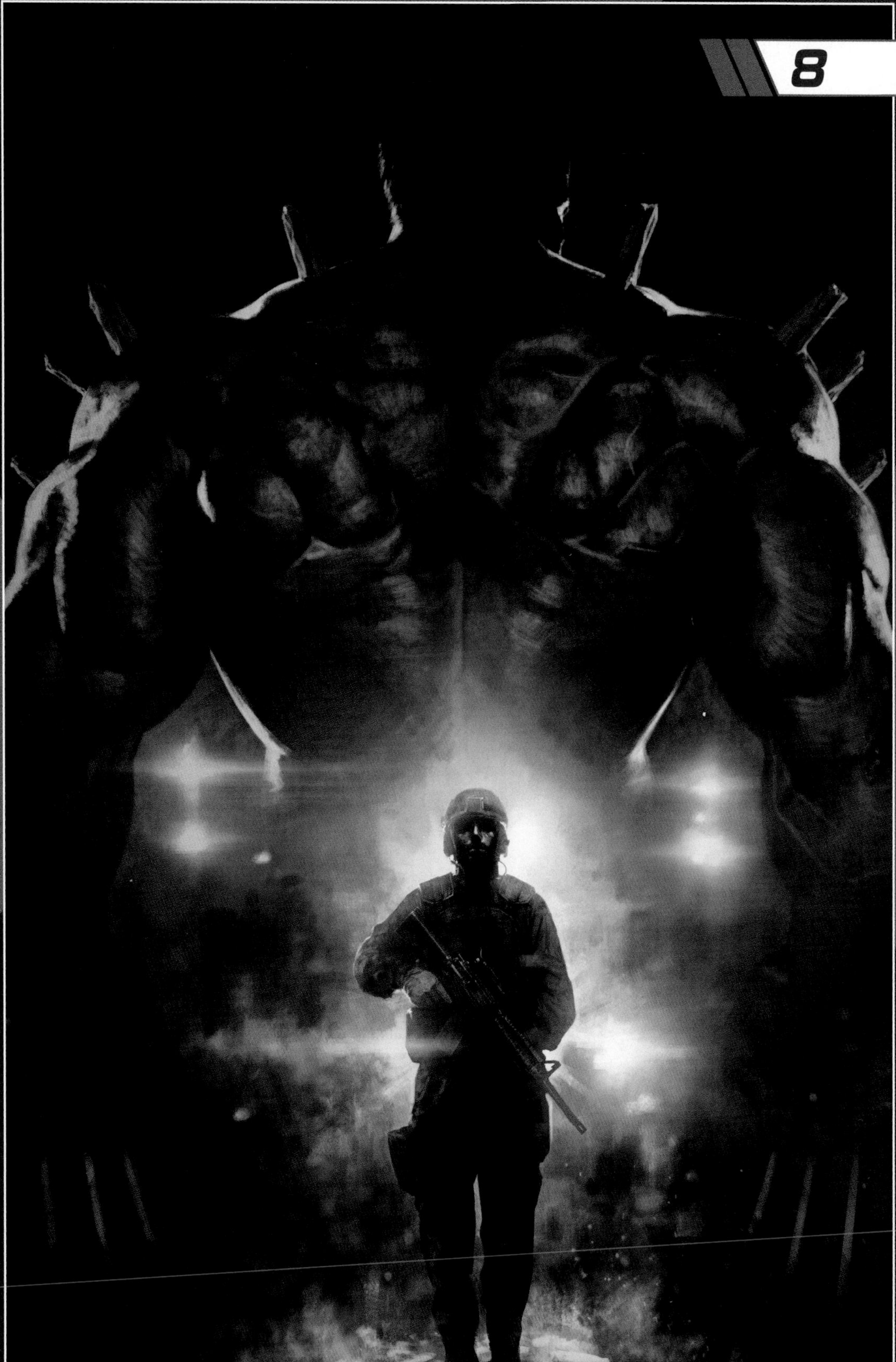

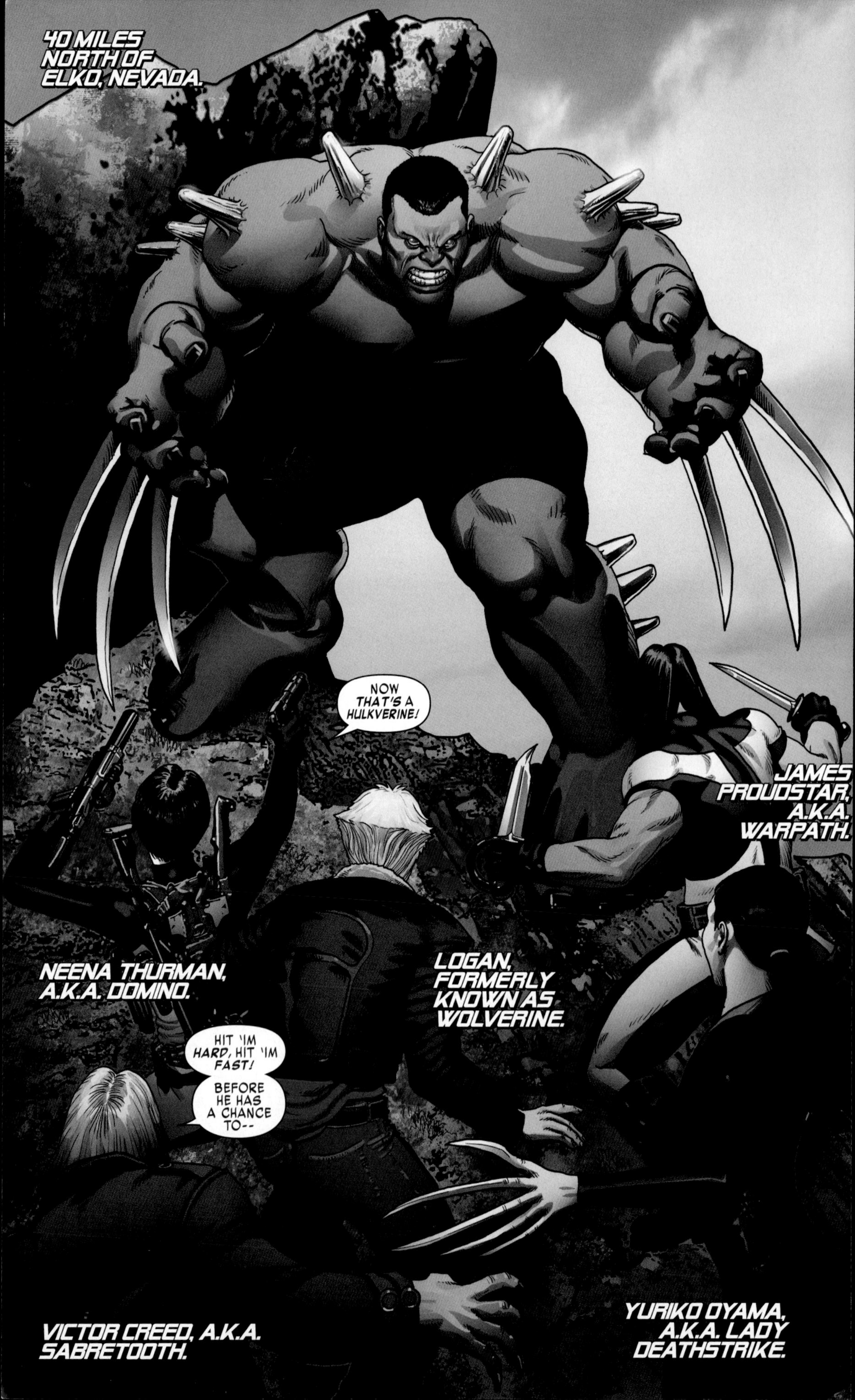
40 MILES NORTH OF ELKO, NEVADA.
NOW THAT'S A HULKVERINE!
JAMES PROUDSTAR, A.K.A. WARPATH.
NEENA THURMAN, A.K.A. DOMINO.
LOGAN, FORMERLY KNOWN AS WOLVERINE.
HIT 'IM HARD, HIT 'IM FAST!
BEFORE HE HAS A CHANCE TO--
VICTOR CREED, A.K.A. SABRETOOTH.
YURIKO OYAMA, A.K.A. LADY DEATHSTRIKE.

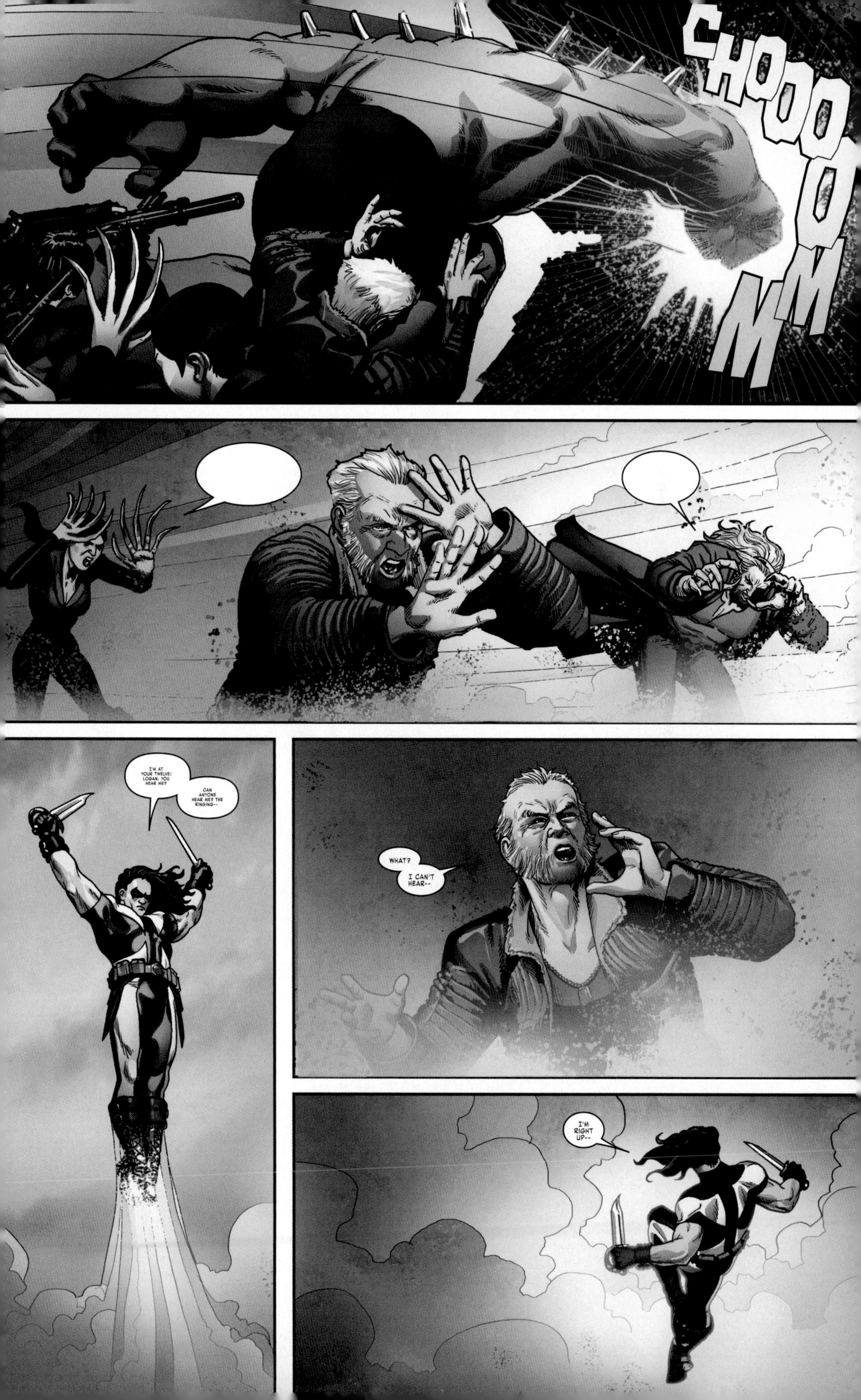
CHOOOOOMMM
I'M AT YOUR TWELVE! LOGAN, YOU HEAR ME?
CAN ANYONE HEAR ME? THE RINGING--
WHAT?
I CAN'T HEAR--
I'M RIGHT UP--

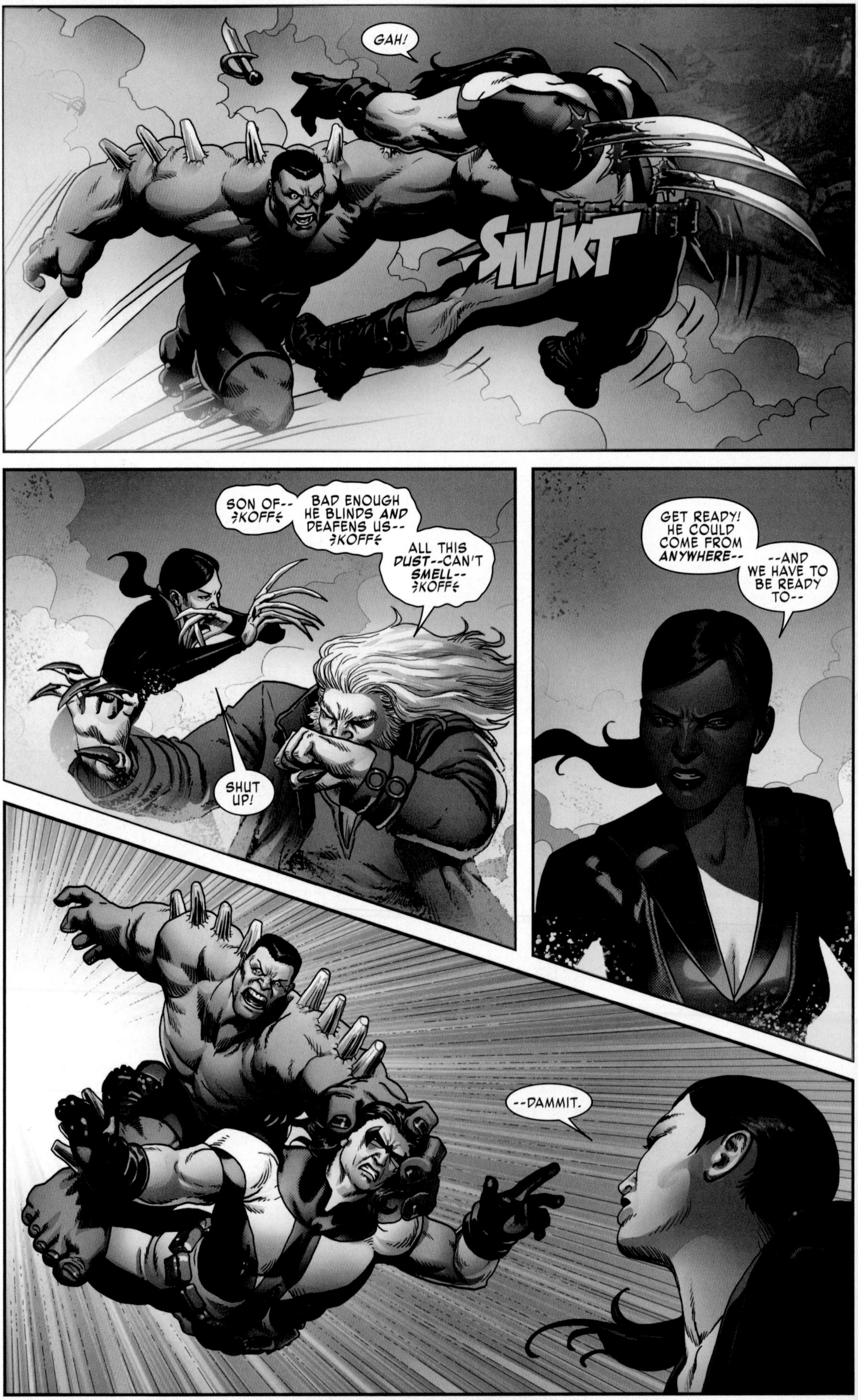
GAH!
SNIKT
SON OF-- ∋KOFF∈
BAD ENOUGH HE BLINDS AND DEAFENS US-- ∋KOFF∈
ALL THIS DUST--CAN'T SMELL-- ∋KOFF∈
SHUT UP!
GET READY! HE COULD COME FROM ANYWHERE--
--AND WE HAVE TO BE READY TO--
--DAMMIT.

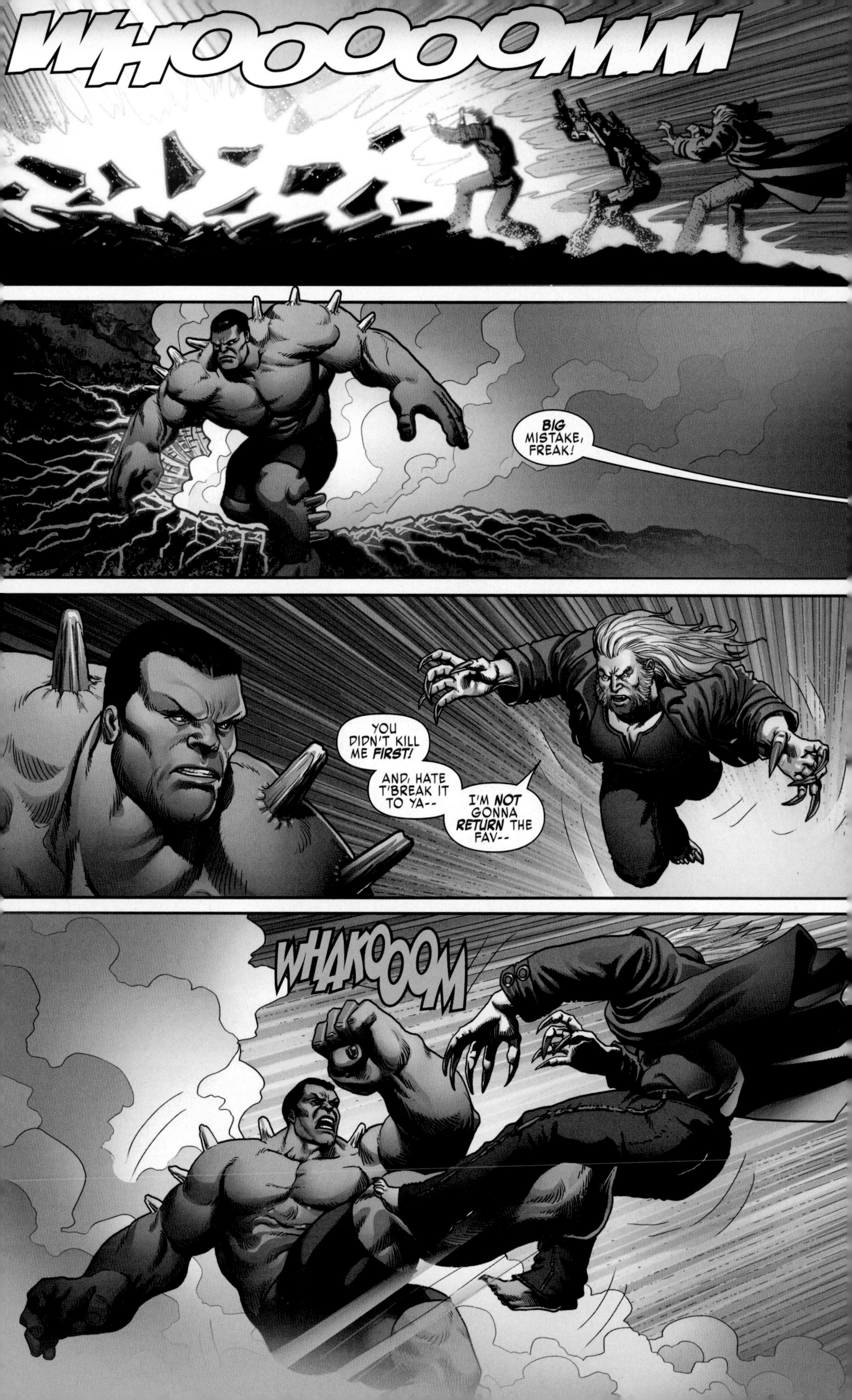
WHOOOOOMM
BIG MISTAKE, FREAK!
YOU DIDN'T KILL ME FIRST!
AND, HATE T'BREAK IT TO YA--
I'M NOT GONNA RETURN THE FAV--
WHAKOOOM

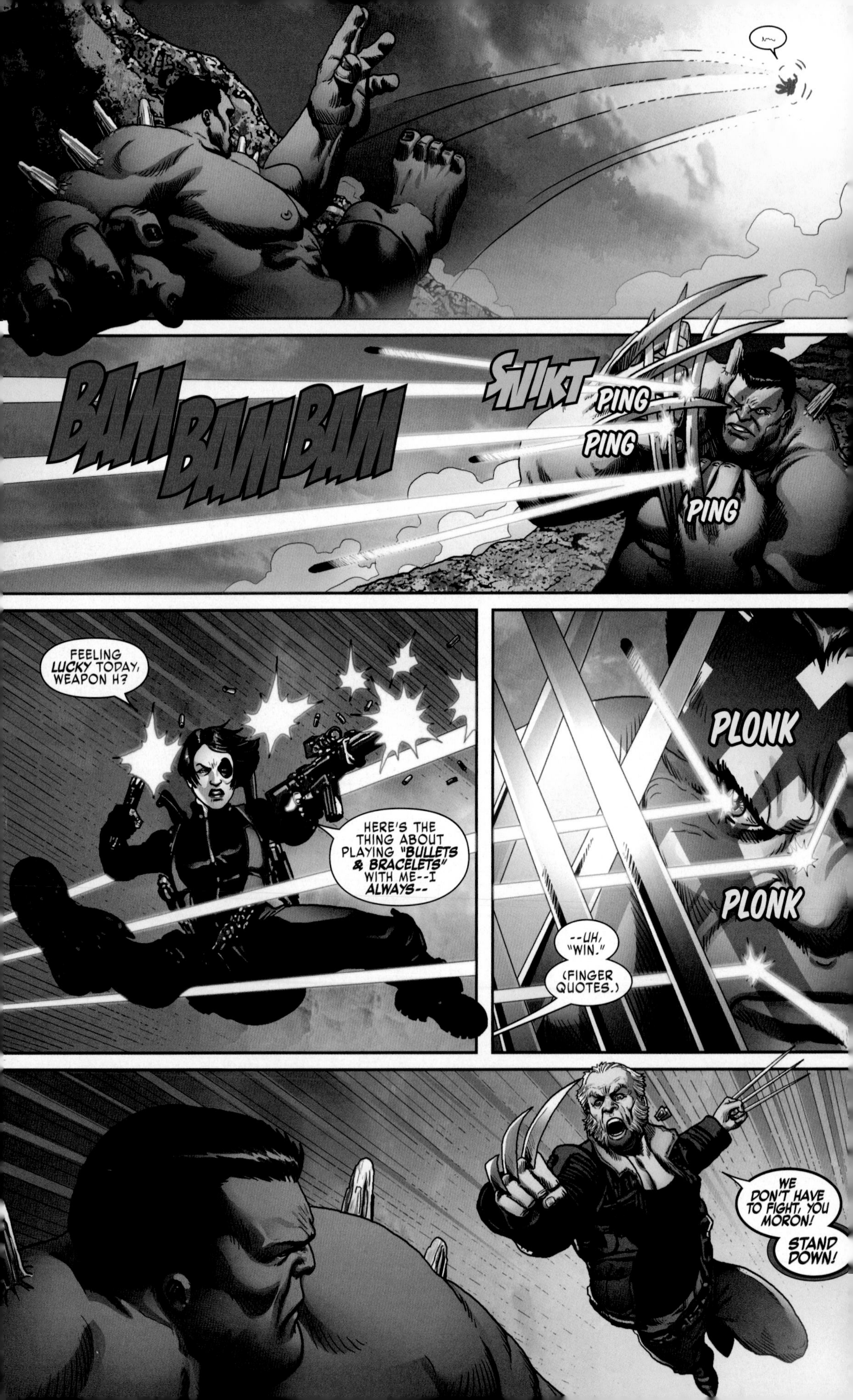

BAM BAM BAM
SNIKT
PING
PING
PING
FEELING LUCKY TODAY, WEAPON H?
HERE'S THE THING ABOUT PLAYING "BULLETS & BRACELETS" WITH ME--I ALWAYS--
PLONK
PLONK
--UH, "WIN."
(FINGER QUOTES.)
WE DON'T HAVE TO FIGHT, YOU MORON!
STAND DOWN!

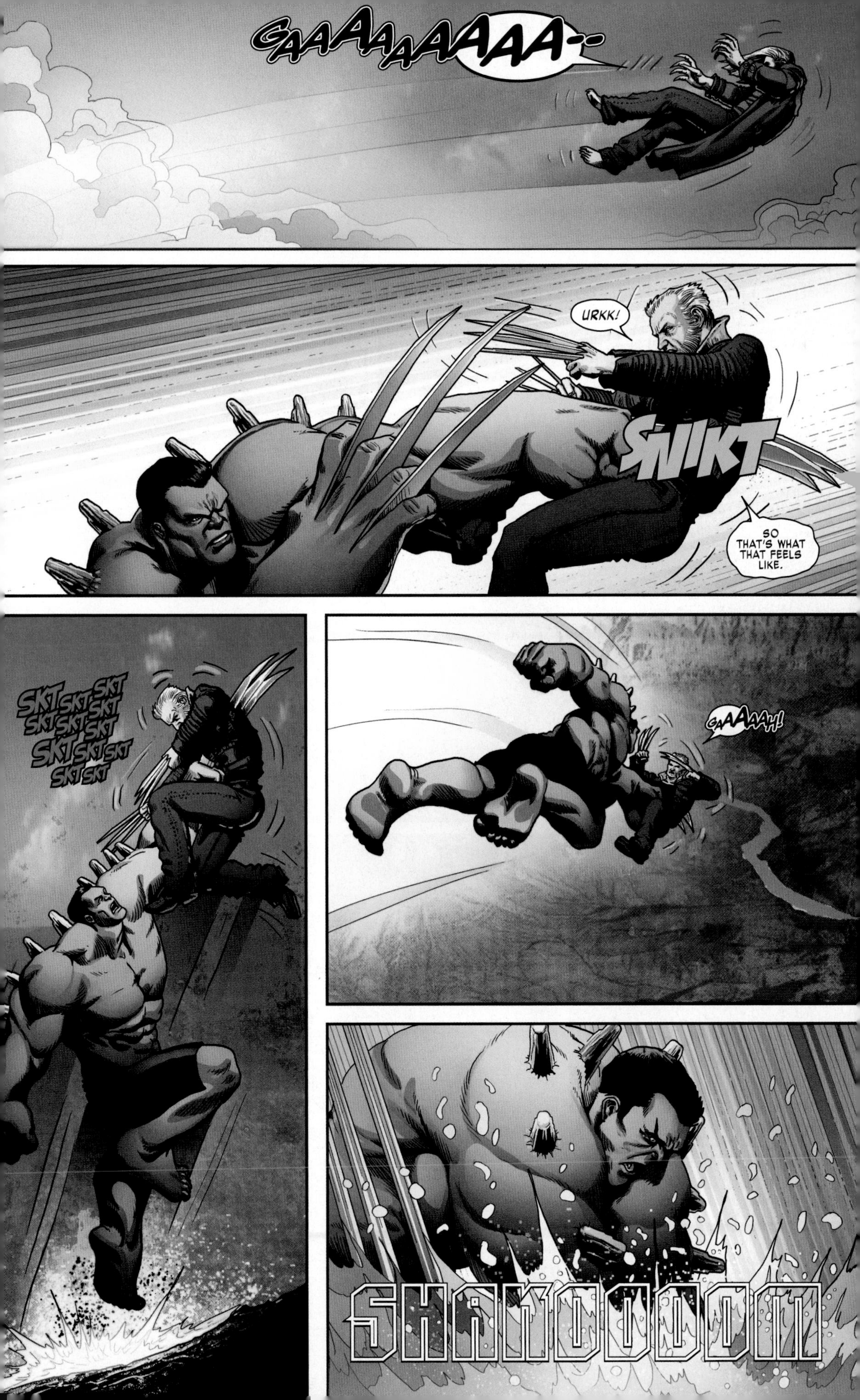
GAAAAAAAAA--
URKK!
SNIKT
SO THAT'S WHAT THAT FEELS LIKE.
SKT SKT SKT SKT SKT SKT SKT SKT SKT SKT SKT SKT
GAAAAAH!
SHAKOOOOM

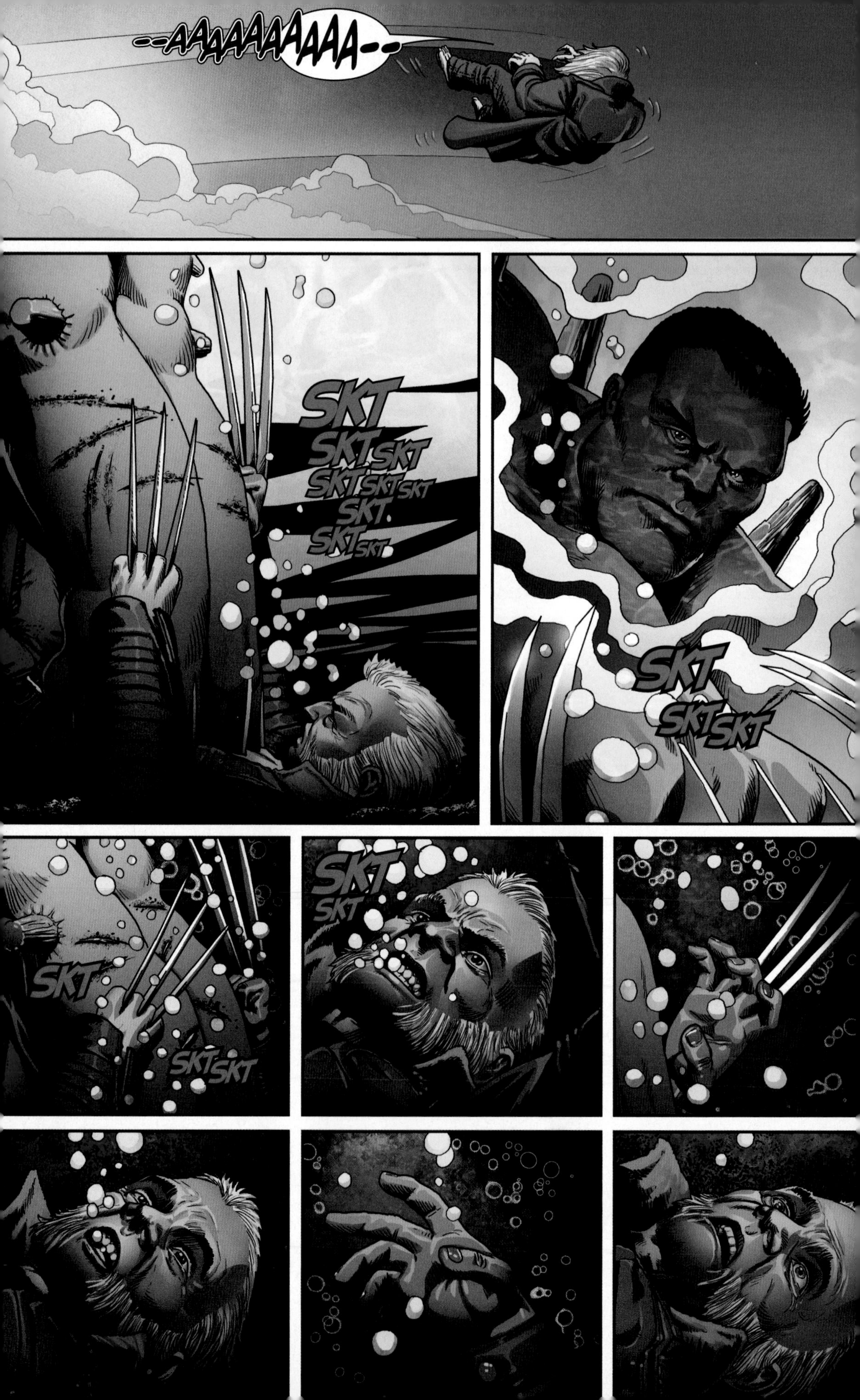
--AAAAAAAAAA--
SKT
SKT SKT
SKT SKT SKT
SKT
SKT SKT
SKT
SKT SKT
SKT
SKT SKT
SKT
SKT

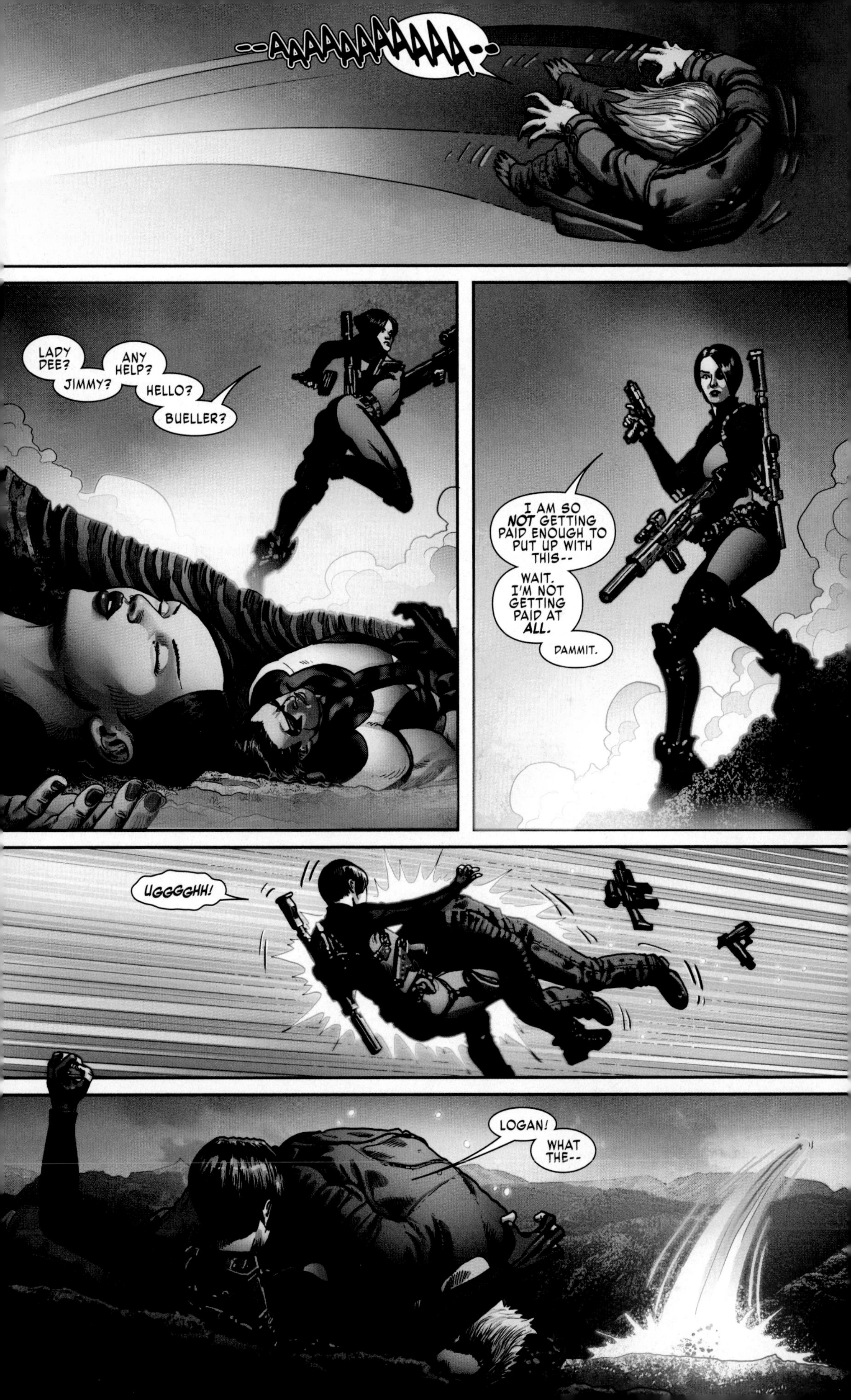
--AAAAAAAAAAA--
LADY DEE?
JIMMY?
ANY HELP?
HELLO?
BUELLER?
I AM SO *NOT* GETTING PAID ENOUGH TO PUT UP WITH THIS--
WAIT. I'M NOT GETTING PAID AT *ALL.*
DAMMIT.
UGGGGHH!
LOGAN!
WHAT THE--

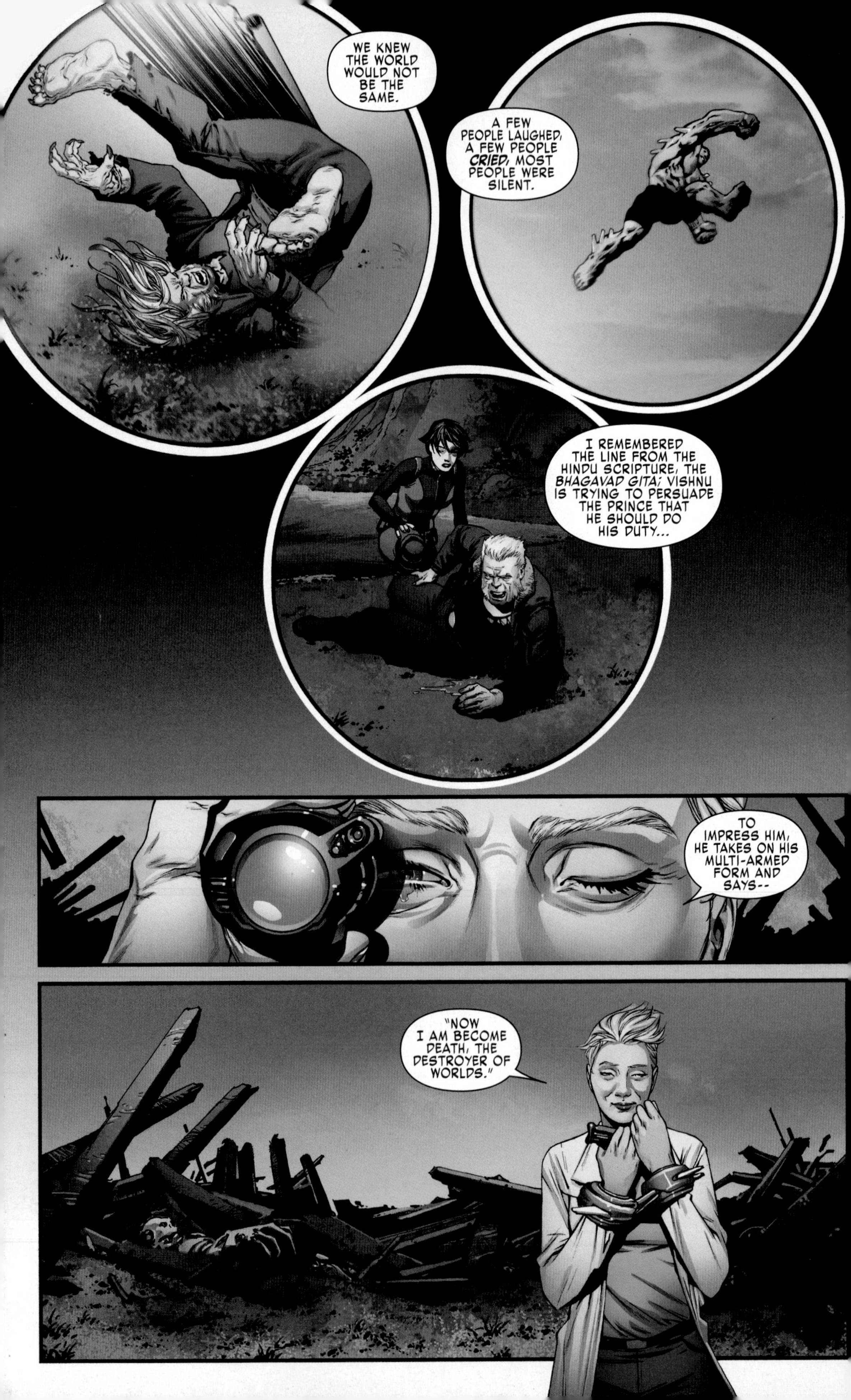
WE KNEW THE WORLD WOULD NOT BE THE SAME.
A FEW PEOPLE LAUGHED, A FEW PEOPLE CRIED, MOST PEOPLE WERE SILENT.
I REMEMBERED THE LINE FROM THE HINDU SCRIPTURE, THE BHAGAVAD GITA; VISHNU IS TRYING TO PERSUADE THE PRINCE THAT HE SHOULD DO HIS DUTY...
TO IMPRESS HIM, HE TAKES ON HIS MULTI-ARMED FORM AND SAYS--
"NOW I AM BECOME DEATH, THE DESTROYER OF WORLDS."

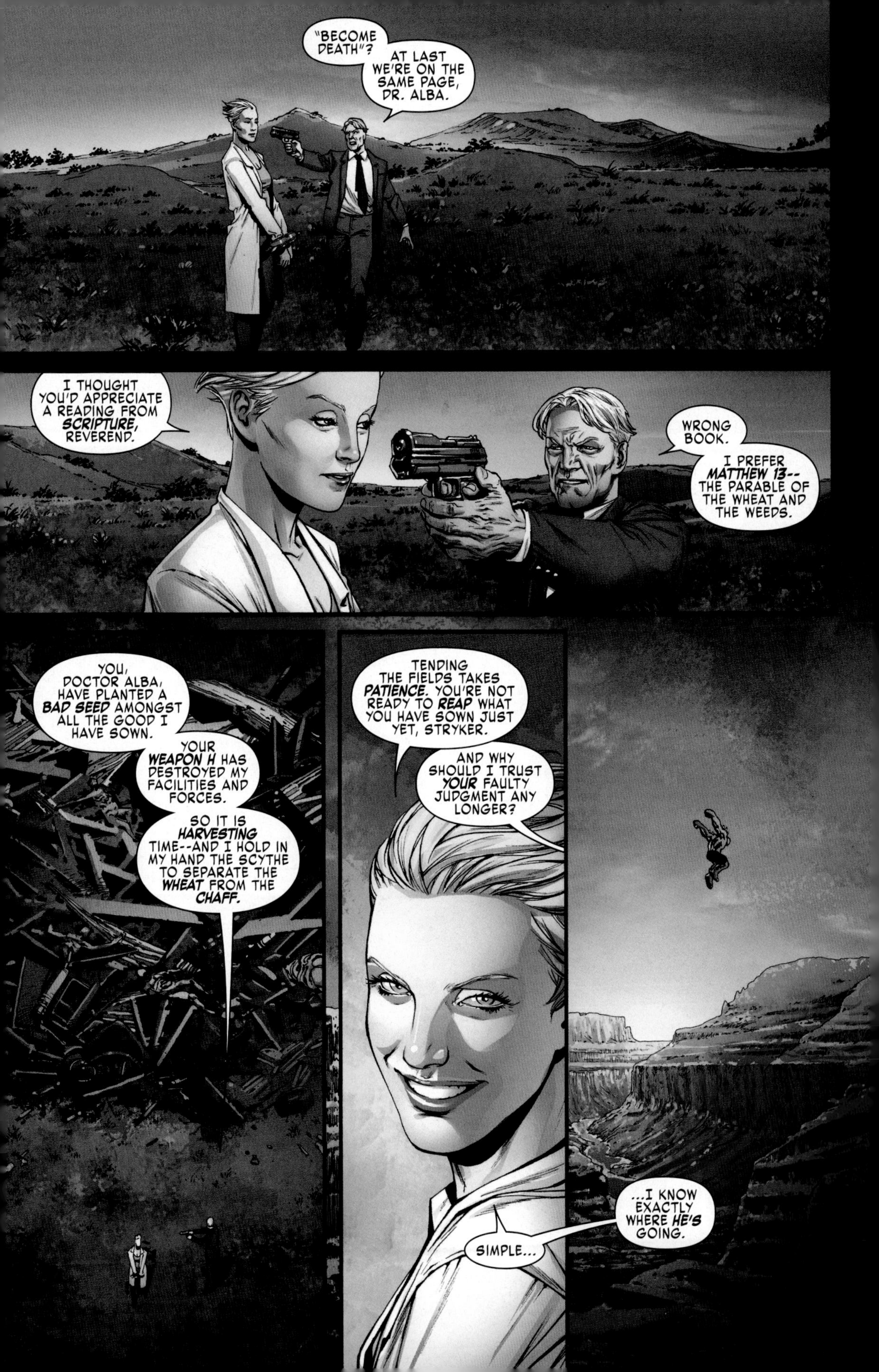
"BECOME DEATH"?
AT LAST WE'RE ON THE SAME PAGE, DR. ALBA.
I THOUGHT YOU'D APPRECIATE A READING FROM SCRIPTURE, REVEREND.
WRONG BOOK.
I PREFER MATTHEW 13-- THE PARABLE OF THE WHEAT AND THE WEEDS.
YOU, DOCTOR ALBA, HAVE PLANTED A BAD SEED AMONGST ALL THE GOOD I HAVE SOWN.
YOUR WEAPON H HAS DESTROYED MY FACILITIES AND FORCES.
SO IT IS HARVESTING TIME--AND I HOLD IN MY HAND THE SCYTHE TO SEPARATE THE WHEAT FROM THE CHAFF.
TENDING THE FIELDS TAKES PATIENCE. YOU'RE NOT READY TO REAP WHAT YOU HAVE SOWN JUST YET, STRYKER.
AND WHY SHOULD I TRUST YOUR FAULTY JUDGMENT ANY LONGER?
SIMPLE...
...I KNOW EXACTLY WHERE HE'S GOING.

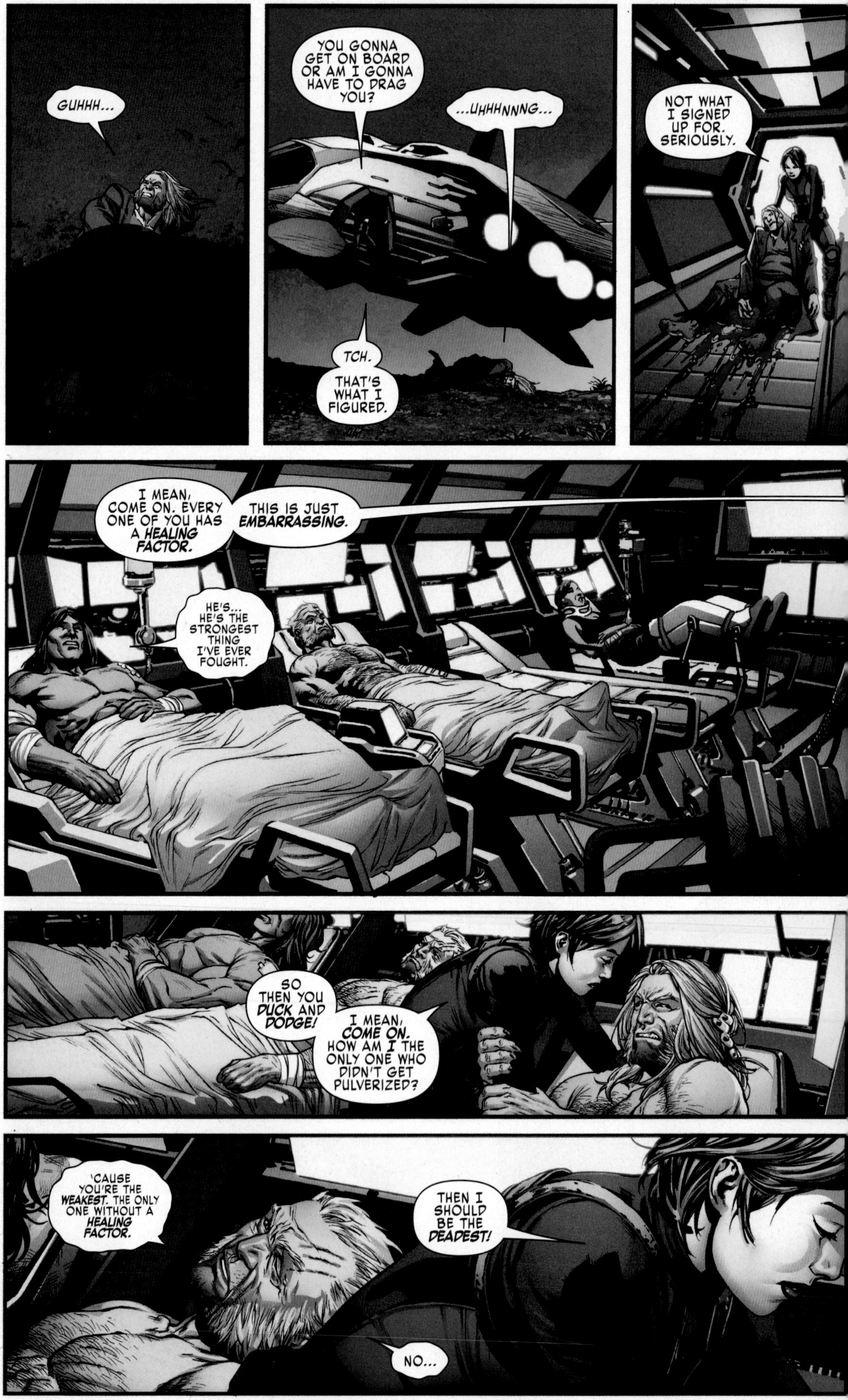
GUHHH...
YOU GONNA GET ON BOARD OR AM I GONNA HAVE TO DRAG YOU?
...UHHHNNNG...
TCH.
THAT'S WHAT I FIGURED.
NOT WHAT I SIGNED UP FOR. SERIOUSLY.
I MEAN, COME ON. EVERY ONE OF YOU HAS A HEALING FACTOR.
THIS IS JUST EMBARRASSING.
HE'S... HE'S THE STRONGEST THING I'VE EVER FOUGHT.
SO THEN YOU DUCK AND DODGE!
I MEAN, COME ON. HOW AM I THE ONLY ONE WHO DIDN'T GET PULVERIZED?
'CAUSE YOU'RE THE WEAKEST. THE ONLY ONE WITHOUT A HEALING FACTOR.
THEN I SHOULD BE THE DEADEST!
NO...

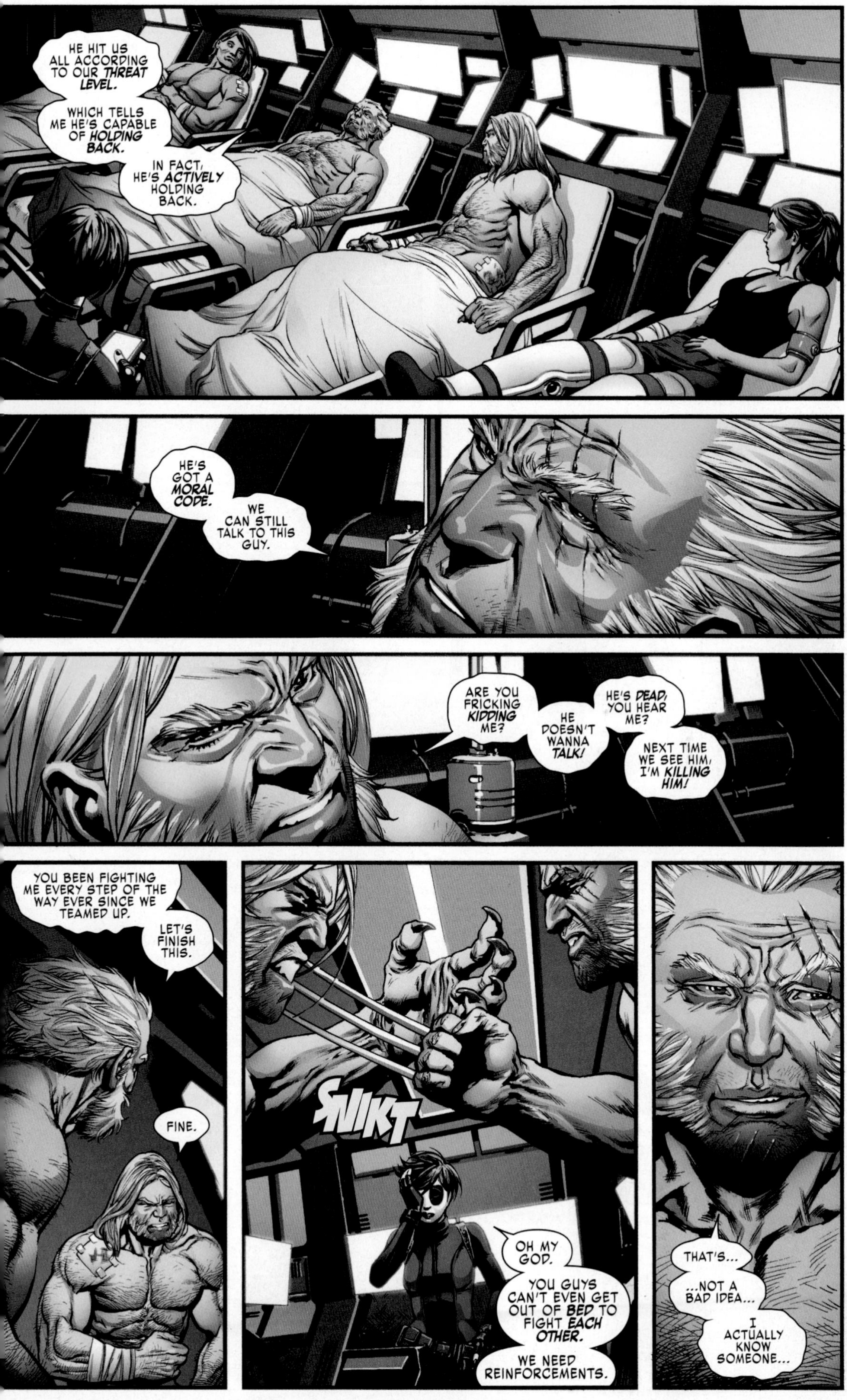
HE HIT US ALL ACCORDING TO OUR THREAT LEVEL.
WHICH TELLS ME HE'S CAPABLE OF HOLDING BACK.
IN FACT, HE'S ACTIVELY HOLDING BACK.
HE'S GOT A MORAL CODE.
WE CAN STILL TALK TO THIS GUY.
ARE YOU FRICKING KIDDING ME?
HE DOESN'T WANNA TALK!
HE'S DEAD, YOU HEAR ME?
NEXT TIME WE SEE HIM, I'M KILLING HIM!
YOU BEEN FIGHTING ME EVERY STEP OF THE WAY EVER SINCE WE TEAMED UP.
LET'S FINISH THIS.
FINE.
SNIKT
OH MY GOD.
YOU GUYS CAN'T EVEN GET OUT OF BED TO FIGHT EACH OTHER.
WE NEED REINFORCEMENTS.
THAT'S...
...NOT A BAD IDEA...
I ACTUALLY KNOW SOMEONE...

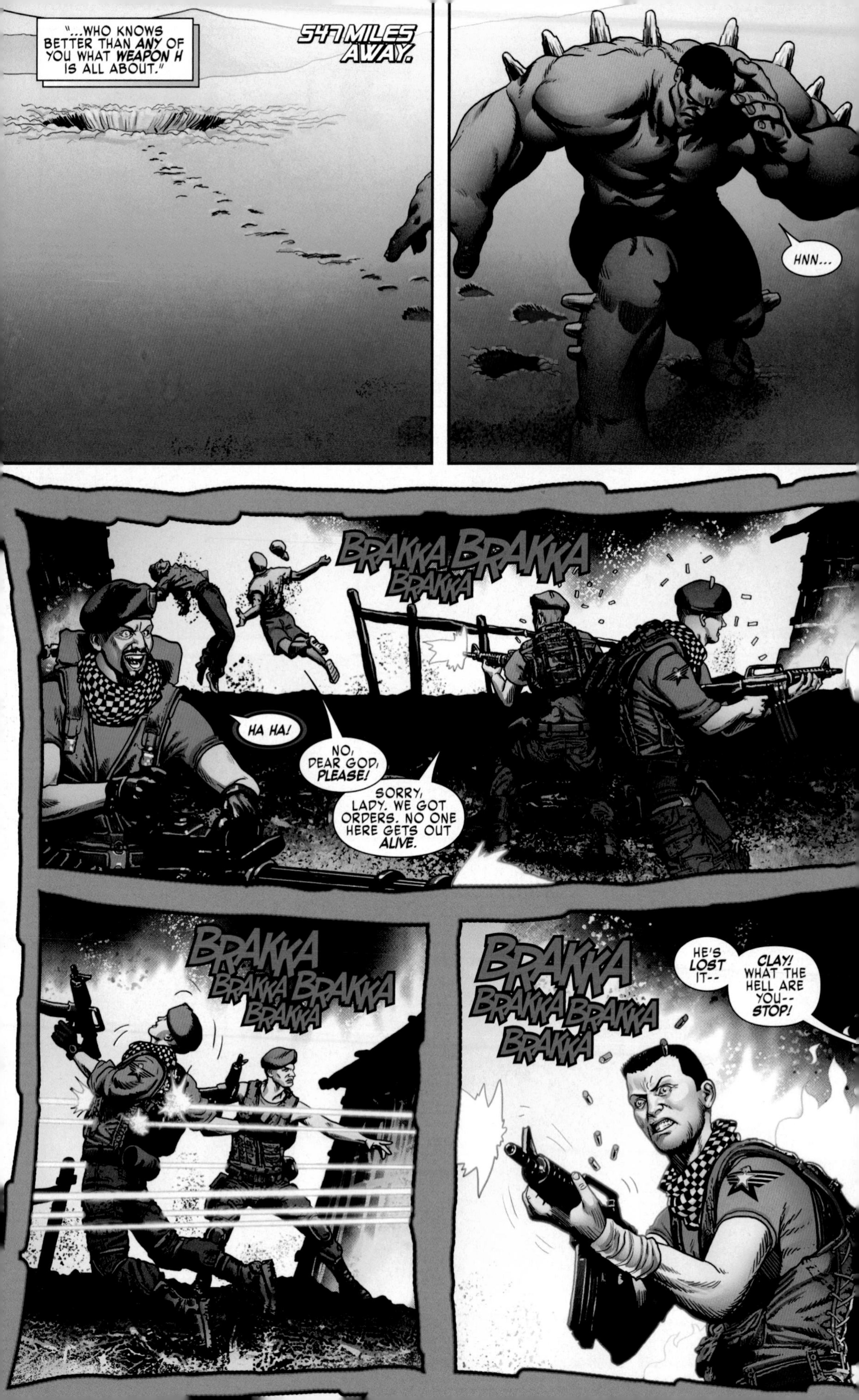
"...WHO KNOWS BETTER THAN ANY OF YOU WHAT WEAPON H IS ALL ABOUT."
547 MILES AWAY.
HNN...
BRAKKA BRAKKA BRAKKA
HA HA!
NO, DEAR GOD, PLEASE!
SORRY, LADY. WE GOT ORDERS. NO ONE HERE GETS OUT ALIVE.
BRAKKA BRAKKA BRAKKA BRAKKA
BRAKKA BRAKKA BRAKKA BRAKKA
HE'S LOST IT--
CLAY! WHAT THE HELL ARE YOU-- STOP!

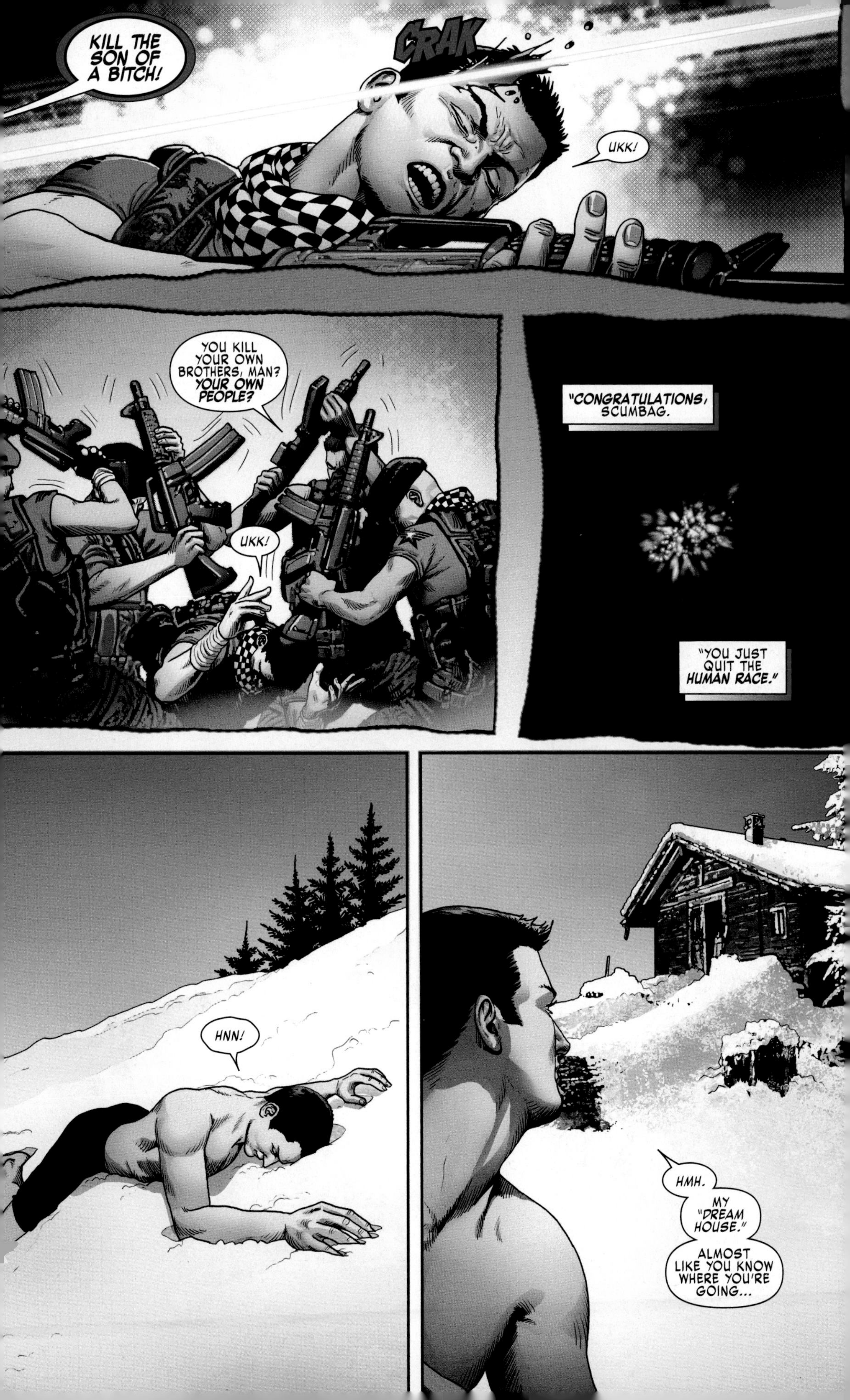
KILL THE SON OF A BITCH!
CRAK
UKK!
YOU KILL YOUR OWN BROTHERS, MAN? YOUR OWN PEOPLE?
UKK!
"CONGRATULATIONS, SCUMBAG.
"YOU JUST QUIT THE HUMAN RACE."
HNN!
HMH.
MY "DREAM HOUSE."
ALMOST LIKE YOU KNOW WHERE YOU'RE GOING...

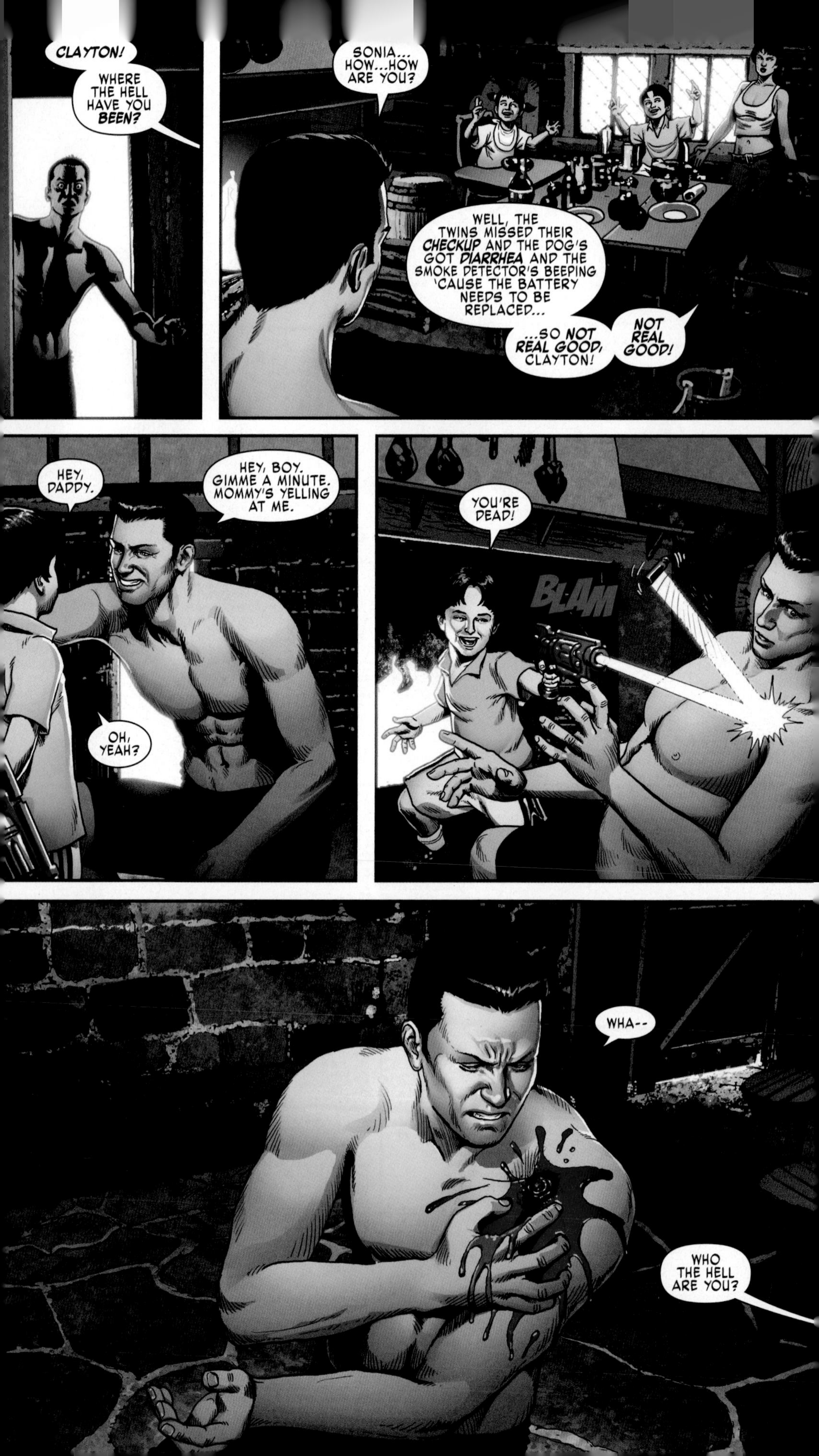
CLAYTON!
WHERE THE HELL HAVE YOU BEEN?
SONIA... HOW...HOW ARE YOU?
WELL, THE TWINS MISSED THEIR CHECKUP AND THE DOG'S GOT DIARRHEA AND THE SMOKE DETECTOR'S BEEPING 'CAUSE THE BATTERY NEEDS TO BE REPLACED...
...SO NOT REAL GOOD, CLAYTON!
NOT REAL GOOD!
HEY, DADDY.
HEY, BOY. GIMME A MINUTE. MOMMY'S YELLING AT ME.
OH, YEAH?
YOU'RE DEAD!
BLAM
WHA--
WHO THE HELL ARE YOU?

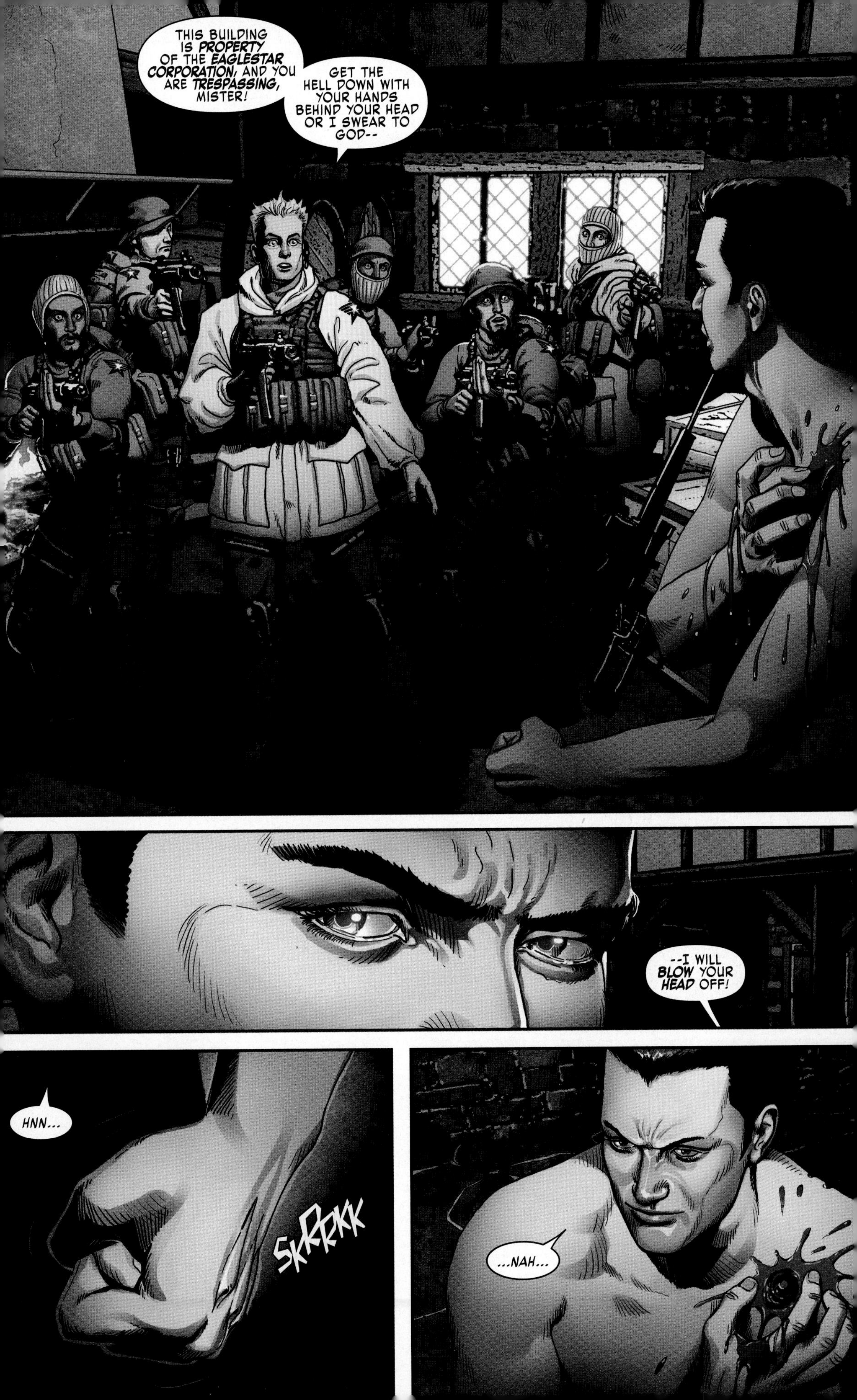
THIS BUILDING IS PROPERTY OF THE EAGLESTAR CORPORATION, AND YOU ARE TRESPASSING, MISTER!
GET THE HELL DOWN WITH YOUR HANDS BEHIND YOUR HEAD OR I SWEAR TO GOD--
--I WILL BLOW YOUR HEAD OFF!
HNN...
SKRRKK
...NAH...

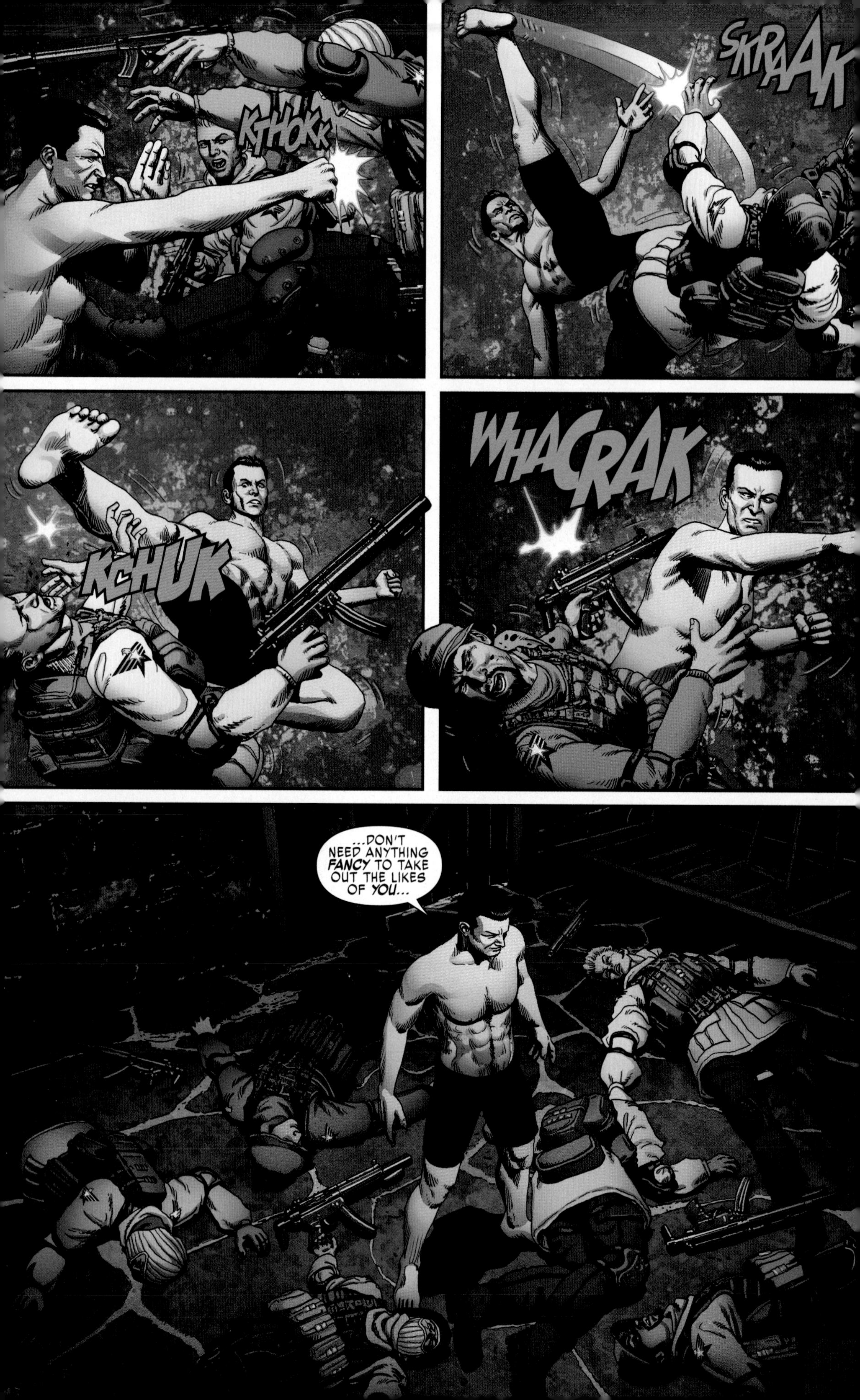
KTHOKK
SKRAAK
KCHUK
WHACRAK
...DON'T NEED ANYTHING FANCY TO TAKE OUT THE LIKES OF YOU...

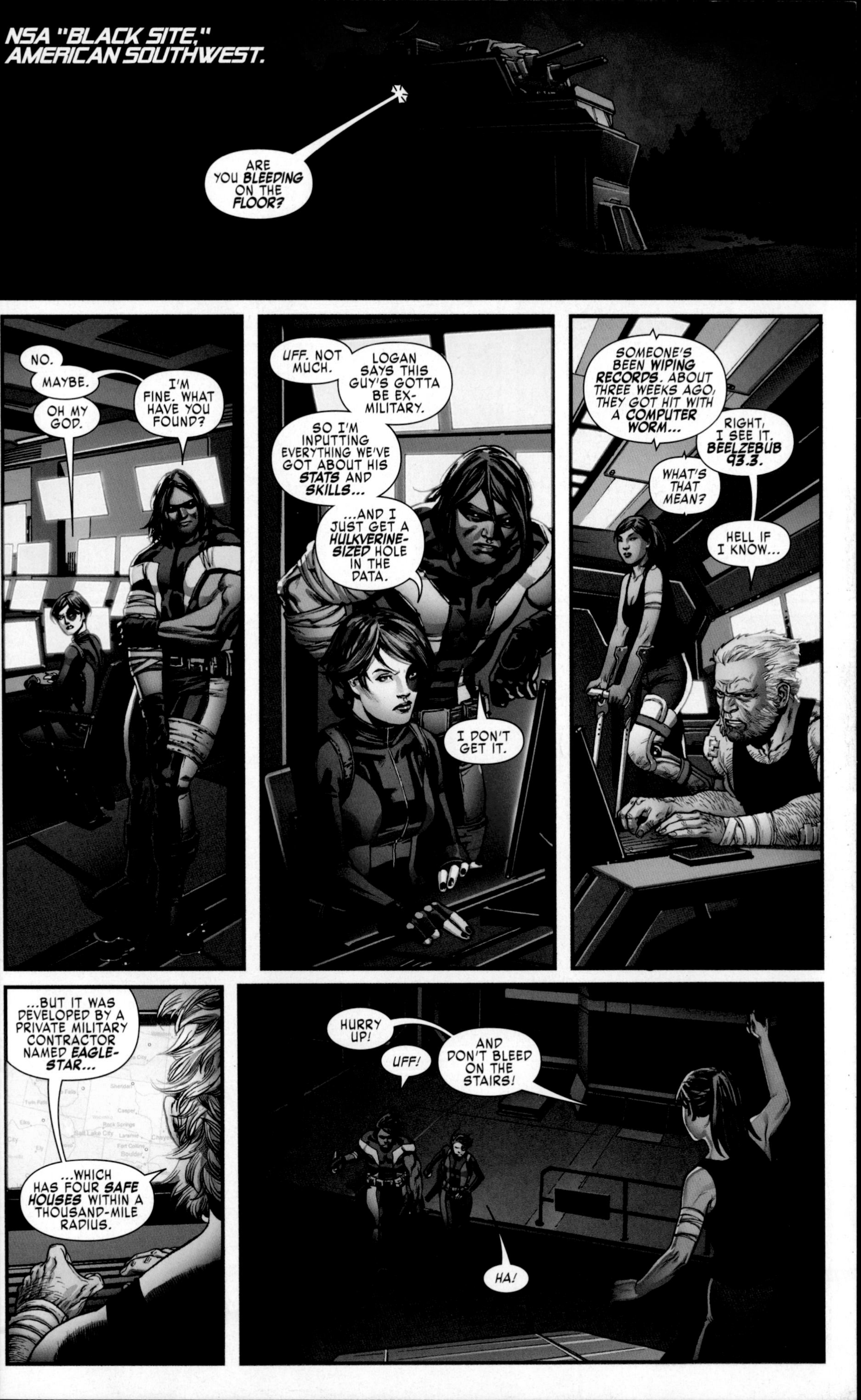
NSA "BLACK SITE," AMERICAN SOUTHWEST.
ARE YOU BLEEDING ON THE FLOOR?
NO.
MAYBE.
OH MY GOD.
I'M FINE. WHAT HAVE YOU FOUND?
UFF. NOT MUCH.
LOGAN SAYS THIS GUY'S GOTTA BE EX-MILITARY.
SO I'M INPUTTING EVERYTHING WE'VE GOT ABOUT HIS STATS AND SKILLS...
...AND I JUST GET A HULKVERINE-SIZED HOLE IN THE DATA.
I DON'T GET IT.
SOMEONE'S BEEN WIPING RECORDS. ABOUT THREE WEEKS AGO, THEY GOT HIT WITH A COMPUTER WORM...
RIGHT, I SEE IT. BEELZEBUB 93.3.
WHAT'S THAT MEAN?
HELL IF I KNOW...
...BUT IT WAS DEVELOPED BY A PRIVATE MILITARY CONTRACTOR NAMED EAGLE-STAR...
...WHICH HAS FOUR SAFE HOUSES WITHIN A THOUSAND-MILE RADIUS.
HURRY UP!
UFF!
AND DON'T BLEED ON THE STAIRS!
HA!

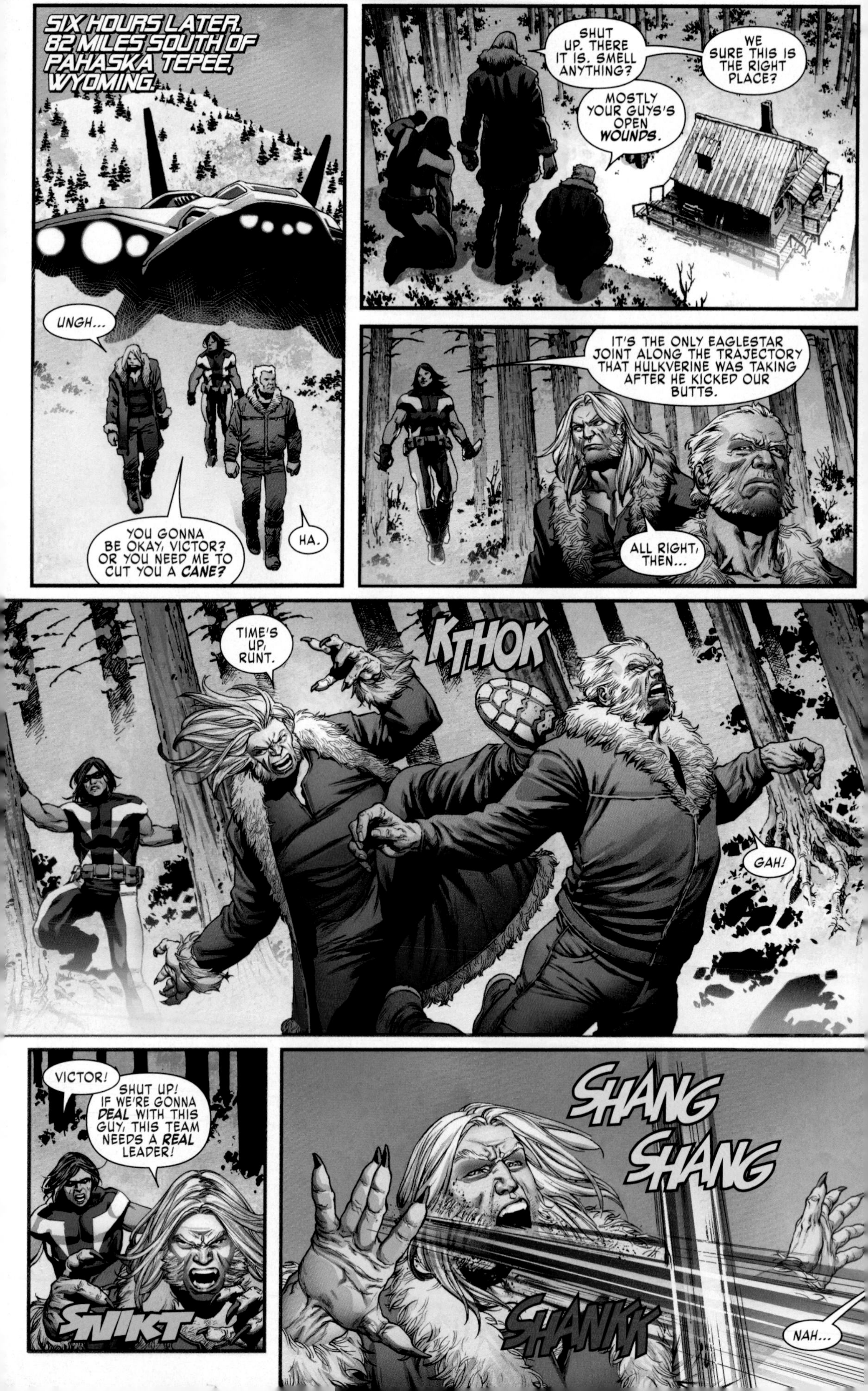
SIX HOURS LATER. 82 MILES SOUTH OF PAHASKA TEPEE, WYOMING.
UNGH...
YOU GONNA BE OKAY, VICTOR? OR YOU NEED ME TO CUT YOU A CANE?
HA.
SHUT UP. THERE IT IS. SMELL ANYTHING?
WE SURE THIS IS THE RIGHT PLACE?
MOSTLY YOUR GUYS'S OPEN WOUNDS.
IT'S THE ONLY EAGLESTAR JOINT ALONG THE TRAJECTORY THAT HULKVERINE WAS TAKING AFTER HE KICKED OUR BUTTS.
ALL RIGHT, THEN...
TIME'S UP, RUNT.
KTHOK
GAH!
VICTOR!
SHUT UP! IF WE'RE GONNA DEAL WITH THIS GUY, THIS TEAM NEEDS A REAL LEADER!
SNIKT
SHANG
SHANG
SHANKK
NAH...

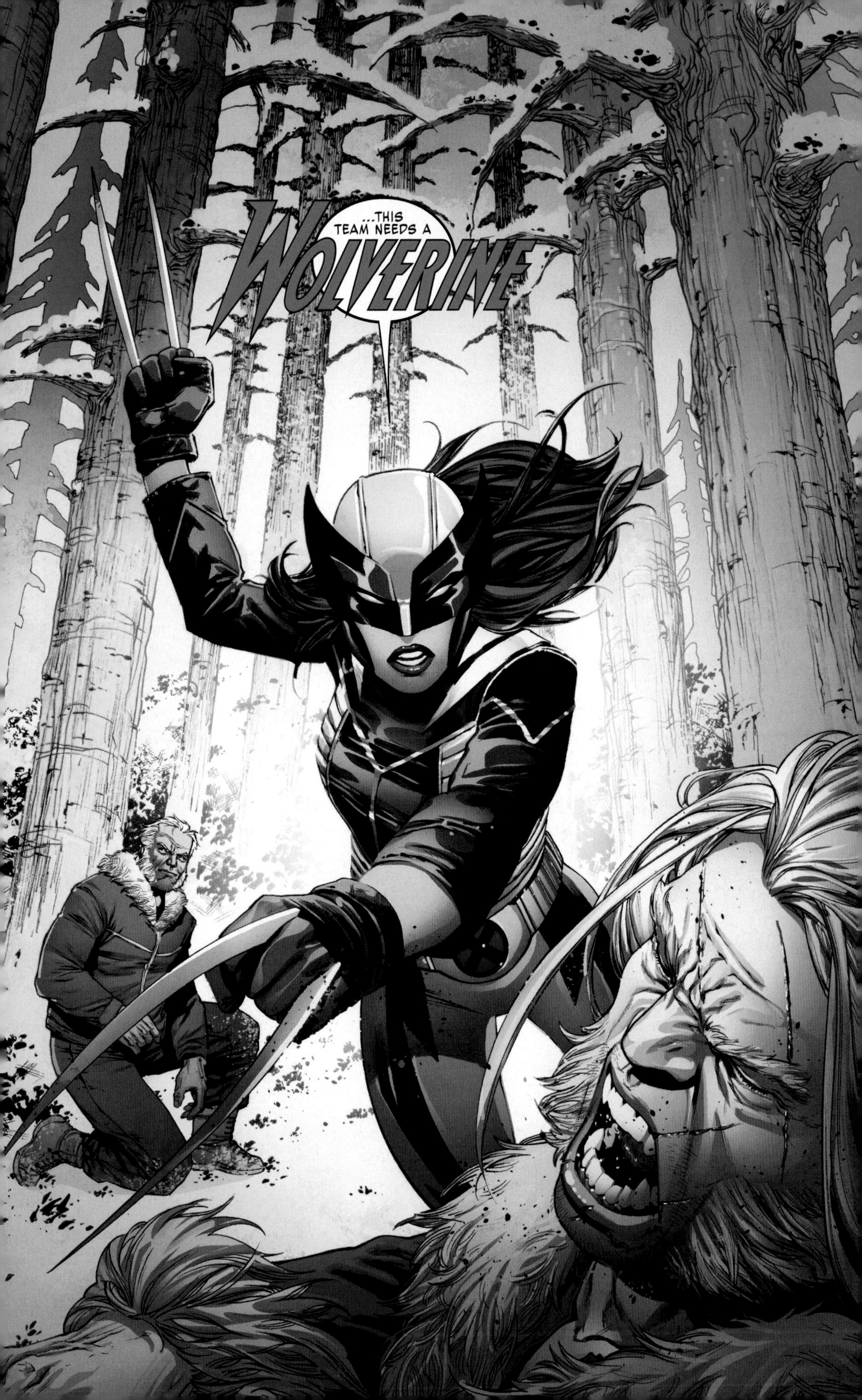
...THIS TEAM NEEDS A
WOLVERINE

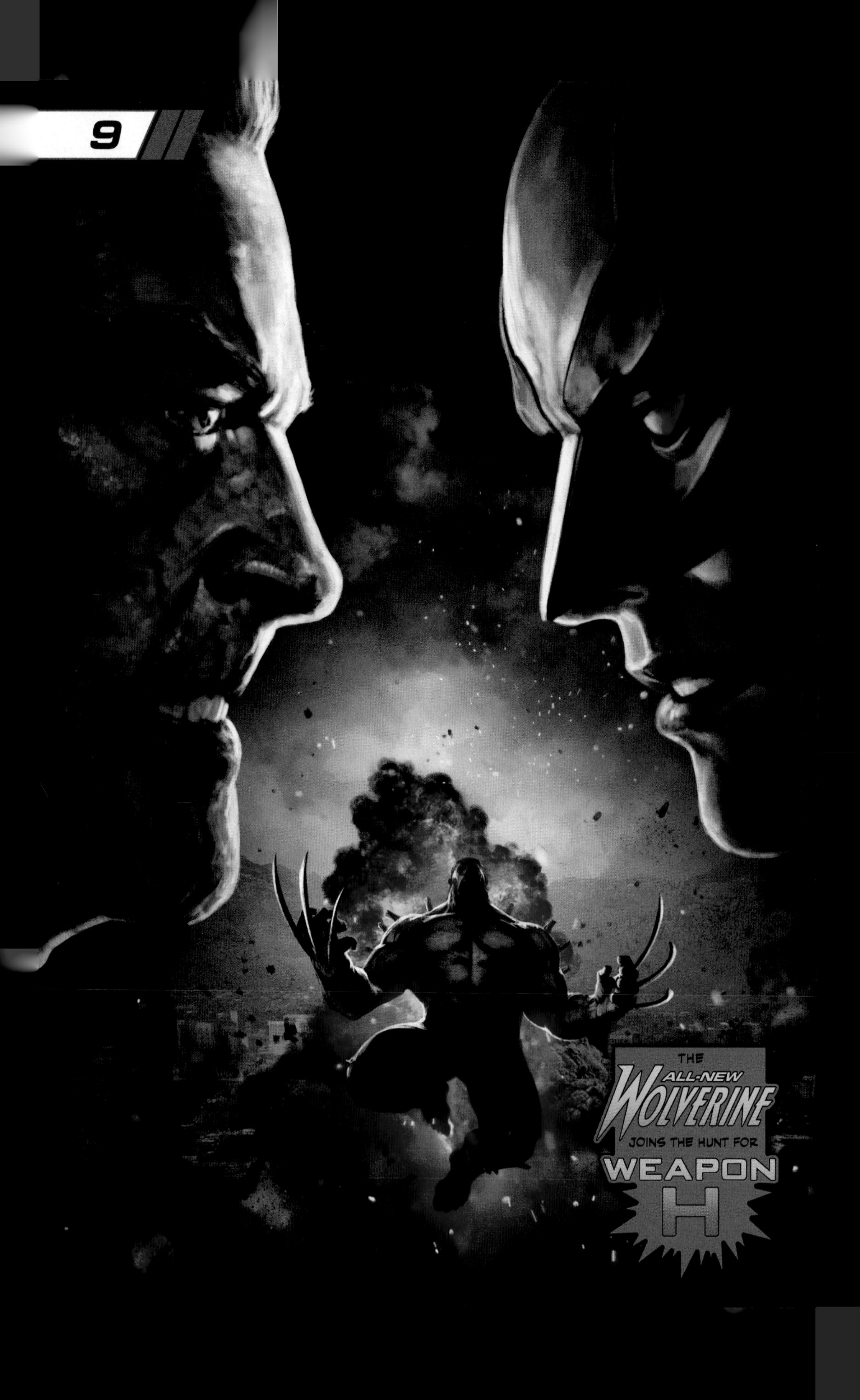
9
THE
ALL-NEW
WOLVERINE
JOINS THE HUNT FOR
WEAPON
H

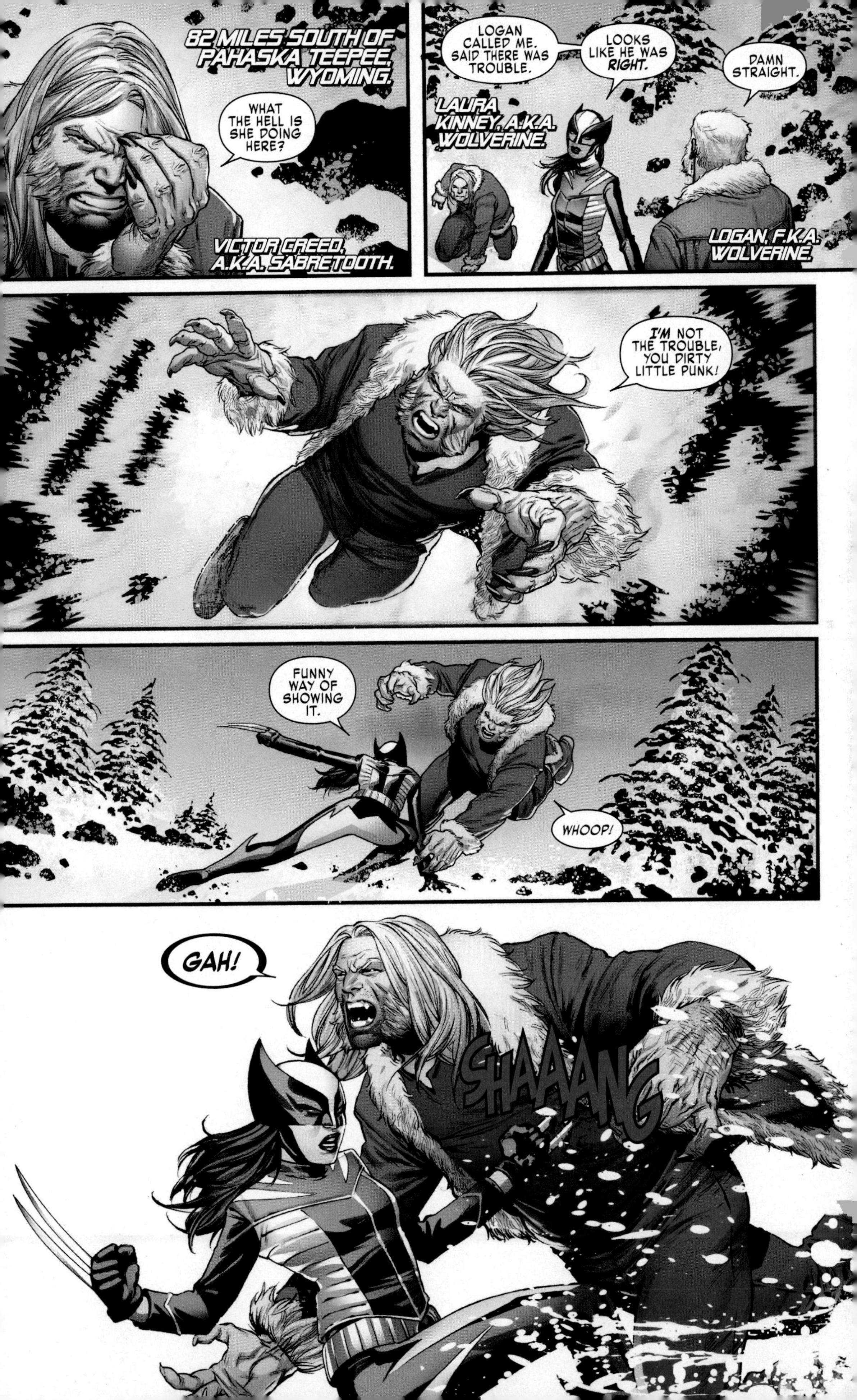
82 MILES SOUTH OF PAHASKA TEEPEE, WYOMING.
WHAT THE HELL IS SHE DOING HERE?
VICTOR CREED, A.K.A. SABRETOOTH.
LOGAN CALLED ME. SAID THERE WAS TROUBLE.
LOOKS LIKE HE WAS RIGHT.
DAMN STRAIGHT.
LAURA KINNEY, A.K.A. WOLVERINE.
LOGAN, F.K.A. WOLVERINE.
I'M NOT THE TROUBLE, YOU DIRTY LITTLE PUNK!
FUNNY WAY OF SHOWING IT.
WHOOP!
GAH!
SHAAANG

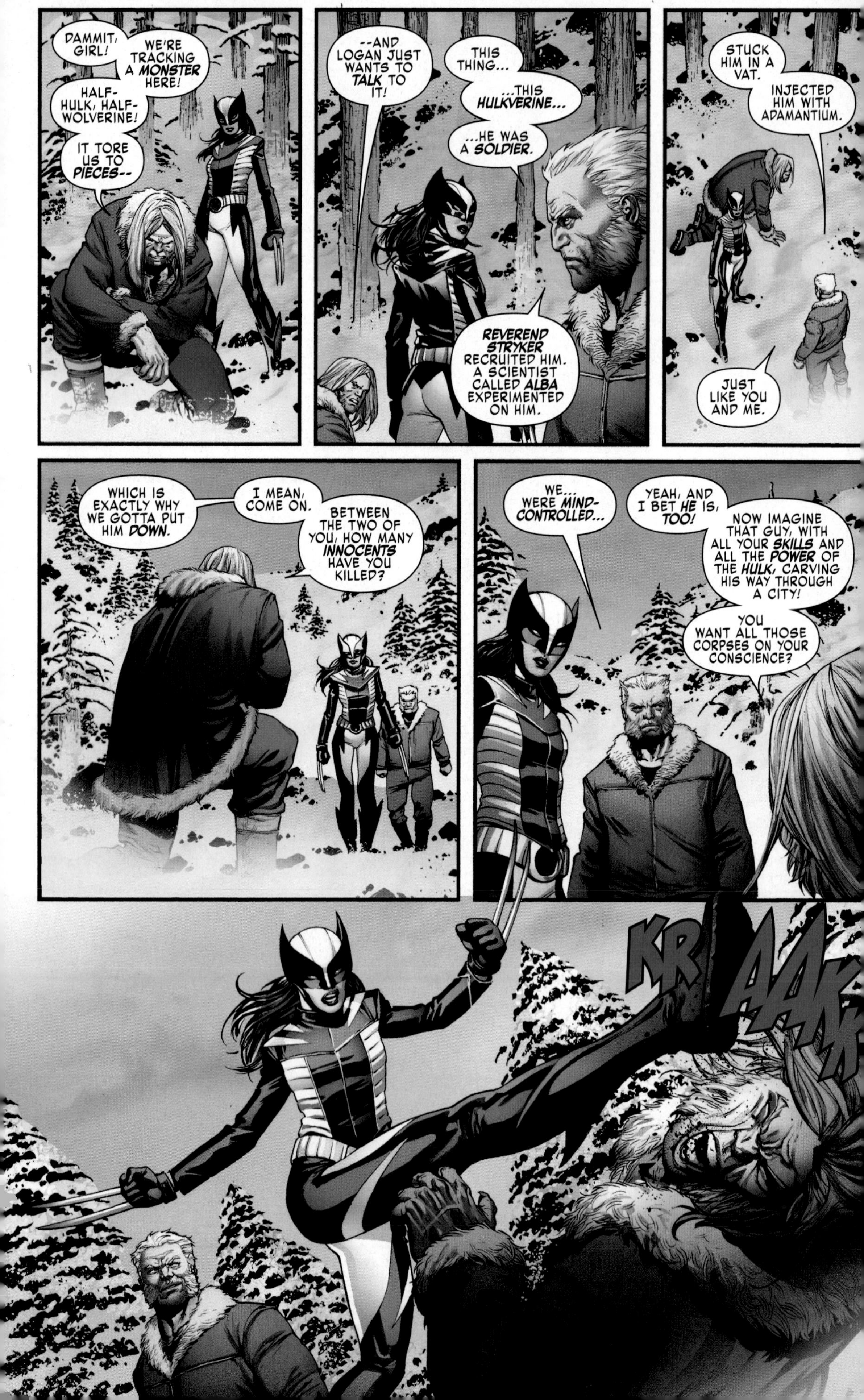

DAMMIT, GIRL!
WE'RE TRACKING A MONSTER HERE!
HALF-HULK, HALF-WOLVERINE!
IT TORE US TO PIECES--
--AND LOGAN JUST WANTS TO TALK TO IT!
THIS THING...
...THIS HULKVERINE...
...HE WAS A SOLDIER.
REVEREND STRYKER RECRUITED HIM. A SCIENTIST CALLED ALBA EXPERIMENTED ON HIM.
STUCK HIM IN A VAT.
INJECTED HIM WITH ADAMANTIUM.
JUST LIKE YOU AND ME.
WHICH IS EXACTLY WHY WE GOTTA PUT HIM DOWN.
I MEAN, COME ON.
BETWEEN THE TWO OF YOU, HOW MANY INNOCENTS HAVE YOU KILLED?
WE... WERE MIND-CONTROLLED...
YEAH, AND I BET HE IS, TOO!
NOW IMAGINE THAT GUY, WITH ALL YOUR SKILLS AND ALL THE POWER OF THE HULK, CARVING HIS WAY THROUGH A CITY!
YOU WANT ALL THOSE CORPSES ON YOUR CONSCIENCE?
KRAAK

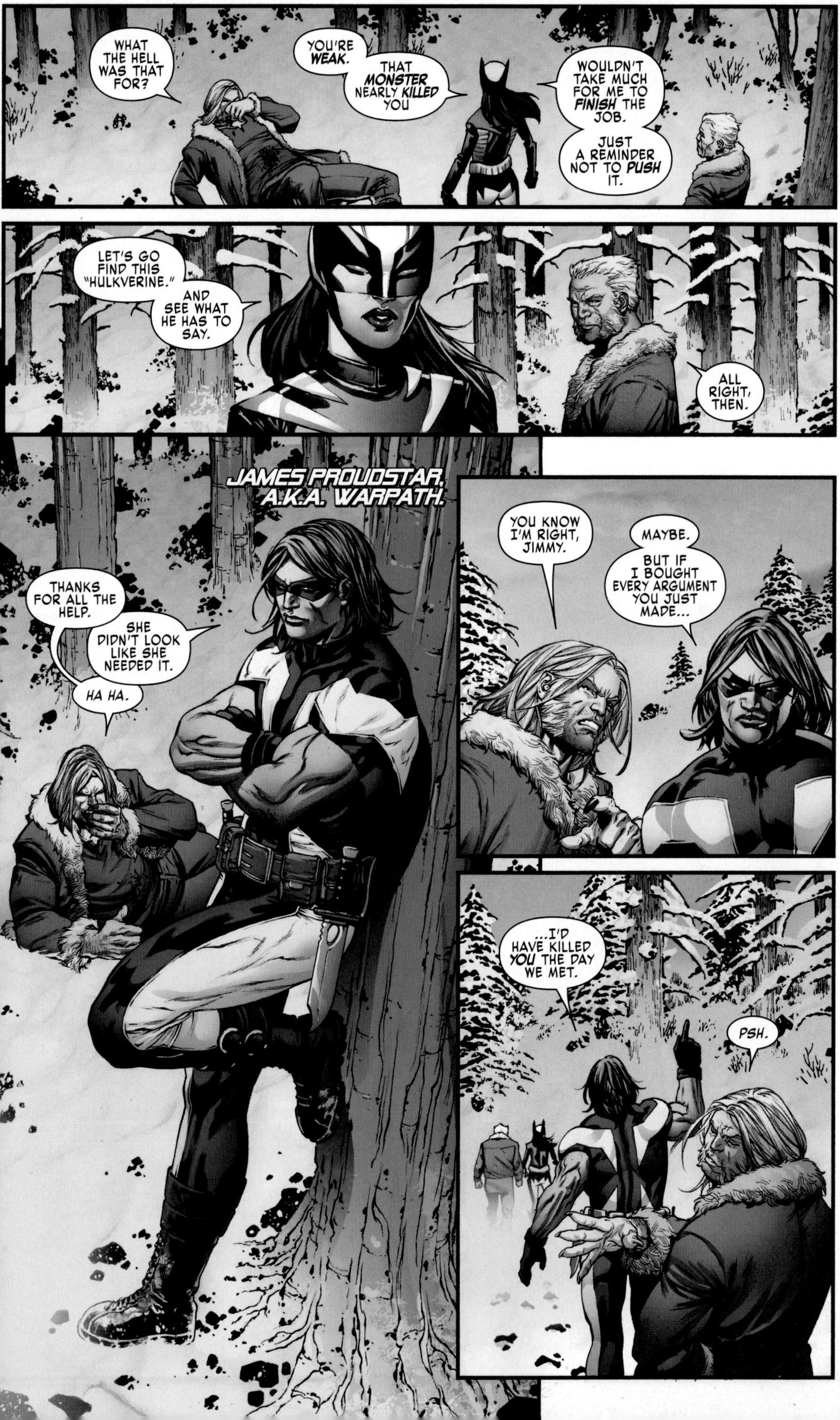
WHAT THE HELL WAS THAT FOR?
YOU'RE WEAK.
THAT MONSTER NEARLY KILLED YOU
WOULDN'T TAKE MUCH FOR ME TO FINISH THE JOB.
JUST A REMINDER NOT TO PUSH IT.
LET'S GO FIND THIS "HULKVERINE."
AND SEE WHAT HE HAS TO SAY.
ALL RIGHT, THEN.
JAMES PROUDSTAR, A.K.A. WARPATH.
THANKS FOR ALL THE HELP.
SHE DIDN'T LOOK LIKE SHE NEEDED IT.
HA HA.
YOU KNOW I'M RIGHT, JIMMY.
MAYBE.
BUT IF I BOUGHT EVERY ARGUMENT YOU JUST MADE...
...I'D HAVE KILLED YOU THE DAY WE MET.
PSH.

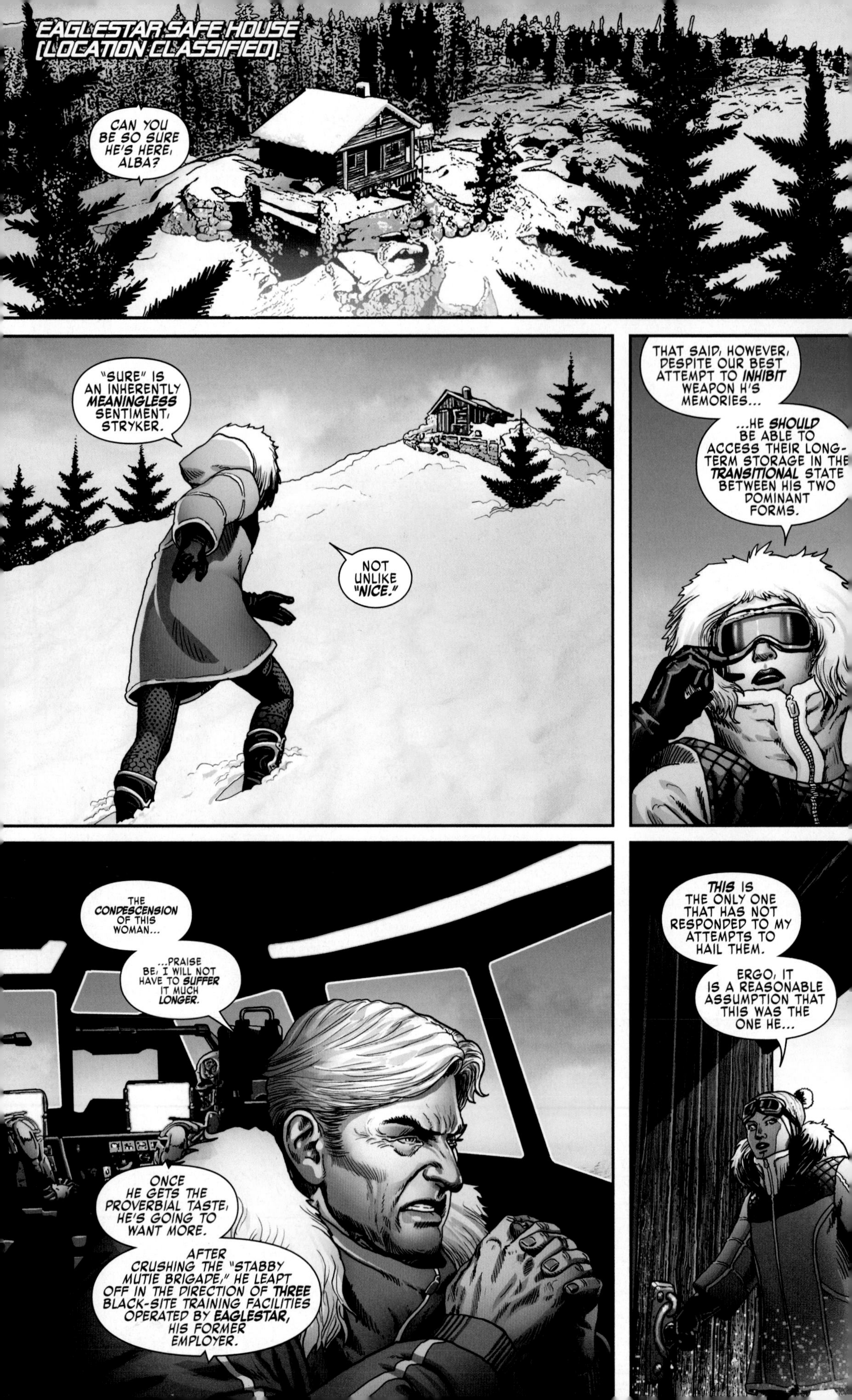
EAGLESTAR SAFE HOUSE [LOCATION CLASSIFIED].
CAN YOU BE SO SURE HE'S HERE, ALBA?
"SURE" IS AN INHERENTLY MEANINGLESS SENTIMENT, STRYKER.
NOT UNLIKE "NICE."
THAT SAID, HOWEVER, DESPITE OUR BEST ATTEMPT TO INHIBIT WEAPON H'S MEMORIES...
...HE SHOULD BE ABLE TO ACCESS THEIR LONG-TERM STORAGE IN THE TRANSITIONAL STATE BETWEEN HIS TWO DOMINANT FORMS.
THE CONDESCENSION OF THIS WOMAN...
...PRAISE BE, I WILL NOT HAVE TO SUFFER IT MUCH LONGER.
ONCE HE GETS THE PROVERBIAL TASTE, HE'S GOING TO WANT MORE.
AFTER CRUSHING THE "STABBY MUTIE BRIGADE," HE LEAPT OFF IN THE DIRECTION OF THREE BLACK-SITE TRAINING FACILITIES OPERATED BY EAGLESTAR, HIS FORMER EMPLOYER.
THIS IS THE ONLY ONE THAT HAS NOT RESPONDED TO MY ATTEMPTS TO HAIL THEM.
ERGO, IT IS A REASONABLE ASSUMPTION THAT THIS WAS THE ONE HE...

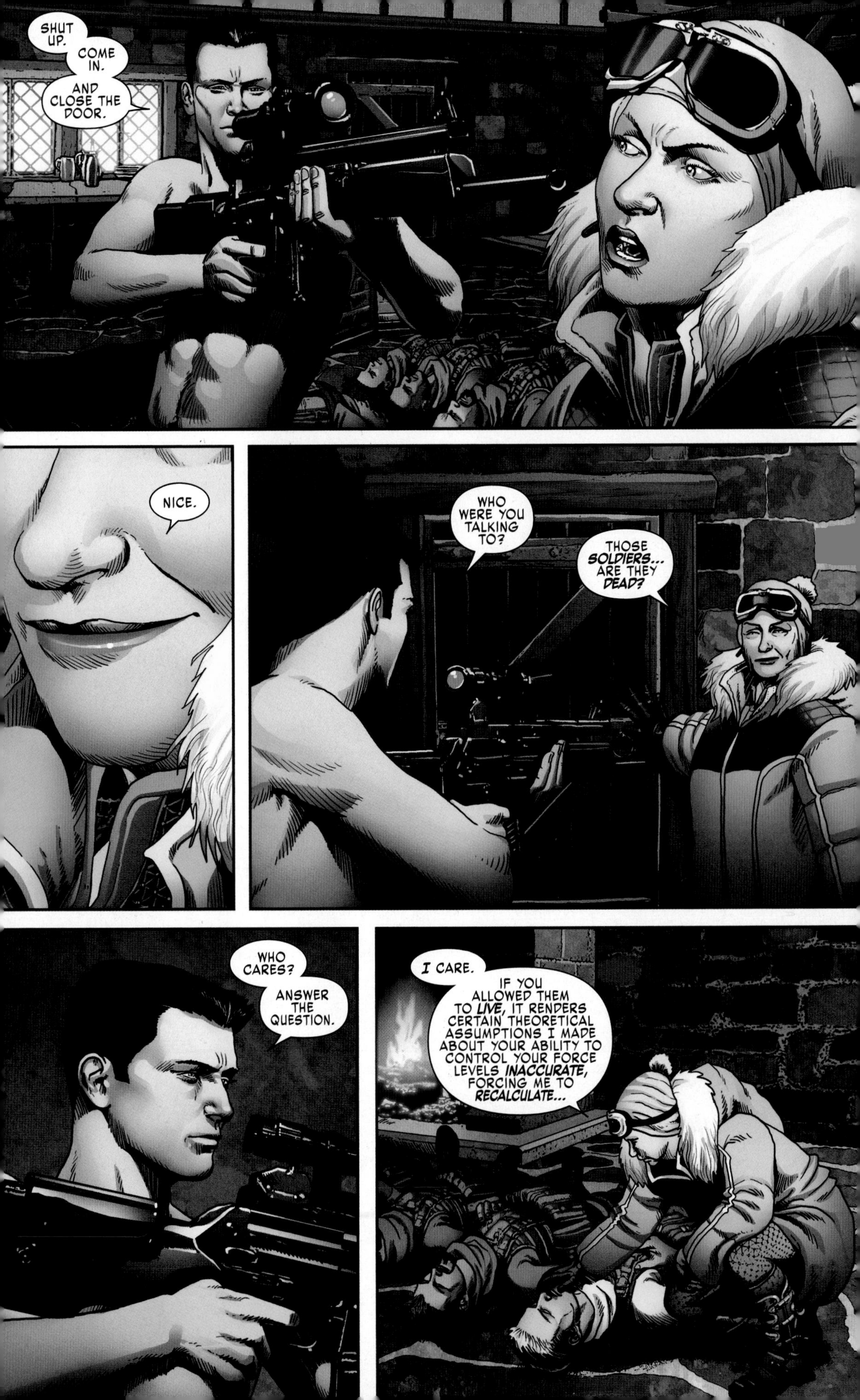
SHUT UP.
COME IN.
AND CLOSE THE DOOR.
NICE.
WHO WERE YOU TALKING TO?
THOSE SOLDIERS... ARE THEY DEAD?
WHO CARES?
ANSWER THE QUESTION.
I CARE.
IF YOU ALLOWED THEM TO LIVE, IT RENDERS CERTAIN THEORETICAL ASSUMPTIONS I MADE ABOUT YOUR ABILITY TO CONTROL YOUR FORCE LEVELS INACCURATE, FORCING ME TO RECALCULATE...

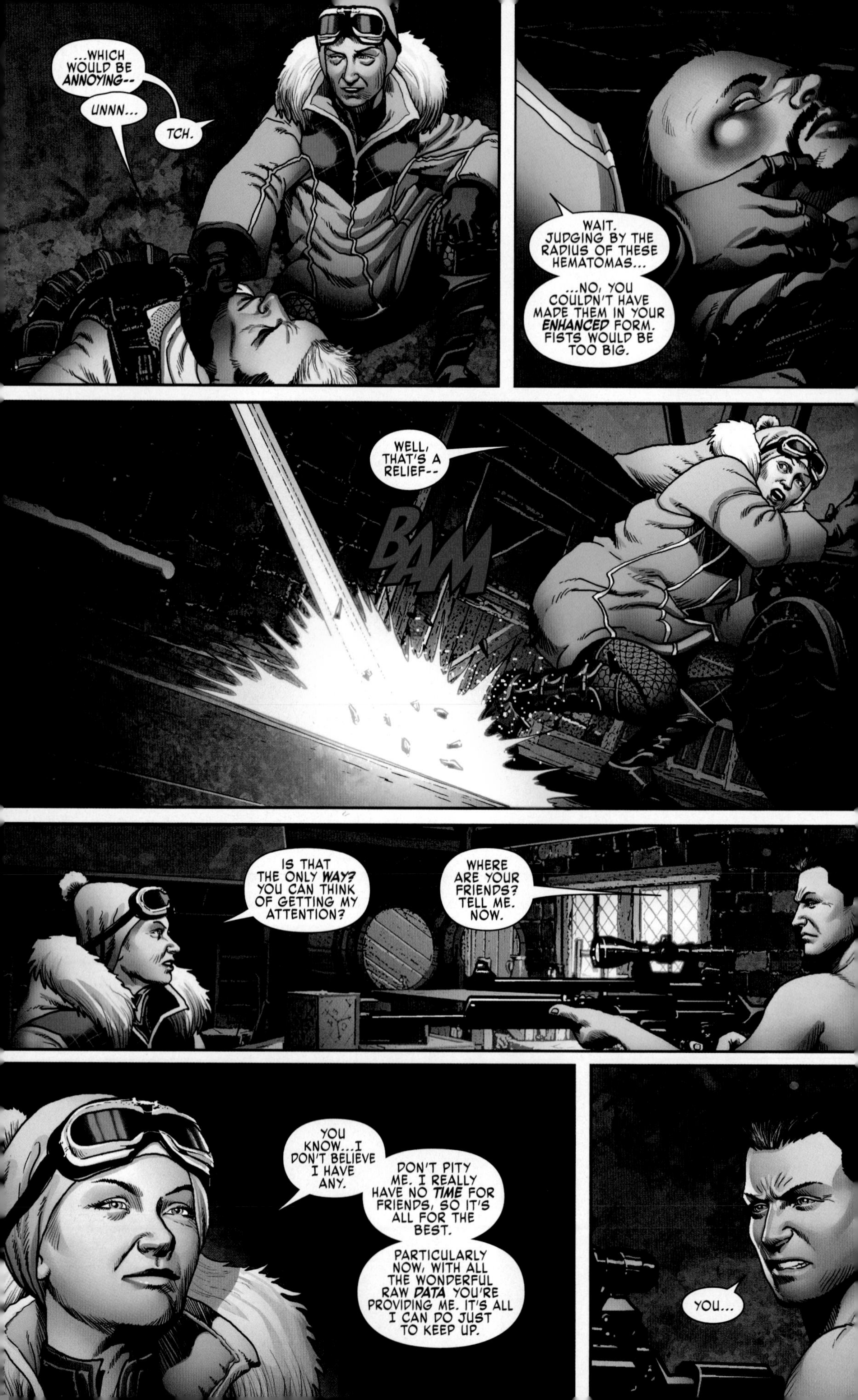
...WHICH WOULD BE ANNOYING--
UNNN...
TCH.
WAIT. JUDGING BY THE RADIUS OF THESE HEMATOMAS...
...NO, YOU COULDN'T HAVE MADE THEM IN YOUR ENHANCED FORM. FISTS WOULD BE TOO BIG.
WELL, THAT'S A RELIEF--
BAM
IS THAT THE ONLY WAY? YOU CAN THINK OF GETTING MY ATTENTION?
WHERE ARE YOUR FRIENDS? TELL ME. NOW.
YOU KNOW...I DON'T BELIEVE I HAVE ANY.
DON'T PITY ME. I REALLY HAVE NO TIME FOR FRIENDS, SO IT'S ALL FOR THE BEST.
PARTICULARLY NOW, WITH ALL THE WONDERFUL RAW DATA YOU'RE PROVIDING ME. IT'S ALL I CAN DO JUST TO KEEP UP.
YOU...

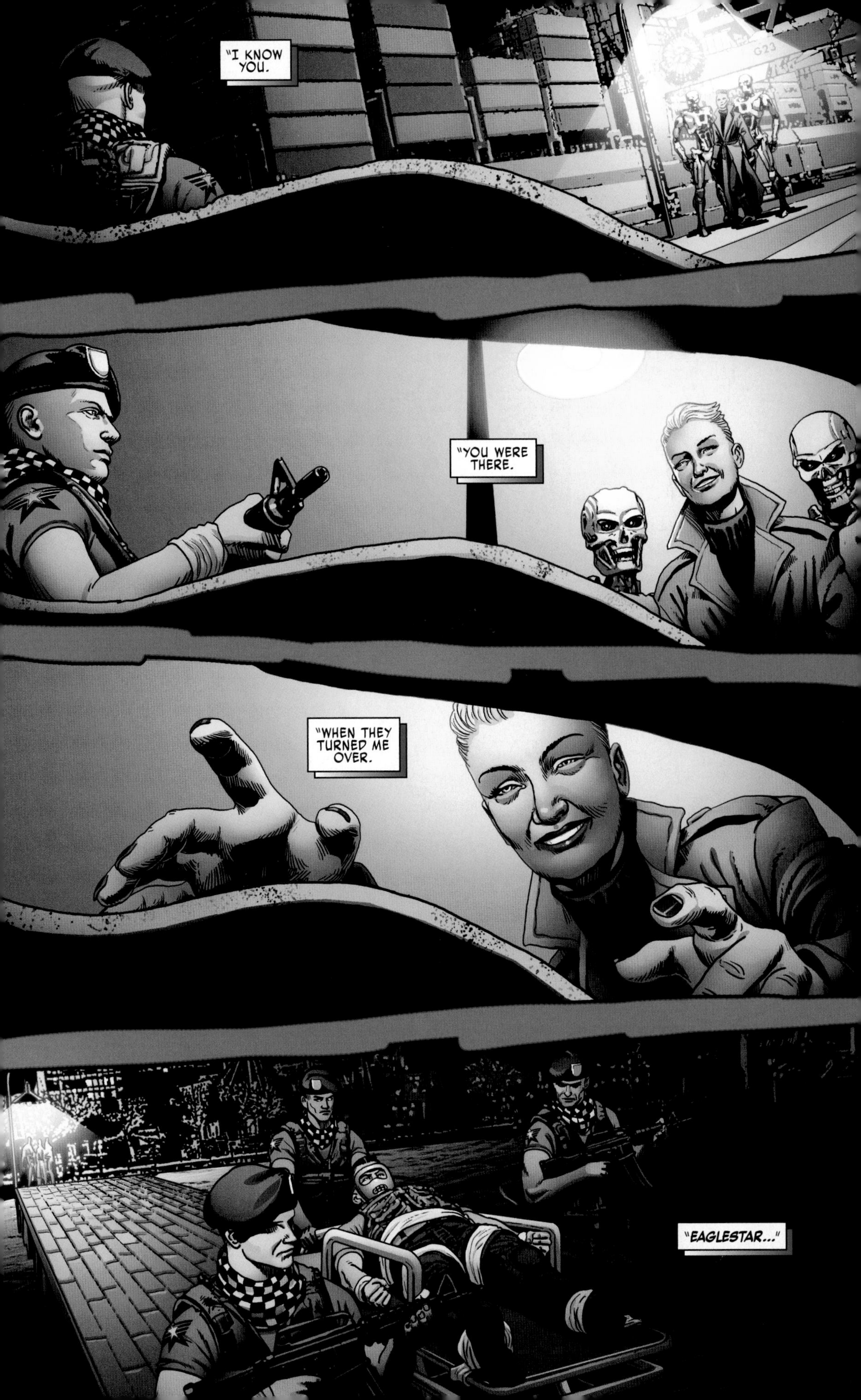
"I KNOW YOU.
G23
"YOU WERE THERE.
"WHEN THEY TURNED ME OVER.
"EAGLESTAR..."

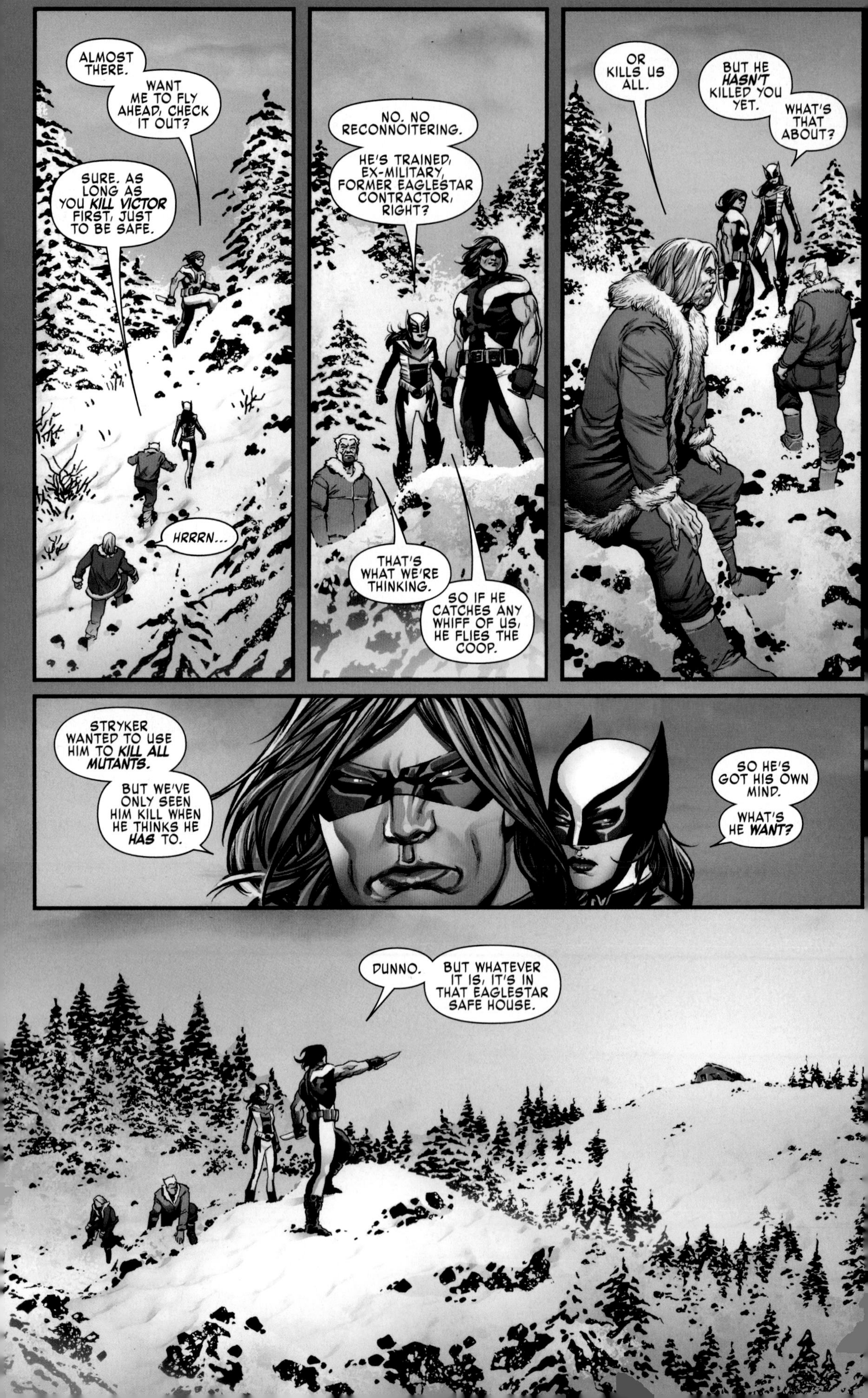
ALMOST THERE.
WANT ME TO FLY AHEAD, CHECK IT OUT?
SURE. AS LONG AS YOU KILL VICTOR FIRST, JUST TO BE SAFE.
HRRRN...
NO. NO RECONNOITERING.
HE'S TRAINED, EX-MILITARY, FORMER EAGLESTAR CONTRACTOR, RIGHT?
THAT'S WHAT WE'RE THINKING.
SO IF HE CATCHES ANY WHIFF OF US, HE FLIES THE COOP.
OR KILLS US ALL.
BUT HE HASN'T KILLED YOU YET.
WHAT'S THAT ABOUT?
STRYKER WANTED TO USE HIM TO KILL ALL MUTANTS.
BUT WE'VE ONLY SEEN HIM KILL WHEN HE THINKS HE HAS TO.
SO HE'S GOT HIS OWN MIND.
WHAT'S HE WANT?
DUNNO.
BUT WHATEVER IT IS, IT'S IN THAT EAGLESTAR SAFE HOUSE.

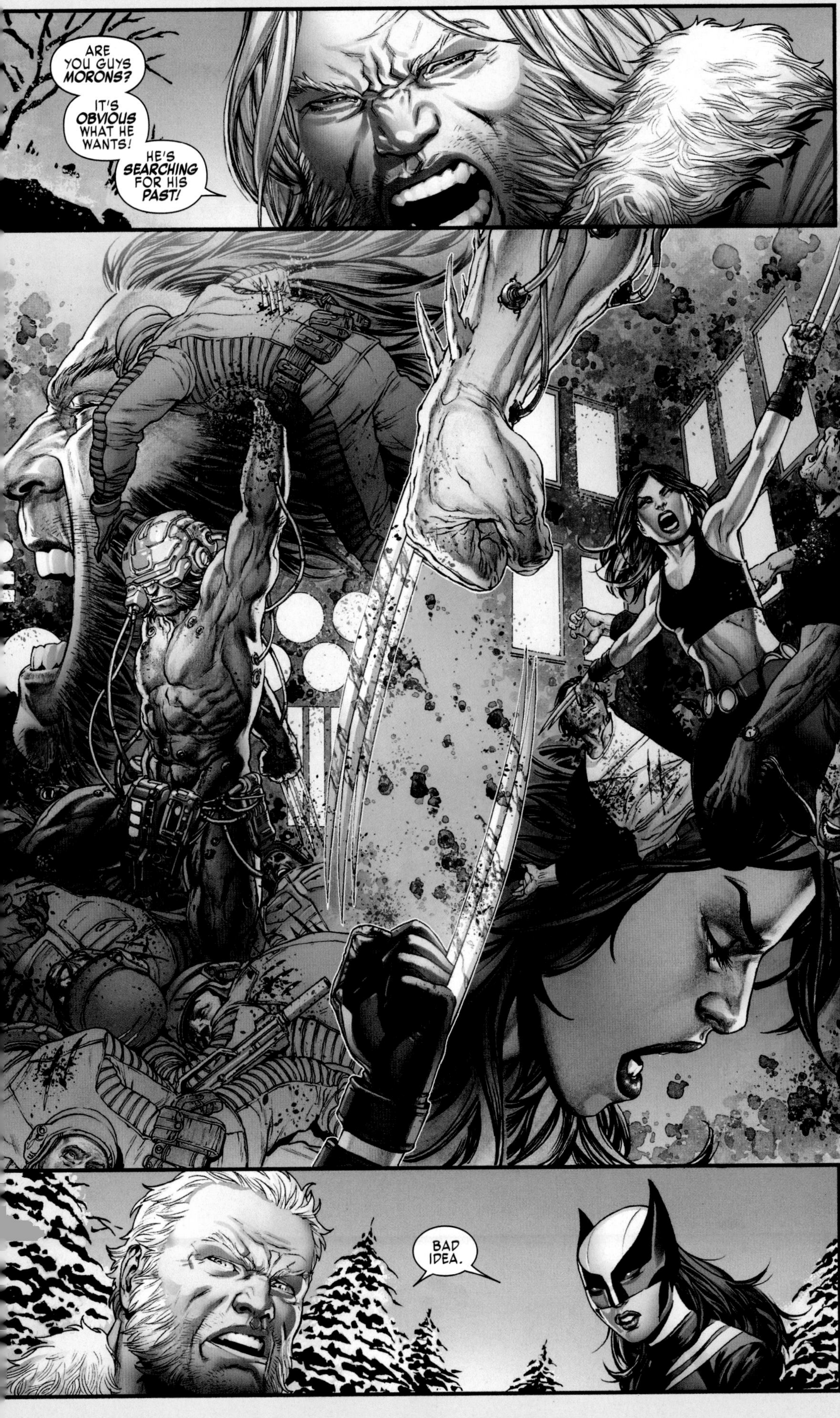
ARE YOU GUYS MORONS?
IT'S OBVIOUS WHAT HE WANTS!
HE'S SEARCHING FOR HIS PAST!
BAD IDEA.

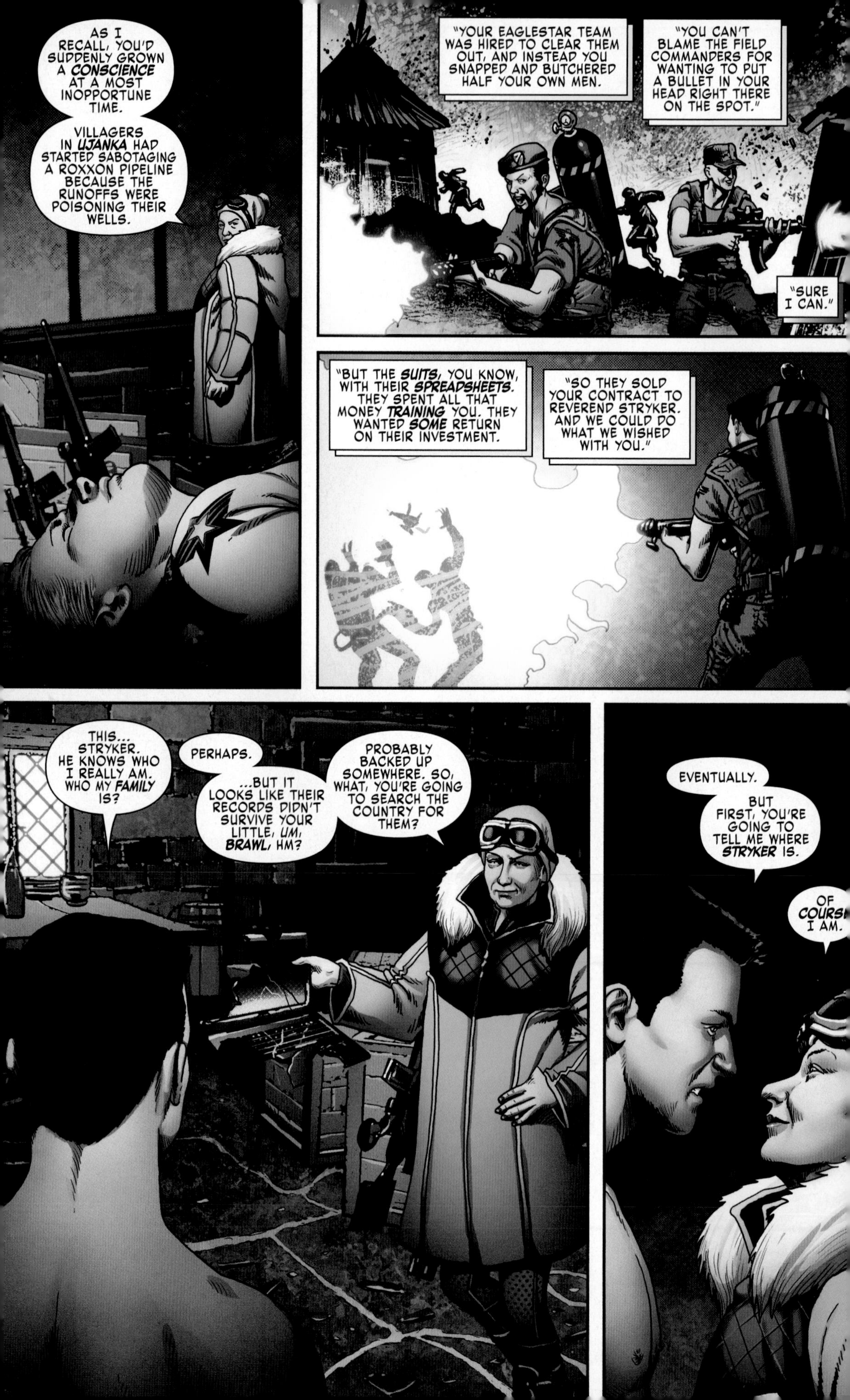
AS I RECALL, YOU'D SUDDENLY GROWN A *CONSCIENCE* AT A MOST INOPPORTUNE TIME.
VILLAGERS IN *UJANKA* HAD STARTED SABOTAGING A ROXXON PIPELINE BECAUSE THE RUNOFFS WERE POISONING THEIR WELLS.
"YOUR EAGLESTAR TEAM WAS HIRED TO CLEAR THEM OUT, AND INSTEAD YOU SNAPPED AND BUTCHERED HALF YOUR OWN MEN.
"YOU CAN'T BLAME THE FIELD COMMANDERS FOR WANTING TO PUT A BULLET IN YOUR HEAD RIGHT THERE ON THE SPOT."
"SURE I CAN."
"BUT THE *SUITS*, YOU KNOW, WITH THEIR *SPREADSHEETS*. THEY SPENT ALL THAT MONEY *TRAINING* YOU. THEY WANTED *SOME* RETURN ON THEIR INVESTMENT.
"SO THEY SOLD YOUR CONTRACT TO REVEREND STRYKER. AND WE COULD DO WHAT WE WISHED WITH YOU."
THIS... STRYKER. HE KNOWS WHO I REALLY AM. WHO MY *FAMILY* IS?
PERHAPS.
...BUT IT LOOKS LIKE THEIR RECORDS DIDN'T SURVIVE YOUR LITTLE, *UM*, *BRAWL*, HM?
PROBABLY BACKED UP SOMEWHERE. SO, WHAT, YOU'RE GOING TO SEARCH THE COUNTRY FOR THEM?
EVENTUALLY.
BUT FIRST, YOU'RE GOING TO TELL ME WHERE *STRYKER* IS.
OF *COURS* I AM.

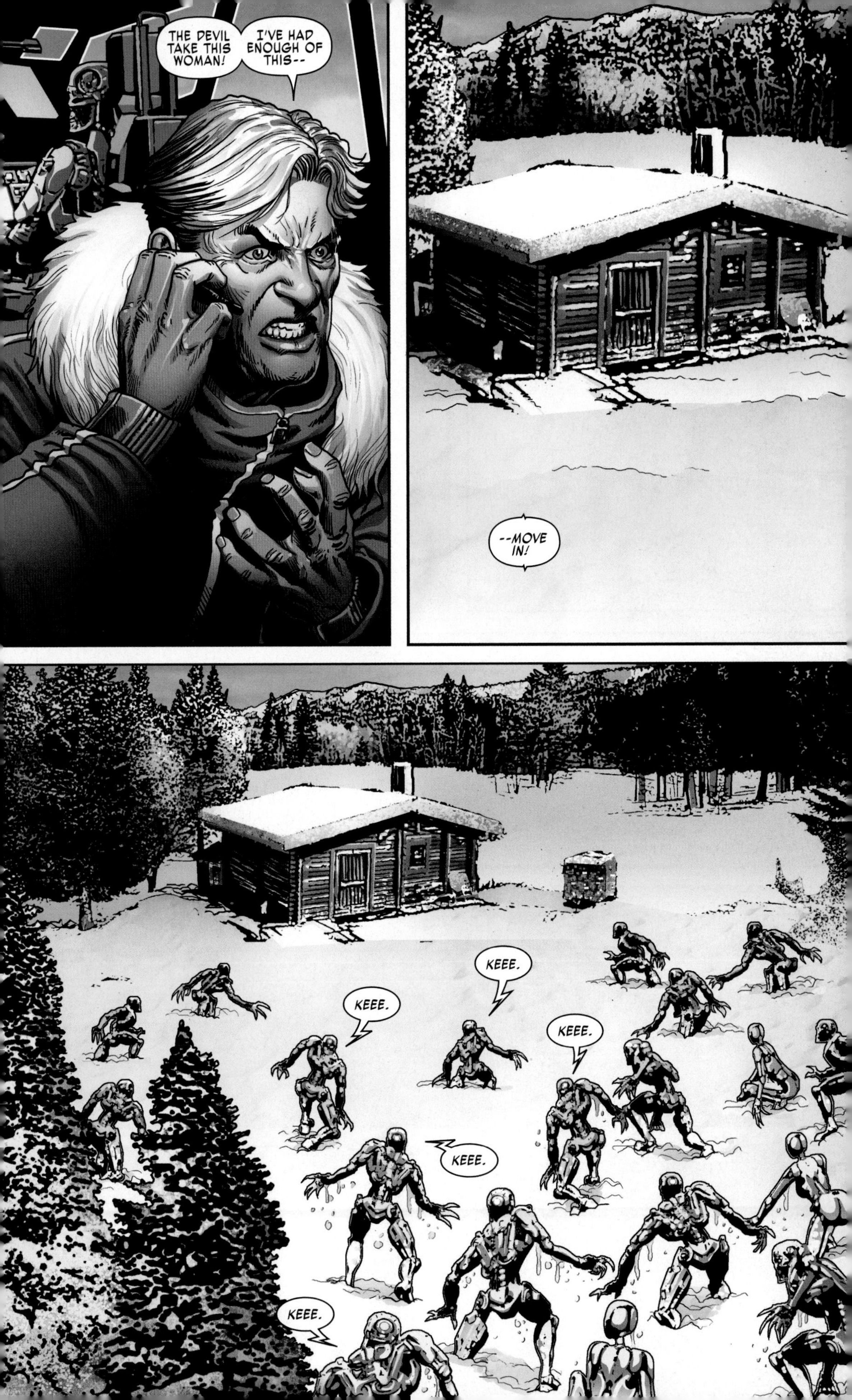
THE DEVIL TAKE THIS WOMAN!
I'VE HAD ENOUGH OF THIS--
--MOVE IN!
KEEE.
KEEE.
KEEE.
KEEE.
KEEE.

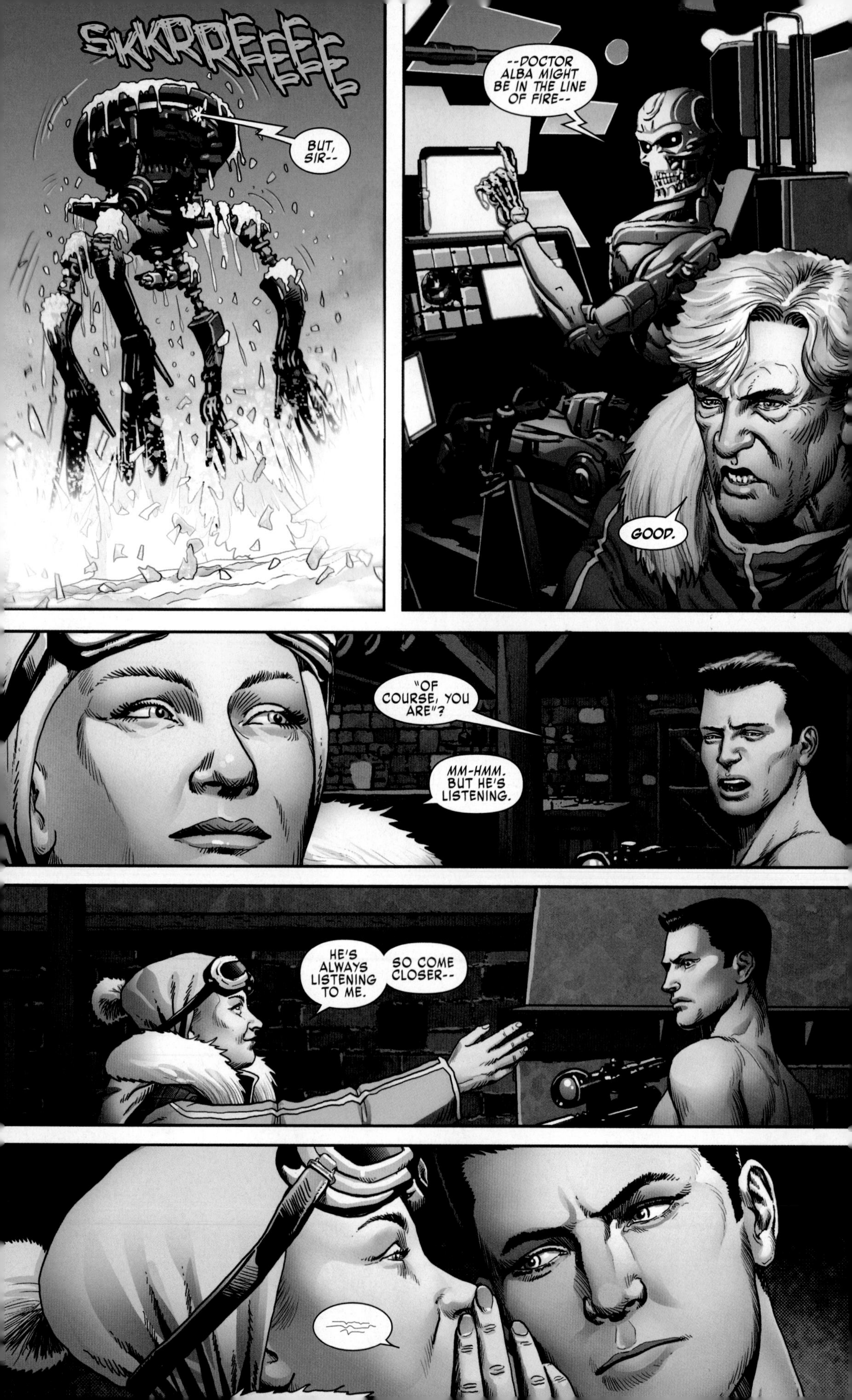
SKKRREEEEE
BUT, SIR--
--DOCTOR ALBA MIGHT BE IN THE LINE OF FIRE--
GOOD.
"OF COURSE, YOU ARE"?
MM-HMM. BUT HE'S LISTENING.
HE'S ALWAYS LISTENING TO ME.
SO COME CLOSER--

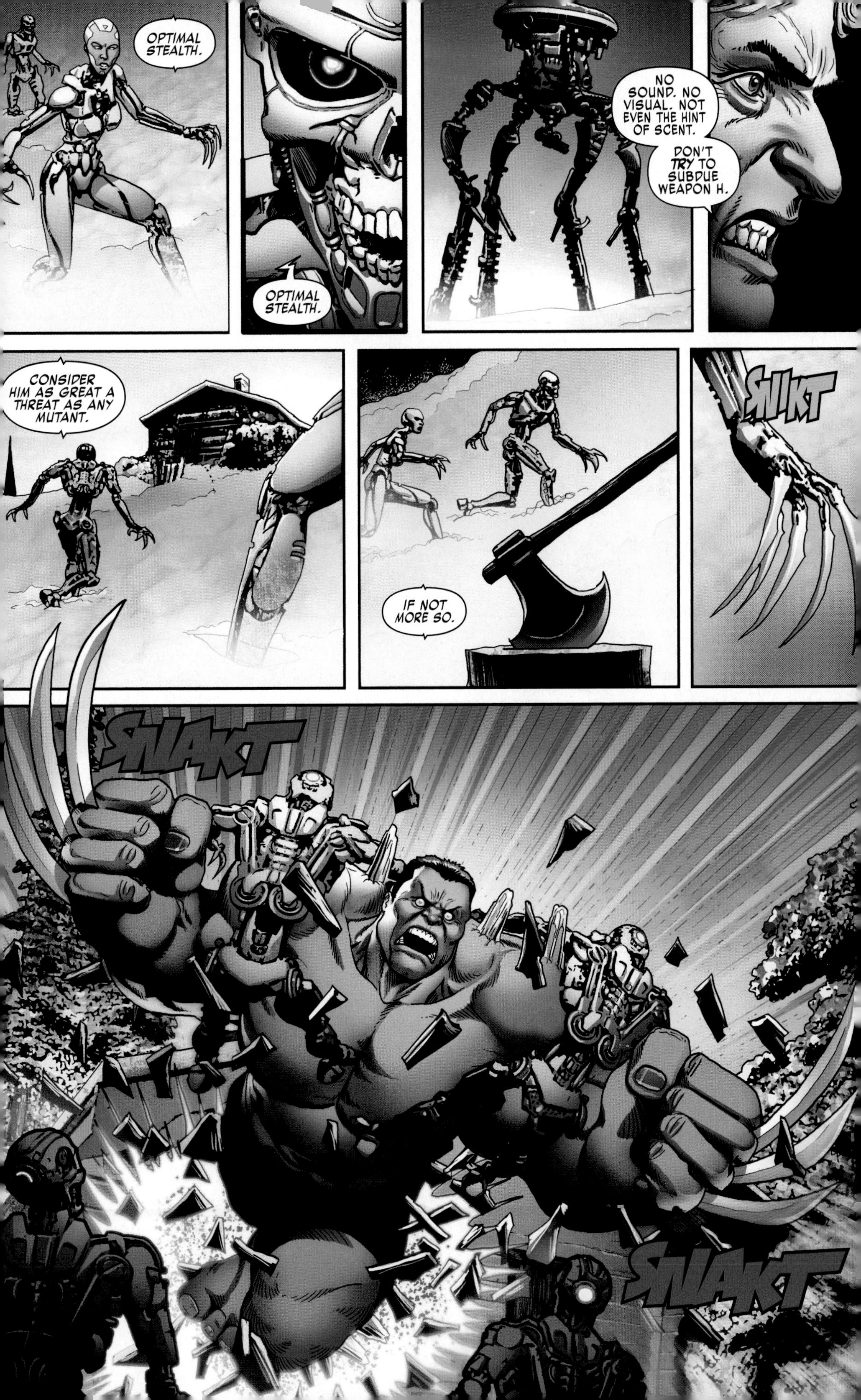
OPTIMAL STEALTH.
OPTIMAL STEALTH.
NO SOUND. NO VISUAL. NOT EVEN THE HINT OF SCENT.
DON'T TRY TO SUBDUE WEAPON H.
CONSIDER HIM AS GREAT A THREAT AS ANY MUTANT.
IF NOT MORE SO.
SNIKT
SNAKT
SNAKT

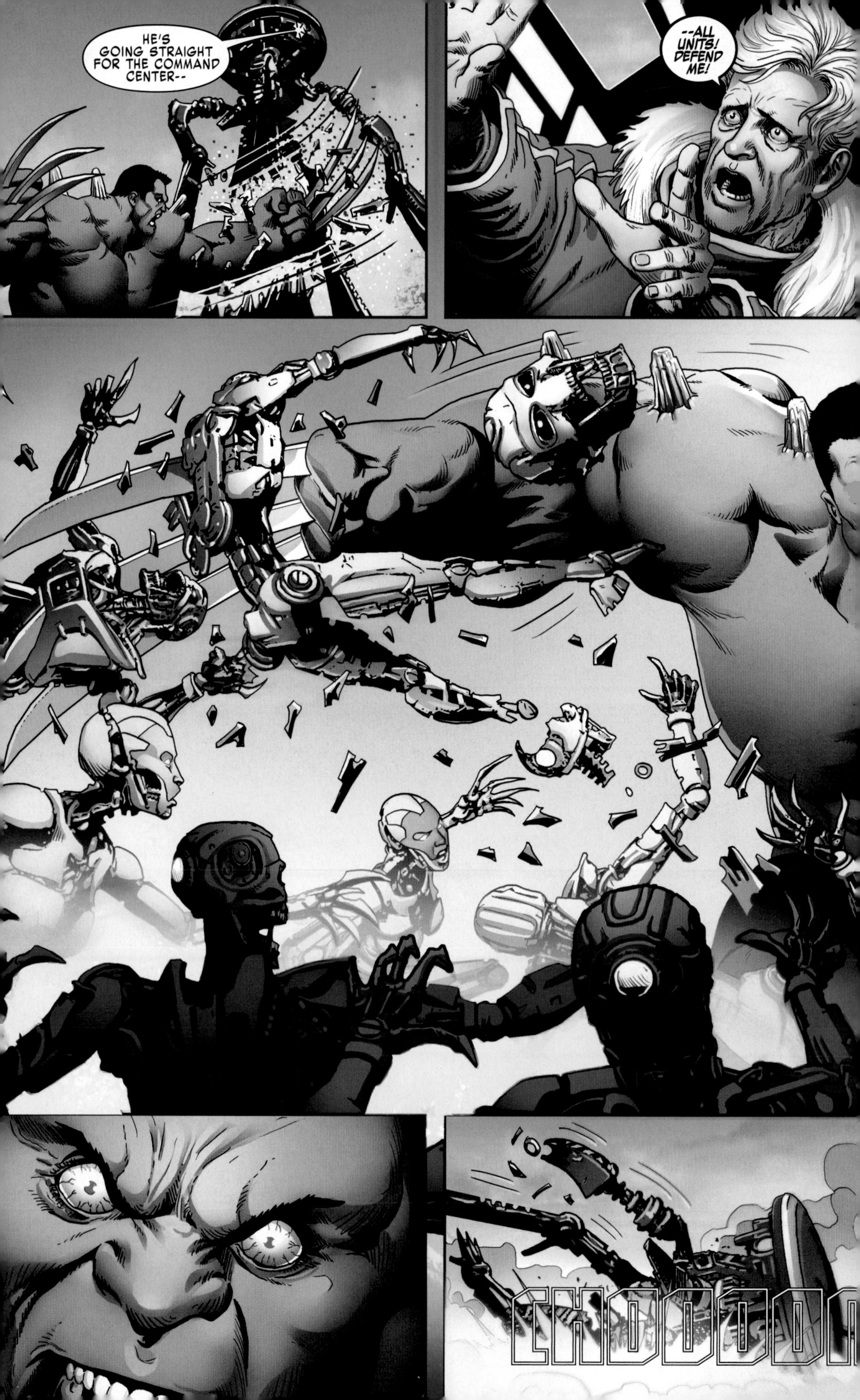
HE'S GOING STRAIGHT FOR THE COMMAND CENTER--
--ALL UNITS! DEFEND ME!

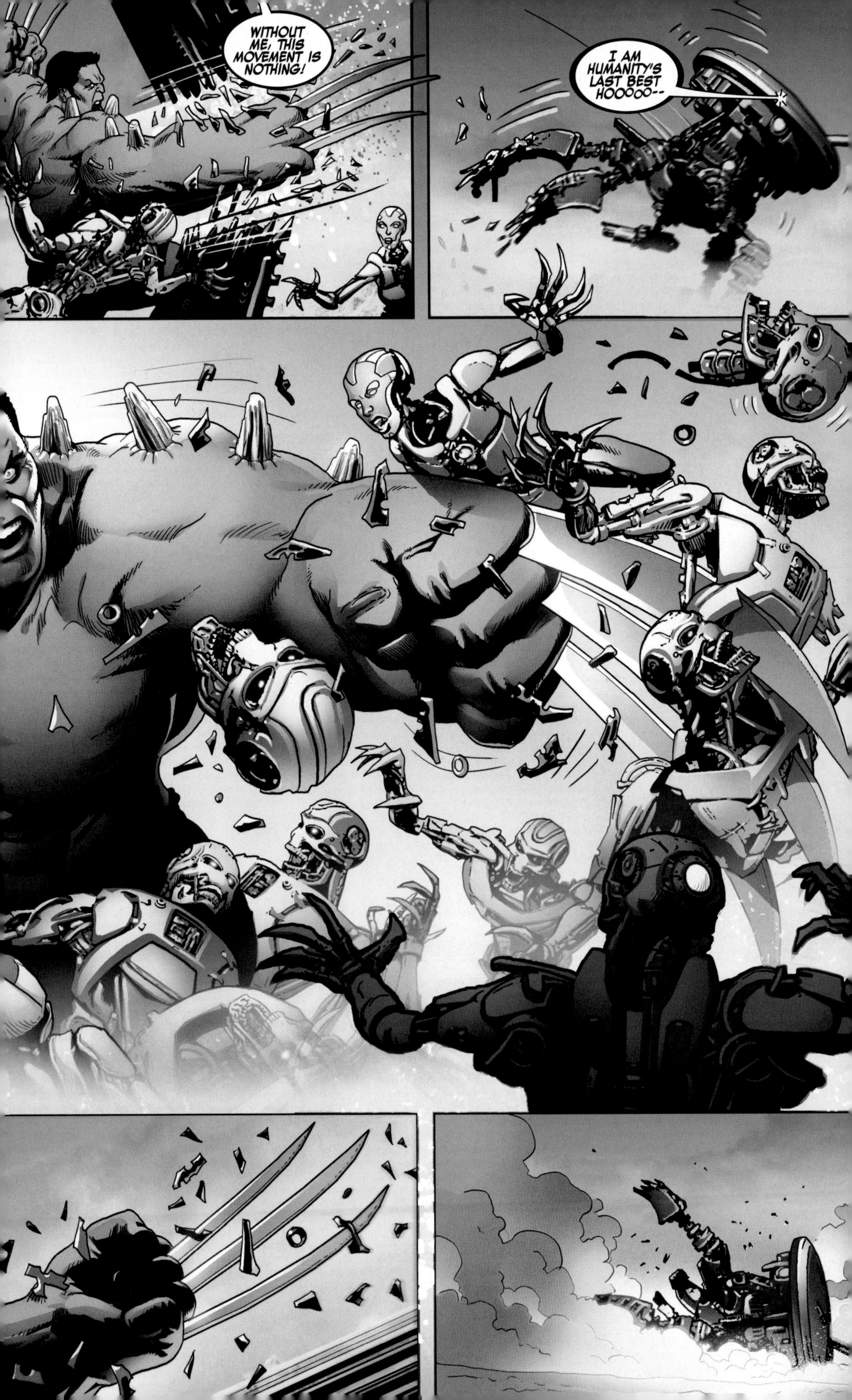
WITHOUT ME, THIS MOVEMENT IS NOTHING!
I AM HUMANITY'S LAST BEST HOOOOO--

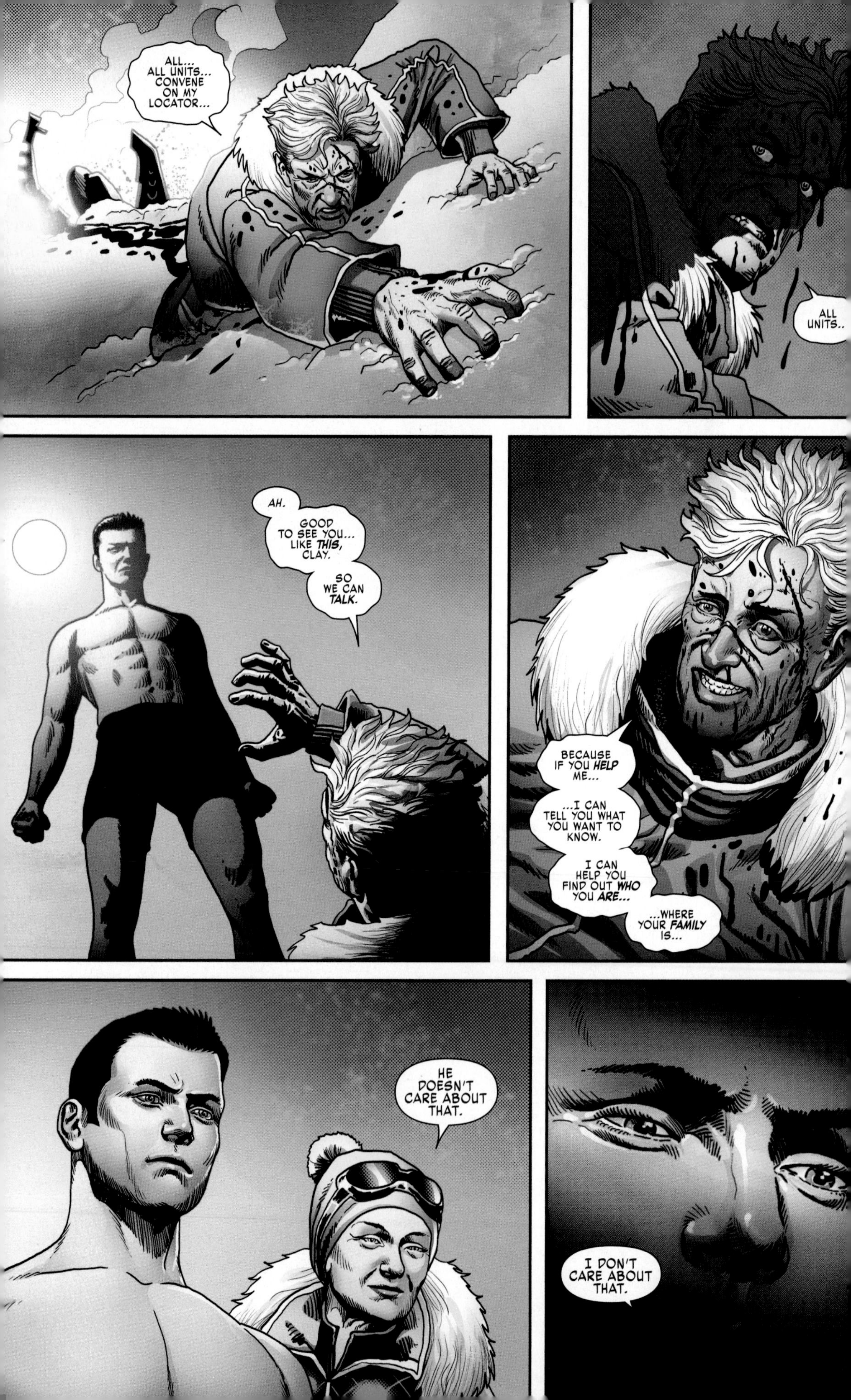
ALL... ALL UNITS... CONVENE ON MY LOCATOR...
ALL UNITS...
AH.
GOOD TO SEE YOU... LIKE THIS, CLAY.
SO WE CAN TALK.
BECAUSE IF YOU HELP ME...
...I CAN TELL YOU WHAT YOU WANT TO KNOW.
I CAN HELP YOU FIND OUT WHO YOU ARE...
...WHERE YOUR FAMILY IS...
HE DOESN'T CARE ABOUT THAT.
I DON'T CARE ABOUT THAT.

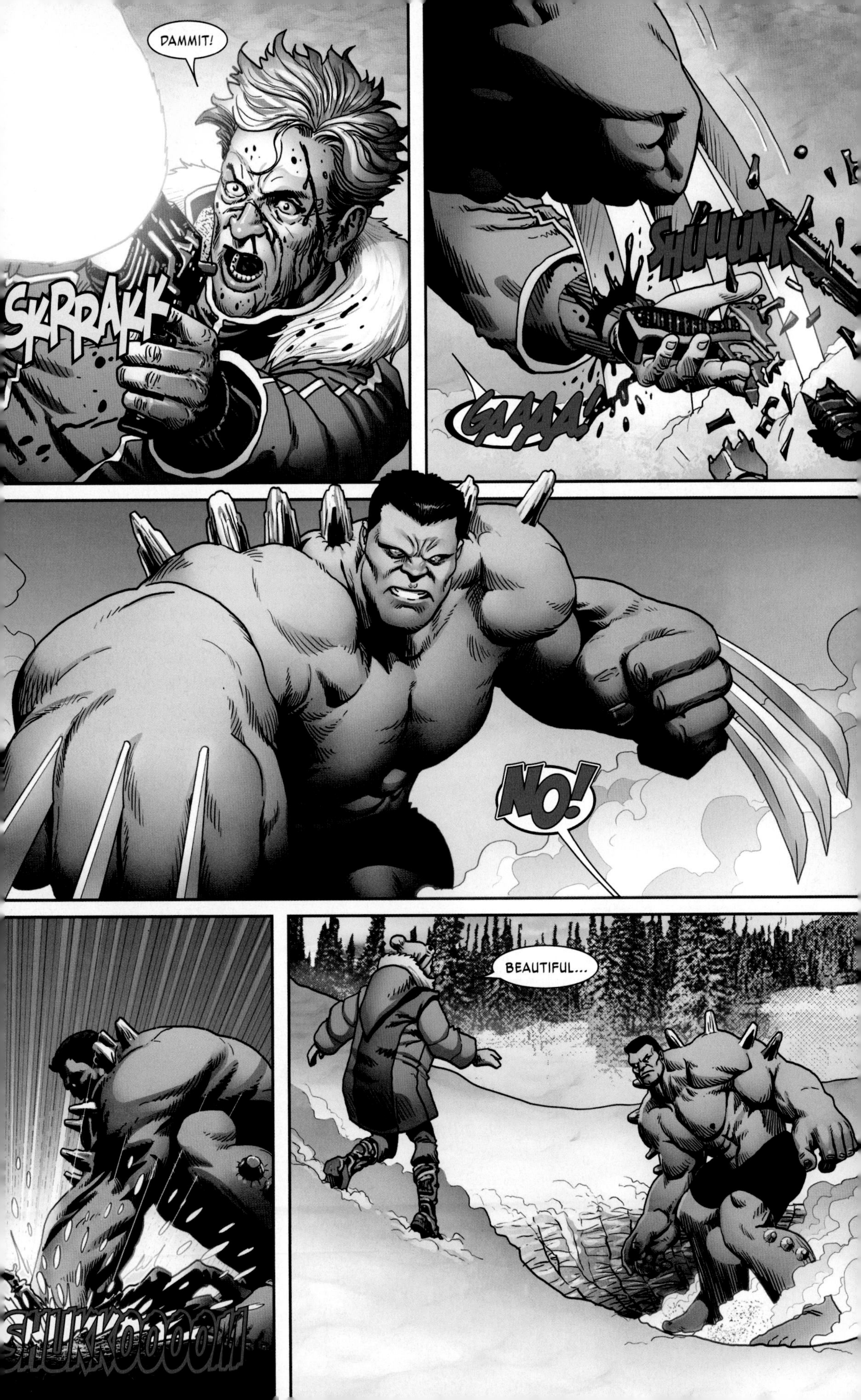
DAMMIT!
SKRRAKK
SHUUUNK
GAAAA!
NO!
SHUKKOOOOM
BEAUTIFUL...

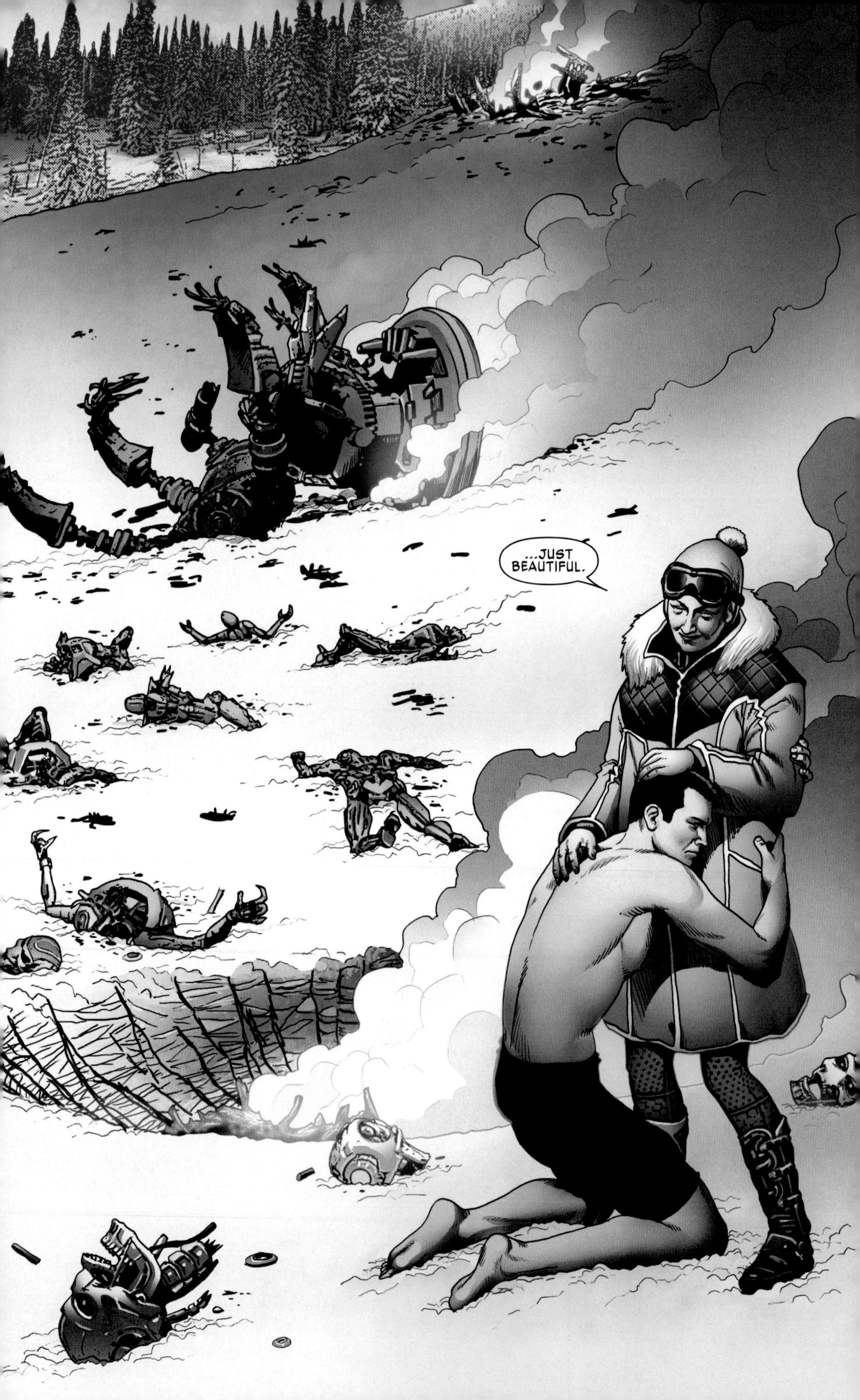
...JUST BEAUTIFUL.

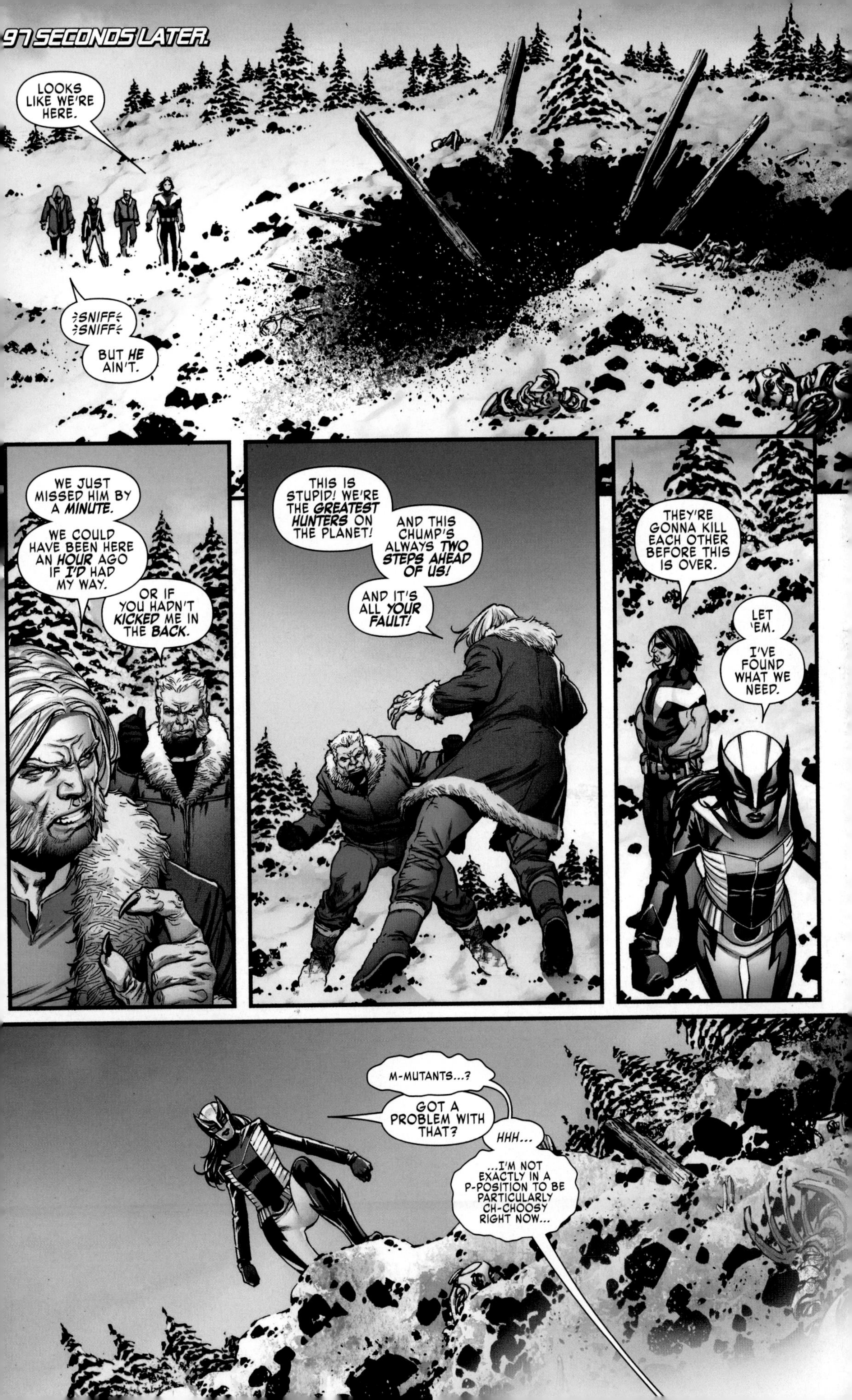
97 SECONDS LATER.
LOOKS LIKE WE'RE HERE.
SNIFF SNIFF
BUT HE AIN'T.
WE JUST MISSED HIM BY A MINUTE.
WE COULD HAVE BEEN HERE AN HOUR AGO IF I'D HAD MY WAY.
OR IF YOU HADN'T KICKED ME IN THE BACK.
THIS IS STUPID! WE'RE THE GREATEST HUNTERS ON THE PLANET!
AND THIS CHUMP'S ALWAYS TWO STEPS AHEAD OF US!
AND IT'S ALL YOUR FAULT!
THEY'RE GONNA KILL EACH OTHER BEFORE THIS IS OVER.
LET 'EM.
I'VE FOUND WHAT WE NEED.
M-MUTANTS...?
GOT A PROBLEM WITH THAT?
HHH...
...I'M NOT EXACTLY IN A P-POSITION TO BE PARTICULARLY CH-CHOOSY RIGHT NOW...

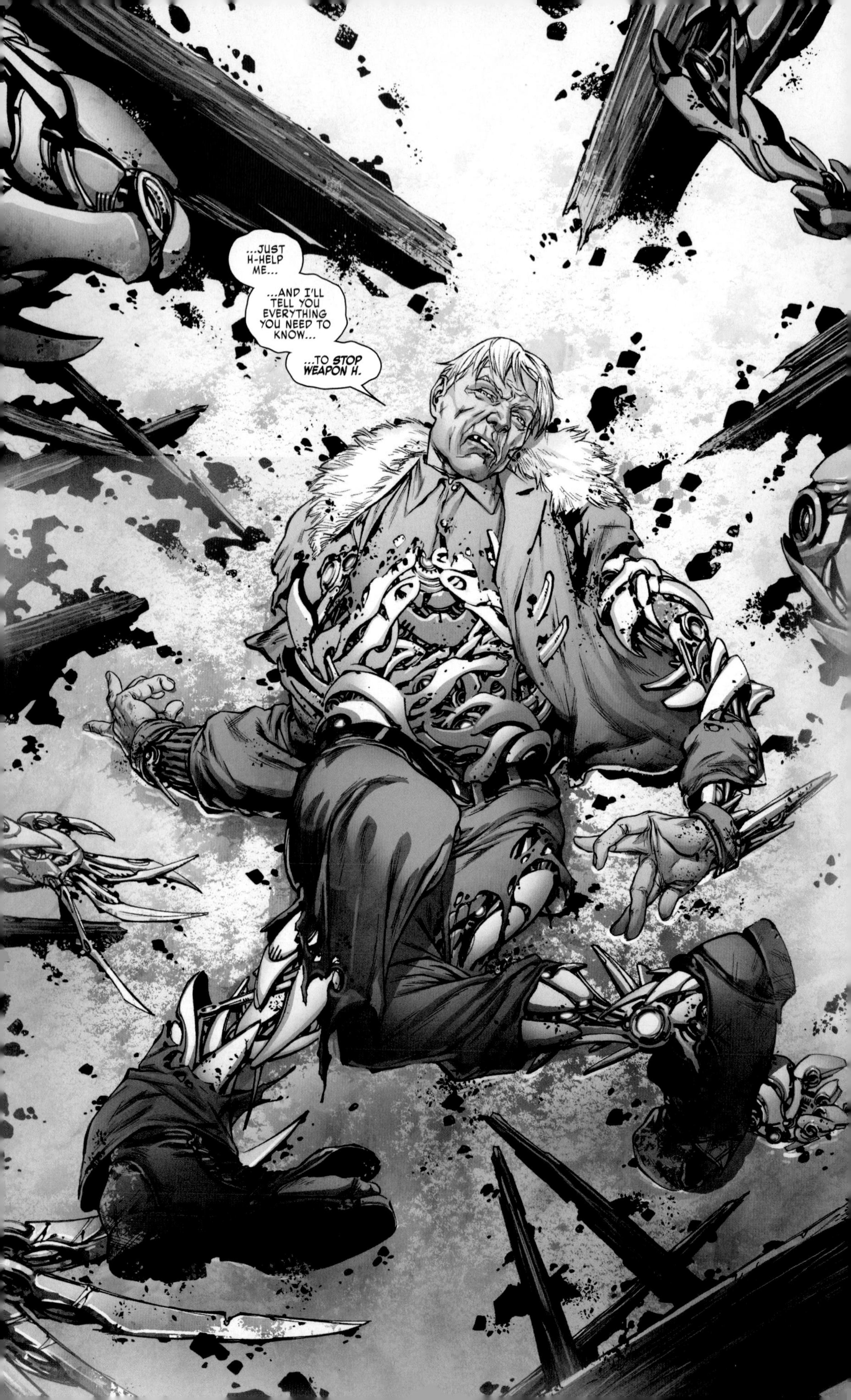
...JUST H-HELP ME...
...AND I'LL TELL YOU EVERYTHING YOU NEED TO KNOW...
...TO **STOP WEAPON H.**

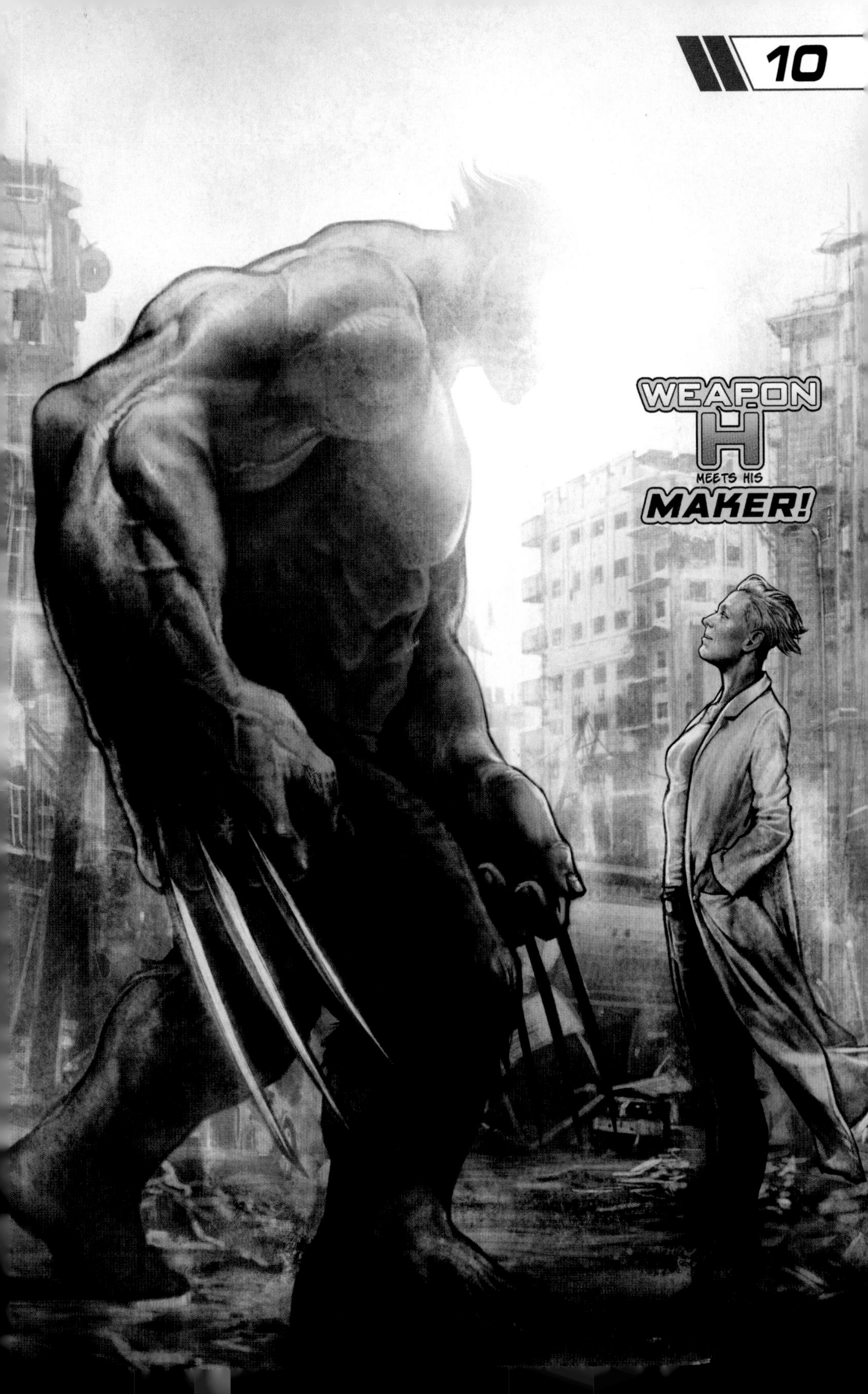
10
WEAPON H
MEETS HIS
MAKER!

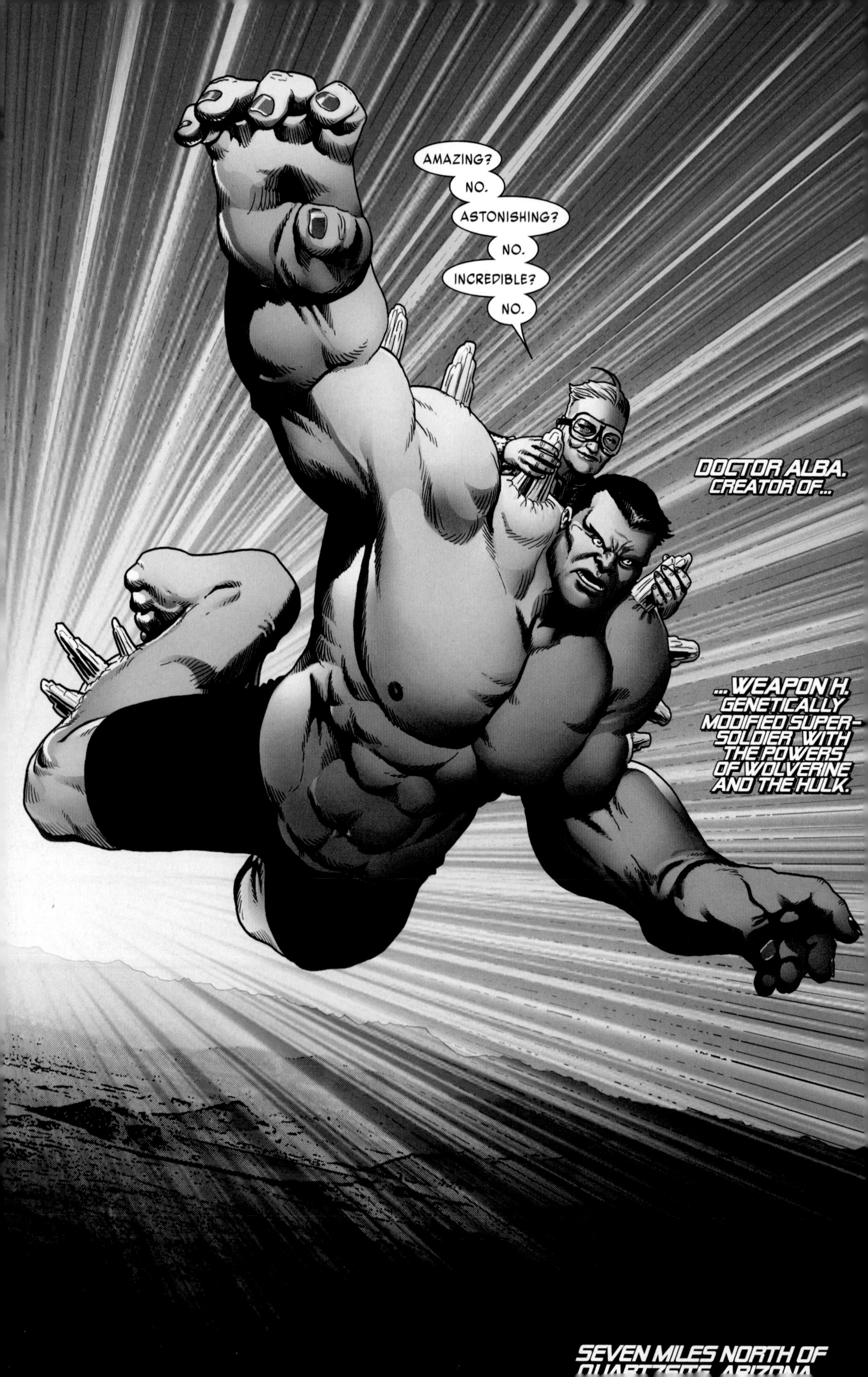

AMAZING?
NO.
ASTONISHING?
NO.
INCREDIBLE?
NO.
DOCTOR ALBA. CREATOR OF...
...WEAPON H. GENETICALLY MODIFIED SUPER-SOLDIER WITH THE POWERS OF WOLVERINE AND THE HULK.
SEVEN MILES NORTH OF

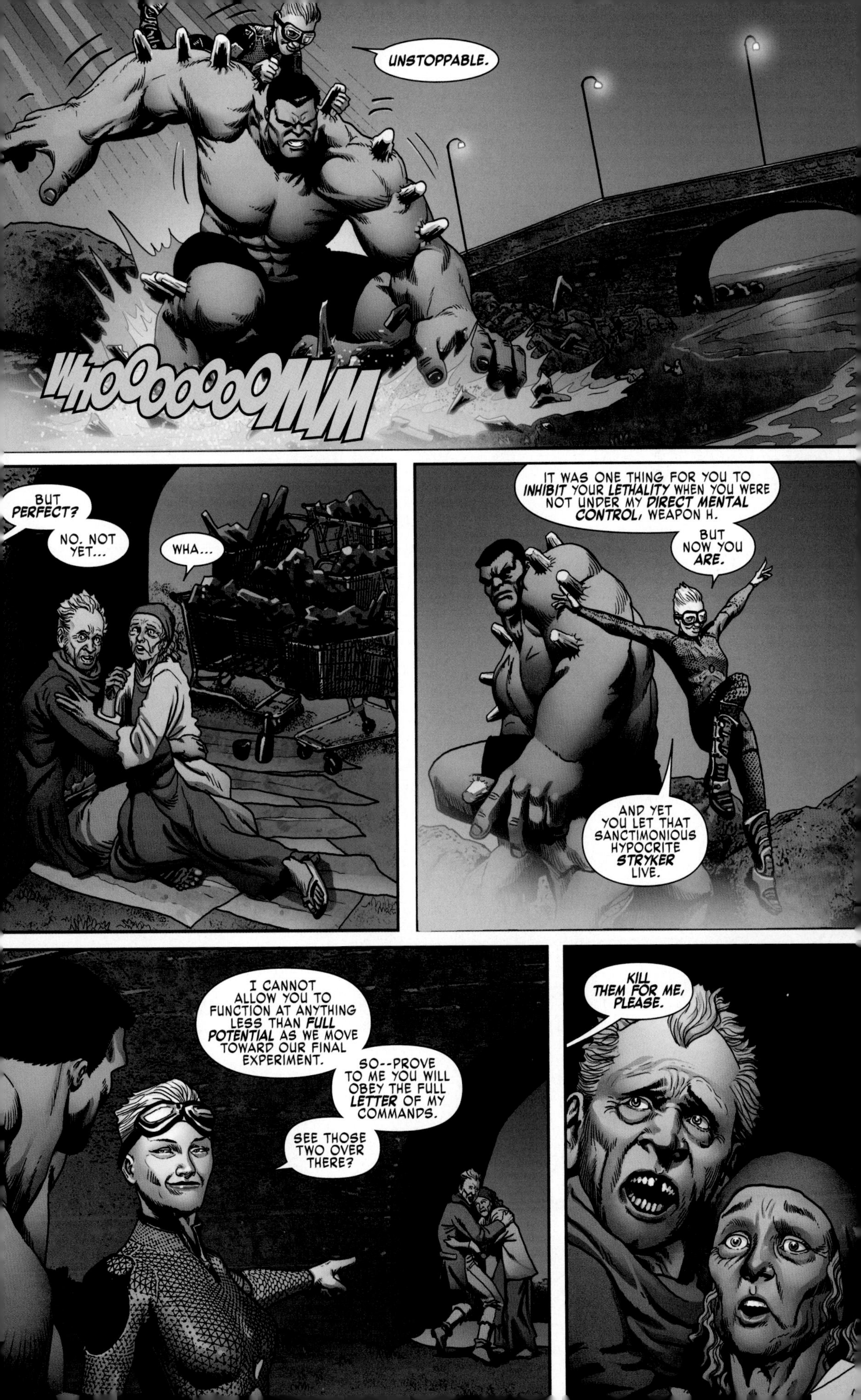
UNSTOPPABLE.
WHOOOOOOOMM
BUT PERFECT?
NO. NOT YET...
WHA...
IT WAS ONE THING FOR YOU TO INHIBIT YOUR LETHALITY WHEN YOU WERE NOT UNDER MY DIRECT MENTAL CONTROL, WEAPON H.
BUT NOW YOU ARE.
AND YET YOU LET THAT SANCTIMONIOUS HYPOCRITE STRYKER LIVE.
I CANNOT ALLOW YOU TO FUNCTION AT ANYTHING LESS THAN FULL POTENTIAL AS WE MOVE TOWARD OUR FINAL EXPERIMENT.
SO--PROVE TO ME YOU WILL OBEY THE FULL LETTER OF MY COMMANDS.
SEE THOSE TWO OVER THERE?
KILL THEM FOR ME, PLEASE.

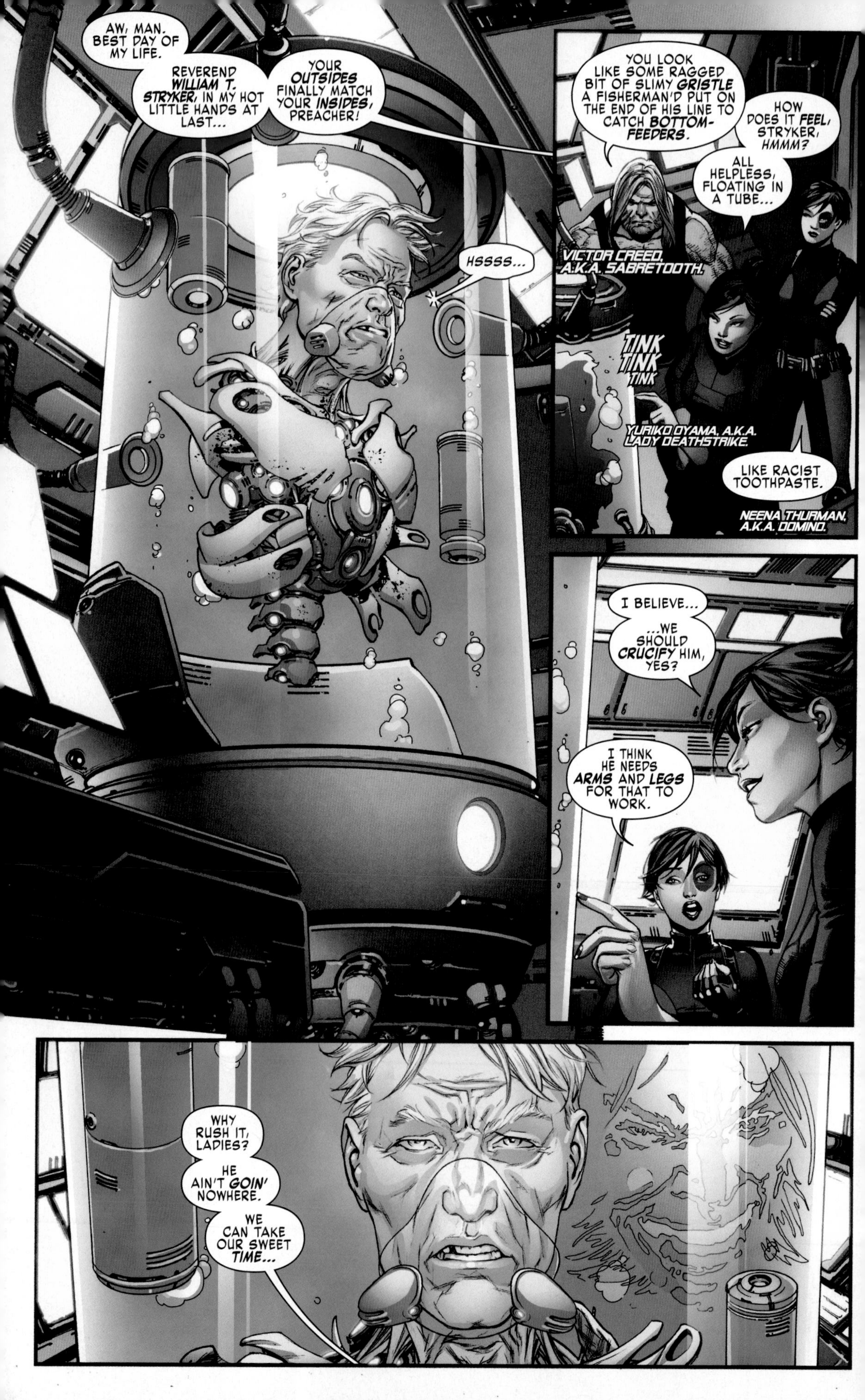
AW, MAN. BEST DAY OF MY LIFE.
REVEREND WILLIAM T. STRYKER, IN MY HOT LITTLE HANDS AT LAST...
YOUR OUTSIDES FINALLY MATCH YOUR INSIDES, PREACHER!
HSSSS...
YOU LOOK LIKE SOME RAGGED BIT OF SLIMY GRISTLE A FISHERMAN'D PUT ON THE END OF HIS LINE TO CATCH BOTTOM-FEEDERS.
VICTOR CREED, A.K.A. SABRETOOTH.
HOW DOES IT FEEL, STRYKER, HMMM?
ALL HELPLESS, FLOATING IN A TUBE...
TINK TINK TINK
YURIKO OYAMA, A.K.A. LADY DEATHSTRIKE.
LIKE RACIST TOOTHPASTE.
NEENA THURMAN, A.K.A. DOMINO.
I BELIEVE...
...WE SHOULD CRUCIFY HIM, YES?
I THINK HE NEEDS ARMS AND LEGS FOR THAT TO WORK.
WHY RUSH IT, LADIES?
HE AIN'T GOIN' NOWHERE.
WE CAN TAKE OUR SWEET TIME...

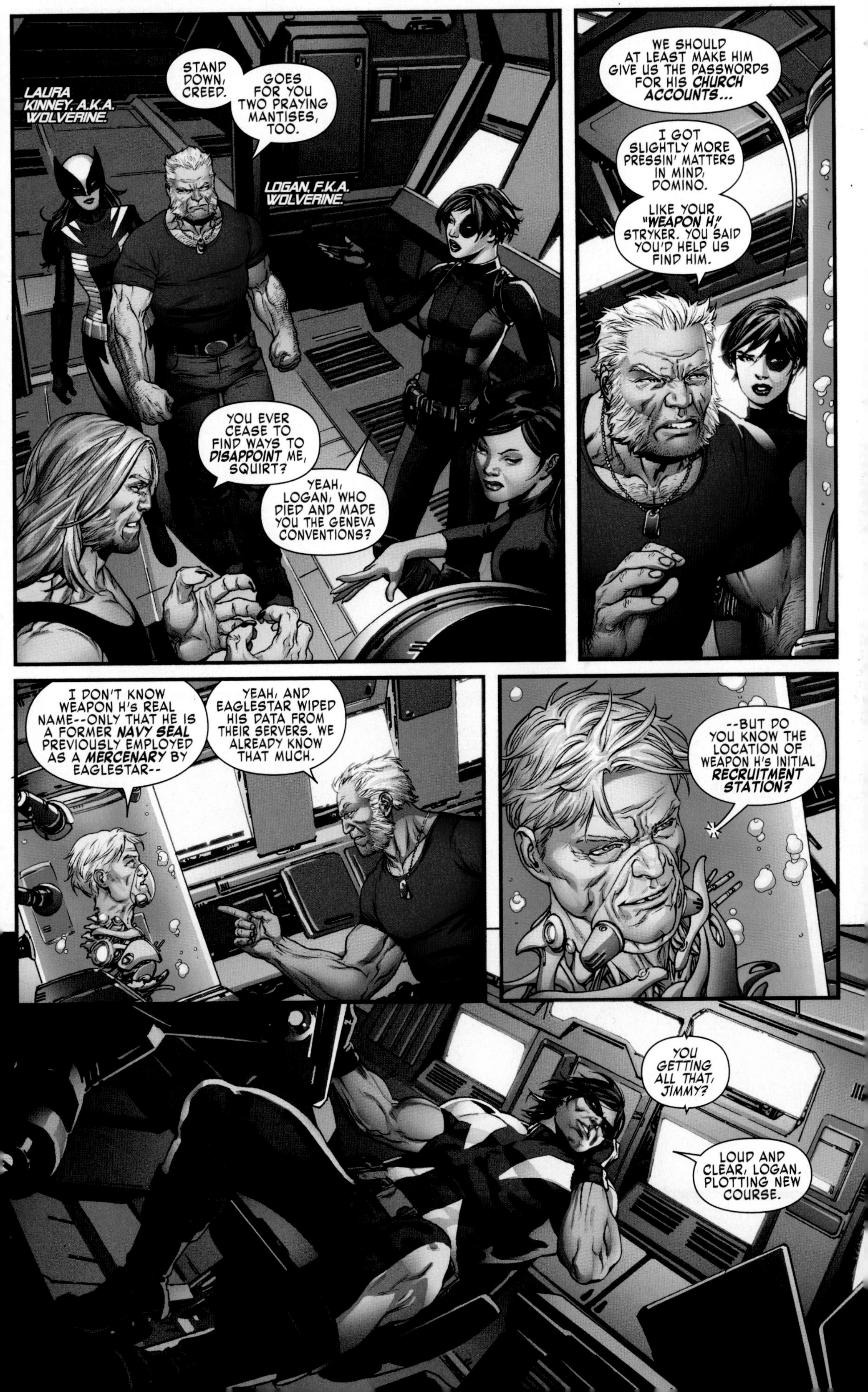
LAURA KINNEY, A.K.A. WOLVERINE.
STAND DOWN, CREED.
GOES FOR YOU TWO PRAYING MANTISES, TOO.
LOGAN, F.K.A. WOLVERINE.
YOU EVER CEASE TO FIND WAYS TO DISAPPOINT ME, SQUIRT?
YEAH, LOGAN, WHO DIED AND MADE YOU THE GENEVA CONVENTIONS?
WE SHOULD AT LEAST MAKE HIM GIVE US THE PASSWORDS FOR HIS CHURCH ACCOUNTS...
I GOT SLIGHTLY MORE PRESSIN' MATTERS IN MIND, DOMINO.
LIKE YOUR "WEAPON H," STRYKER. YOU SAID YOU'D HELP US FIND HIM.
I DON'T KNOW WEAPON H's REAL NAME--ONLY THAT HE IS A FORMER NAVY SEAL PREVIOUSLY EMPLOYED AS A MERCENARY BY EAGLESTAR--
YEAH, AND EAGLESTAR WIPED HIS DATA FROM THEIR SERVERS. WE ALREADY KNOW THAT MUCH.
--BUT DO YOU KNOW THE LOCATION OF WEAPON H's INITIAL RECRUITMENT STATION?
YOU GETTING ALL THAT, JIMMY?
LOUD AND CLEAR, LOGAN. PLOTTING NEW COURSE.

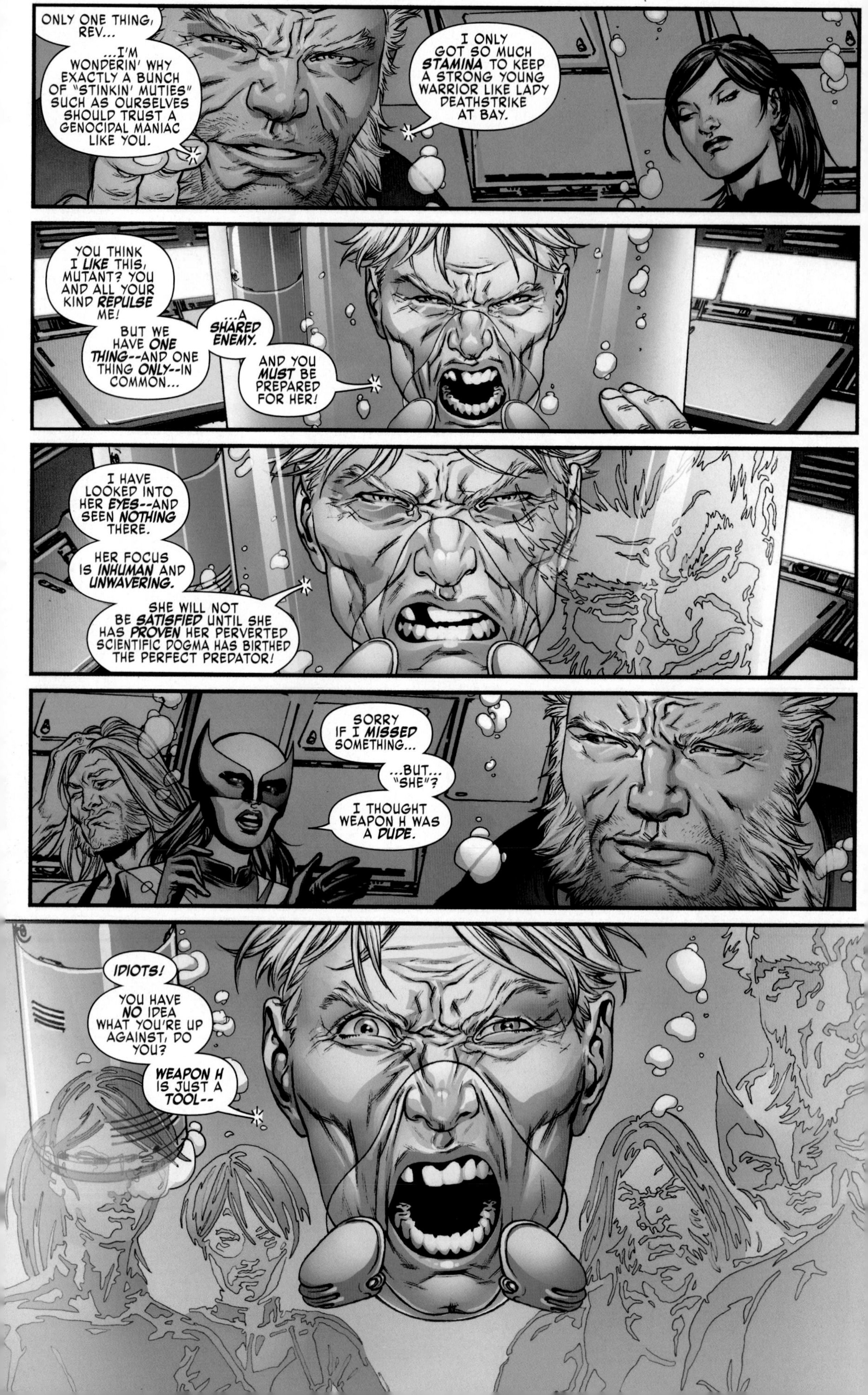

ONLY ONE THING, REV...
...I'M WONDERIN' WHY EXACTLY A BUNCH OF "STINKIN' MUTIES" SUCH AS OURSELVES SHOULD TRUST A GENOCIDAL MANIAC LIKE YOU.
I ONLY GOT SO MUCH STAMINA TO KEEP A STRONG YOUNG WARRIOR LIKE LADY DEATHSTRIKE AT BAY.
YOU THINK I LIKE THIS, MUTANT? YOU AND ALL YOUR KIND REPULSE ME!
BUT WE HAVE ONE THING--AND ONE THING ONLY--IN COMMON...
...A SHARED ENEMY.
AND YOU MUST BE PREPARED FOR HER!
I HAVE LOOKED INTO HER EYES--AND SEEN NOTHING THERE.
HER FOCUS IS INHUMAN AND UNWAVERING.
SHE WILL NOT BE SATISFIED UNTIL SHE HAS PROVEN HER PERVERTED SCIENTIFIC DOGMA HAS BIRTHED THE PERFECT PREDATOR!
SORRY IF I MISSED SOMETHING...
...BUT... "SHE"?
I THOUGHT WEAPON H WAS A DUDE.
IDIOTS!
YOU HAVE NO IDEA WHAT YOU'RE UP AGAINST, DO YOU?
WEAPON H IS JUST A TOOL--

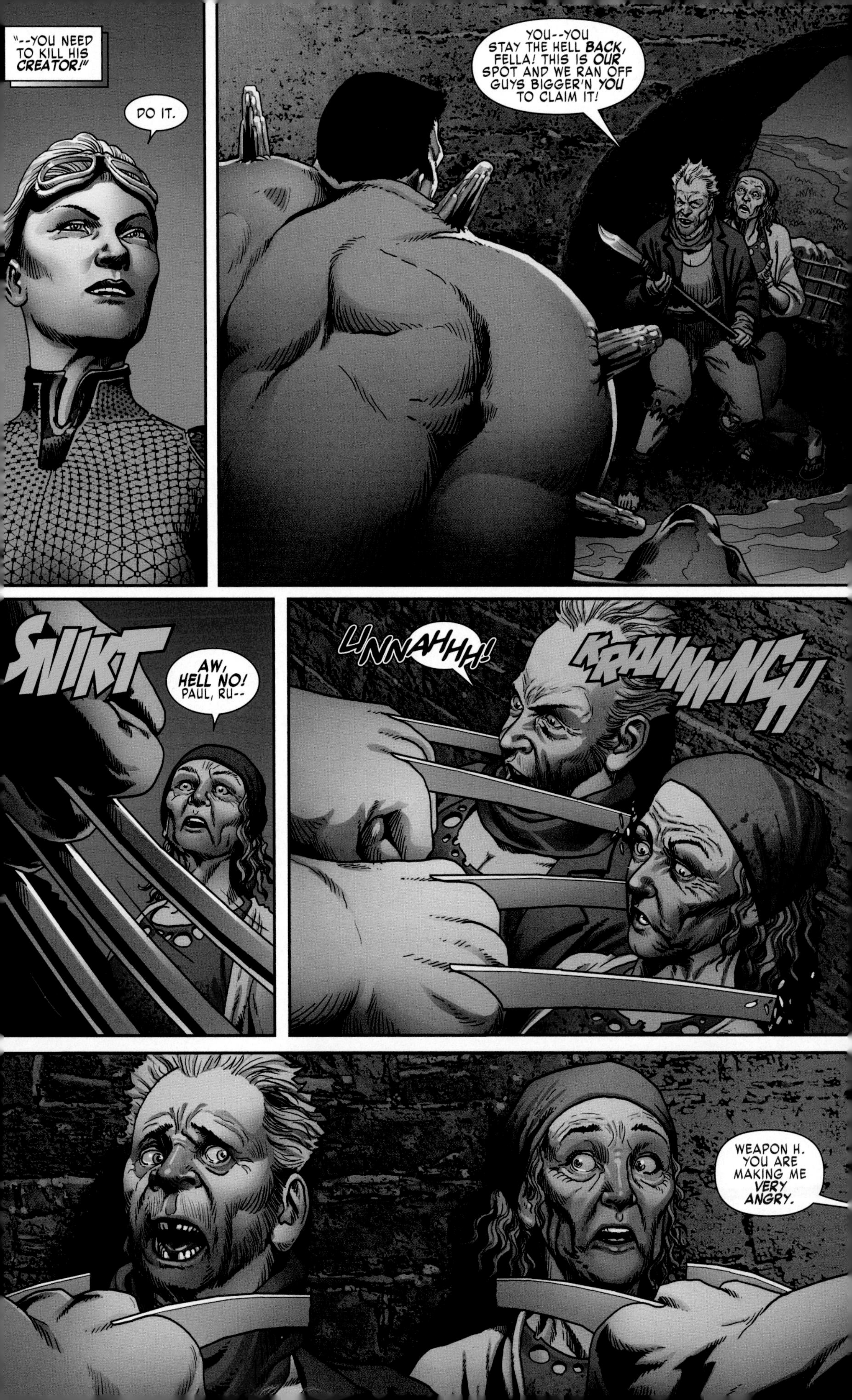
"--YOU NEED TO KILL HIS CREATOR!"
DO IT.
YOU--YOU STAY THE HELL BACK, FELLA! THIS IS OUR SPOT AND WE RAN OFF GUYS BIGGER'N YOU TO CLAIM IT!
SNIKT
AW, HELL NO! PAUL, RU--
UNNAHHH!
KRANNNNCH
WEAPON H. YOU ARE MAKING ME VERY ANGRY.

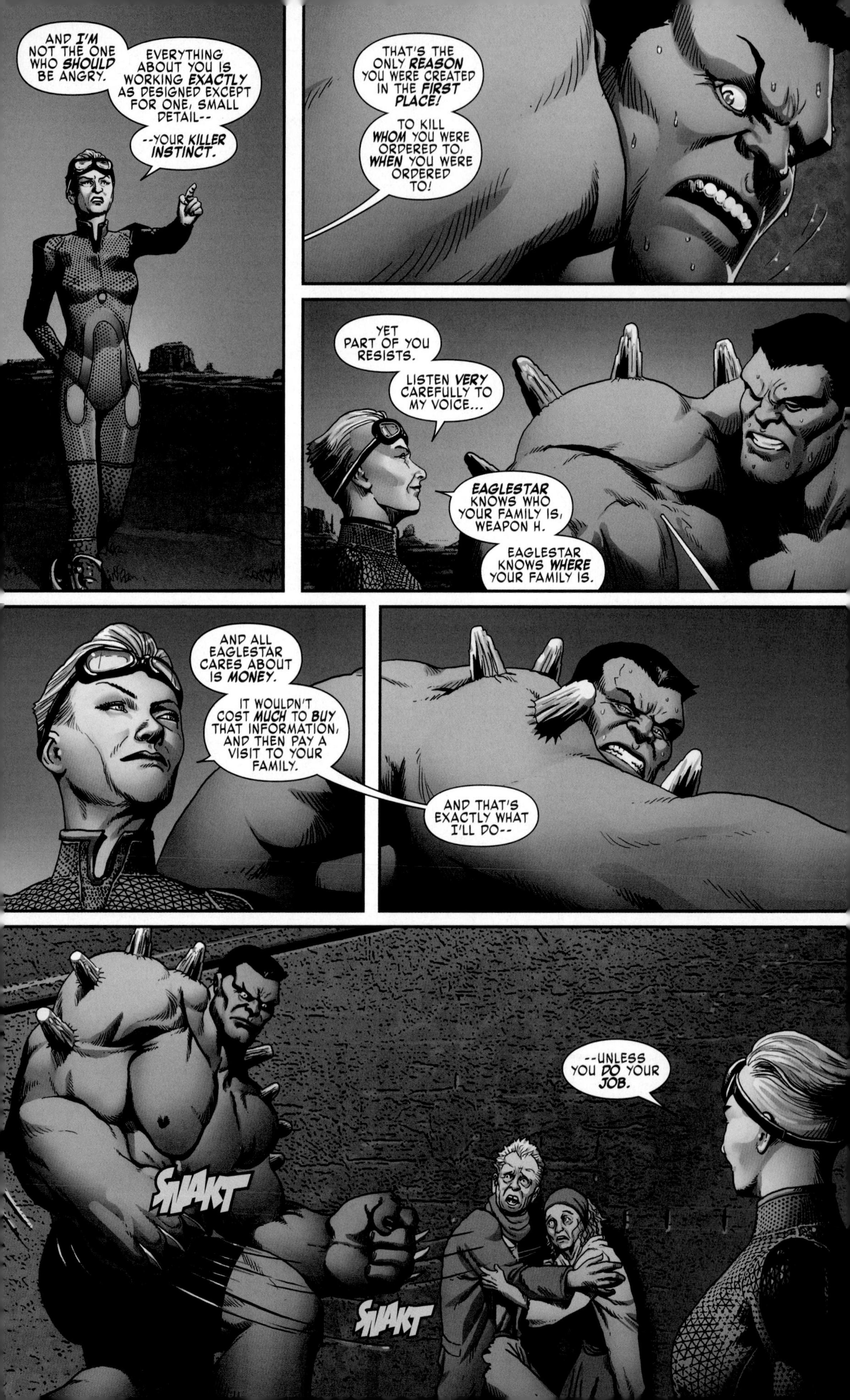
AND I'M NOT THE ONE WHO SHOULD BE ANGRY.
EVERYTHING ABOUT YOU IS WORKING EXACTLY AS DESIGNED EXCEPT FOR ONE, SMALL DETAIL--
--YOUR KILLER INSTINCT.
THAT'S THE ONLY REASON YOU WERE CREATED IN THE FIRST PLACE!
TO KILL WHOM YOU WERE ORDERED TO, WHEN YOU WERE ORDERED TO!
YET PART OF YOU RESISTS.
LISTEN VERY CAREFULLY TO MY VOICE...
EAGLESTAR KNOWS WHO YOUR FAMILY IS, WEAPON H.
EAGLESTAR KNOWS WHERE YOUR FAMILY IS.
AND ALL EAGLESTAR CARES ABOUT IS MONEY.
IT WOULDN'T COST MUCH TO BUY THAT INFORMATION, AND THEN PAY A VISIT TO YOUR FAMILY.
AND THAT'S EXACTLY WHAT I'LL DO--
--UNLESS YOU DO YOUR JOB.
SNAKT
SNAKT

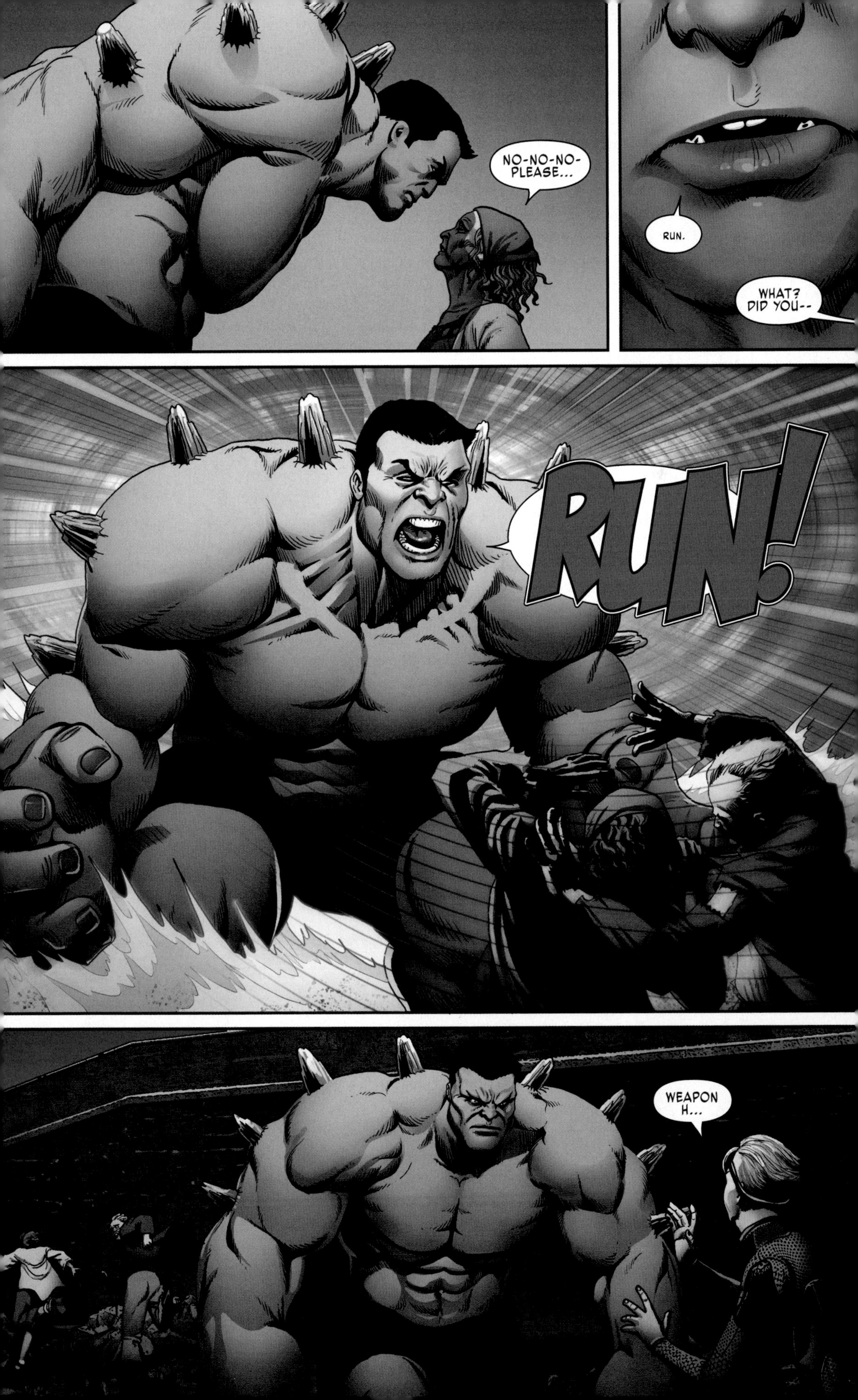

NO-NO-NO-PLEASE...
RUN.
WHAT? DID YOU--
RUN!
WEAPON H...

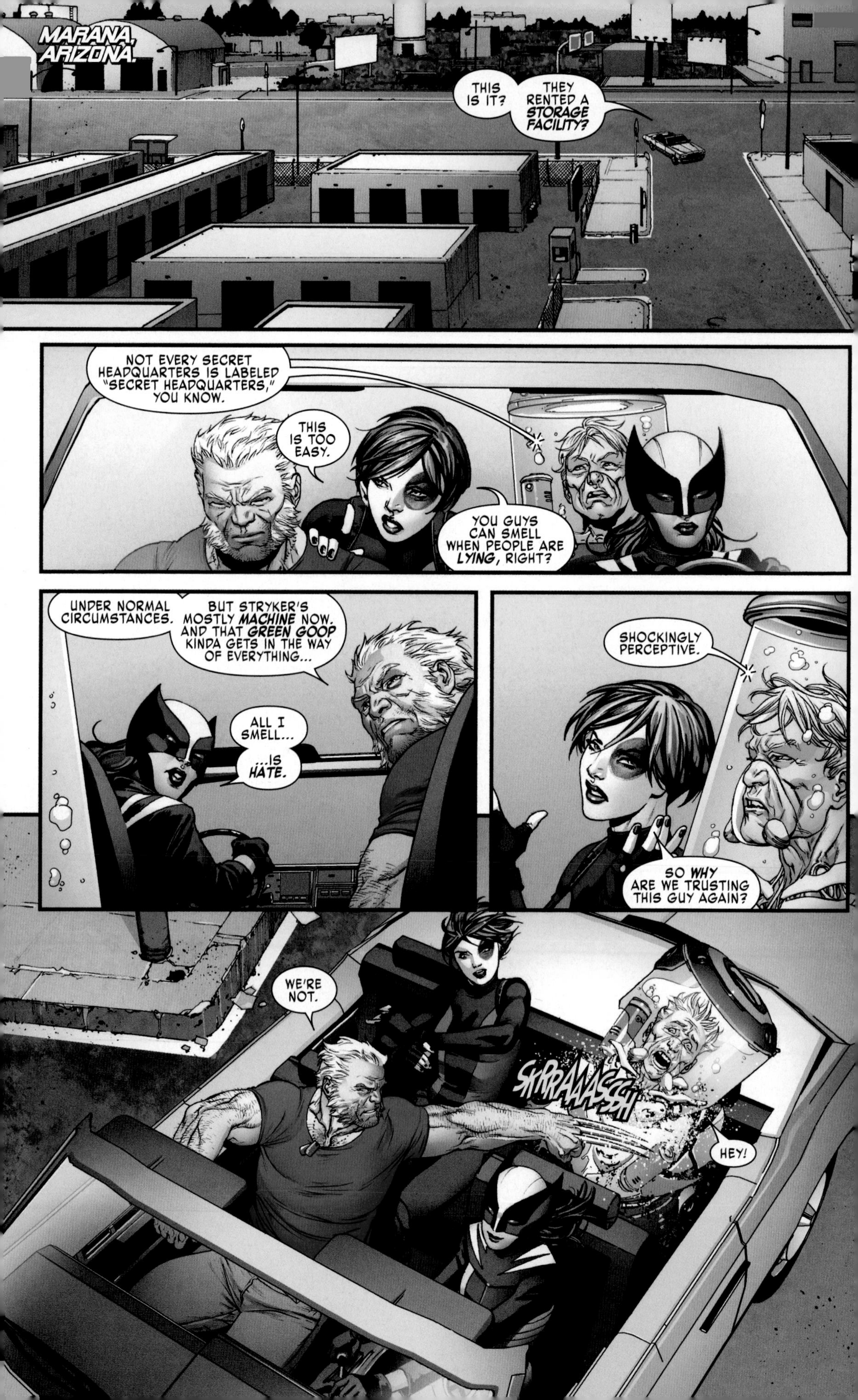
MARANA, ARIZONA.
THIS IS IT?
THEY RENTED A STORAGE FACILITY?
NOT EVERY SECRET HEADQUARTERS IS LABELED "SECRET HEADQUARTERS," YOU KNOW.
THIS IS TOO EASY.
YOU GUYS CAN SMELL WHEN PEOPLE ARE LYING, RIGHT?
UNDER NORMAL CIRCUMSTANCES.
BUT STRYKER'S MOSTLY MACHINE NOW. AND THAT GREEN GOOP KINDA GETS IN THE WAY OF EVERYTHING...
ALL I SMELL...
...IS HATE.
SHOCKINGLY PERCEPTIVE.
SO WHY ARE WE TRUSTING THIS GUY AGAIN?
WE'RE NOT.
SKRRAAAASCCH
HEY!

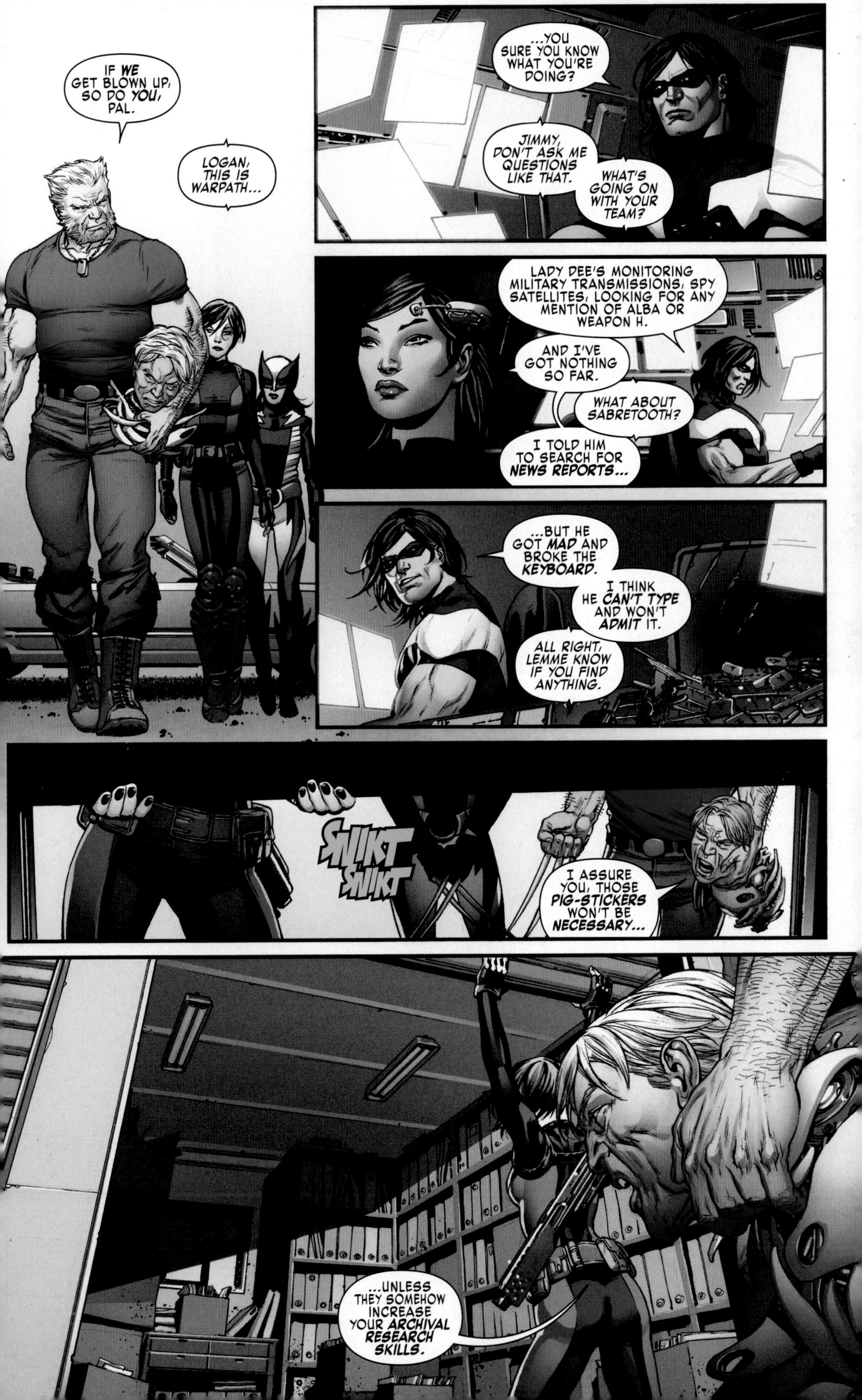

IF WE GET BLOWN UP, SO DO YOU, PAL.
LOGAN, THIS IS WARPATH...
...YOU SURE YOU KNOW WHAT YOU'RE DOING?
JIMMY, DON'T ASK ME QUESTIONS LIKE THAT.
WHAT'S GOING ON WITH YOUR TEAM?
LADY DEE'S MONITORING MILITARY TRANSMISSIONS, SPY SATELLITES, LOOKING FOR ANY MENTION OF ALBA OR WEAPON H.
AND I'VE GOT NOTHING SO FAR.
WHAT ABOUT SABRETOOTH?
I TOLD HIM TO SEARCH FOR NEWS REPORTS...
...BUT HE GOT MAD AND BROKE THE KEYBOARD.
I THINK HE CAN'T TYPE AND WON'T ADMIT IT.
ALL RIGHT, LEMME KNOW IF YOU FIND ANYTHING.
SNIKT
SNIKT
I ASSURE YOU, THOSE PIG-STICKERS WON'T BE NECESSARY...
...UNLESS THEY SOMEHOW INCREASE YOUR ARCHIVAL RESEARCH SKILLS.

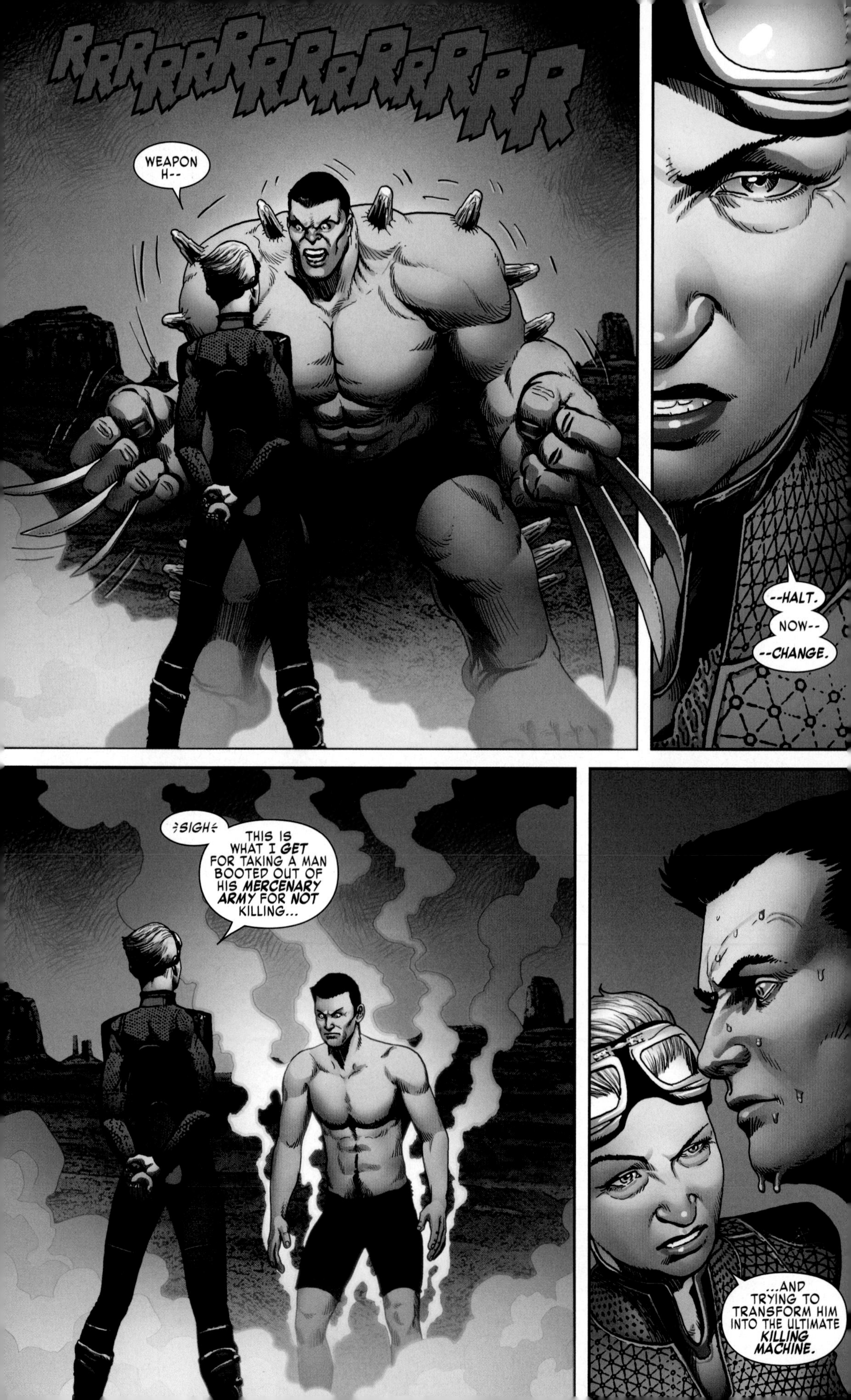
RRRRRRRRRRRRRRRRR
WEAPON H--
--HALT.
NOW--
--CHANGE.
SIGH
THIS IS WHAT I GET FOR TAKING A MAN BOOTED OUT OF HIS MERCENARY ARMY FOR NOT KILLING...
...AND TRYING TO TRANSFORM HIM INTO THE ULTIMATE KILLING MACHINE.

HONESTLY, I'D RATHER BE SHOOTING SOMEONE.

HELL, I'D RATHER BE GETTING SHOT.

HERE IT IS.

MISSION TO WEST AFRICA...

TEAM WAS SUPPOSED TO TAKE OUT A VILLAGE THAT WAS SUSPECTED OF SABOTAGING AN OIL PIPELINE...

...BUT ONE MERC REFUSED ORDERS.

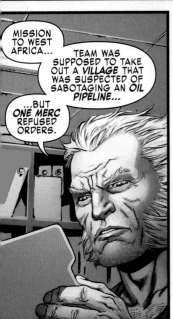

THAT'S THE ONE. HE SHOT UP HIS OWN PLATOON IN ORDER TO SAVE THE VILLAGERS.

HE WAS EAGLESTAR'S BEST TRAINED KILLER.

BUT THEY COULDN'T TRUST HIM AFTER THAT.

SO YOU BOUGHT HIM?

ALBA NEEDED TEST SUBJECTS...

...I WAS DUBIOUS. I ONLY WANTED TO USE TRUE BELIEVERS. RECRUITS WHO UNDERSTOOD OUR MISSION TO KILL MUTANTS.

I GUESS I APPRECIATE THE HONESTY...

...BUT IF YOU WANNA LIVE, YOU BETTER LEARN HOW TO READ YOUR AUDIENCE A LITTLE BETTER.

SO... HE HAS A MIND OF HIS OWN.

WELL. HAD, ANYWAY.

WHAT'S HIS NAME?

THEY DON'T GIVE HIS BACKGROUND OR BIO...NOT ENOUGH DETAIL...

IT'S ENOUGH FOR ME.

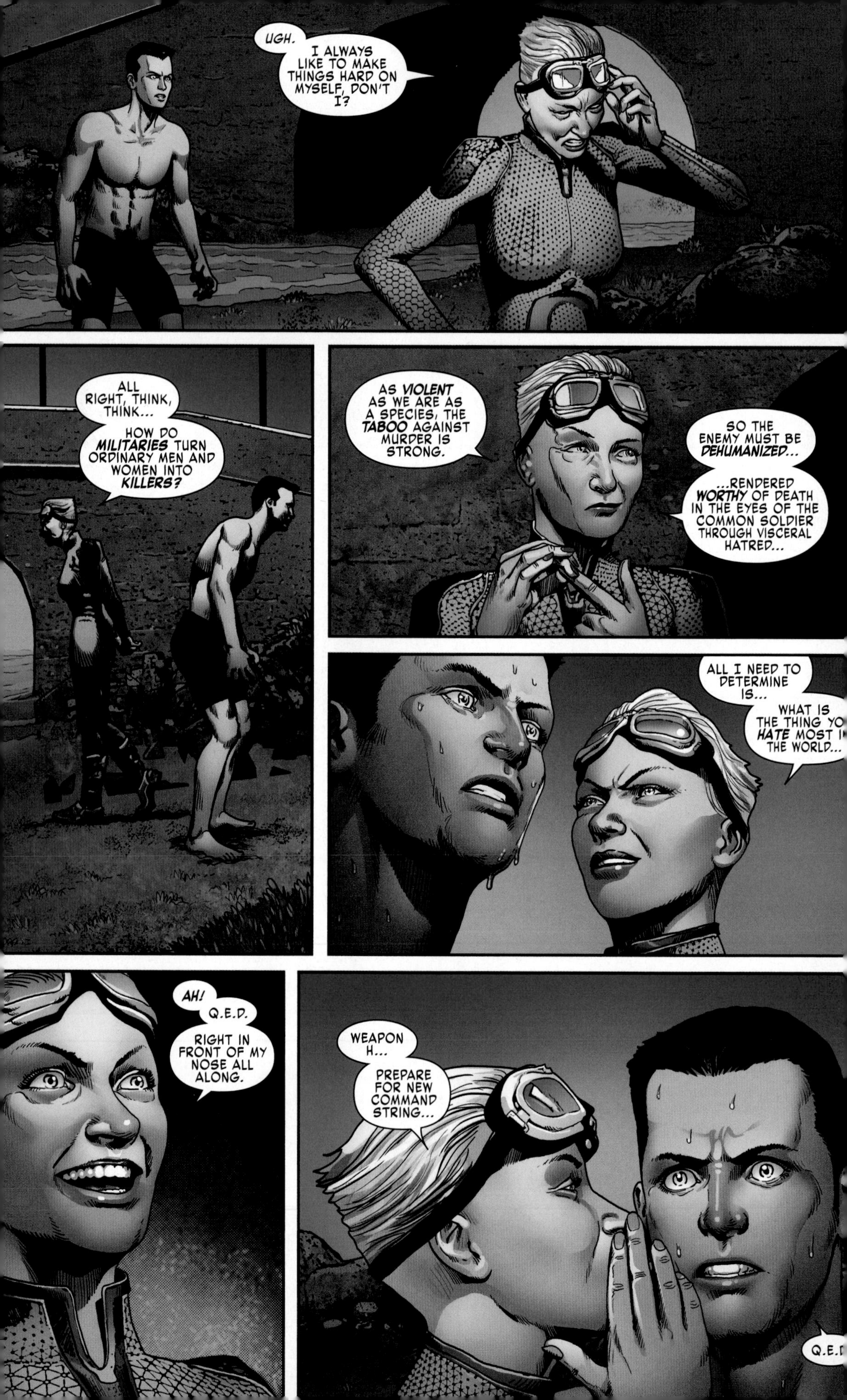
UGH.
I ALWAYS LIKE TO MAKE THINGS HARD ON MYSELF, DON'T I?
ALL RIGHT, THINK, THINK...
HOW DO MILITARIES TURN ORDINARY MEN AND WOMEN INTO KILLERS?
AS VIOLENT AS WE ARE AS A SPECIES, THE TABOO AGAINST MURDER IS STRONG.
SO THE ENEMY MUST BE DEHUMANIZED...
...RENDERED WORTHY OF DEATH IN THE EYES OF THE COMMON SOLDIER THROUGH VISCERAL HATRED...
ALL I NEED TO DETERMINE IS...
WHAT IS THE THING YO HATE MOST I THE WORLD...
AH!
Q.E.D.
RIGHT IN FRONT OF MY NOSE ALL ALONG.
WEAPON H...
PREPARE FOR NEW COMMAND STRING...
Q.E.D

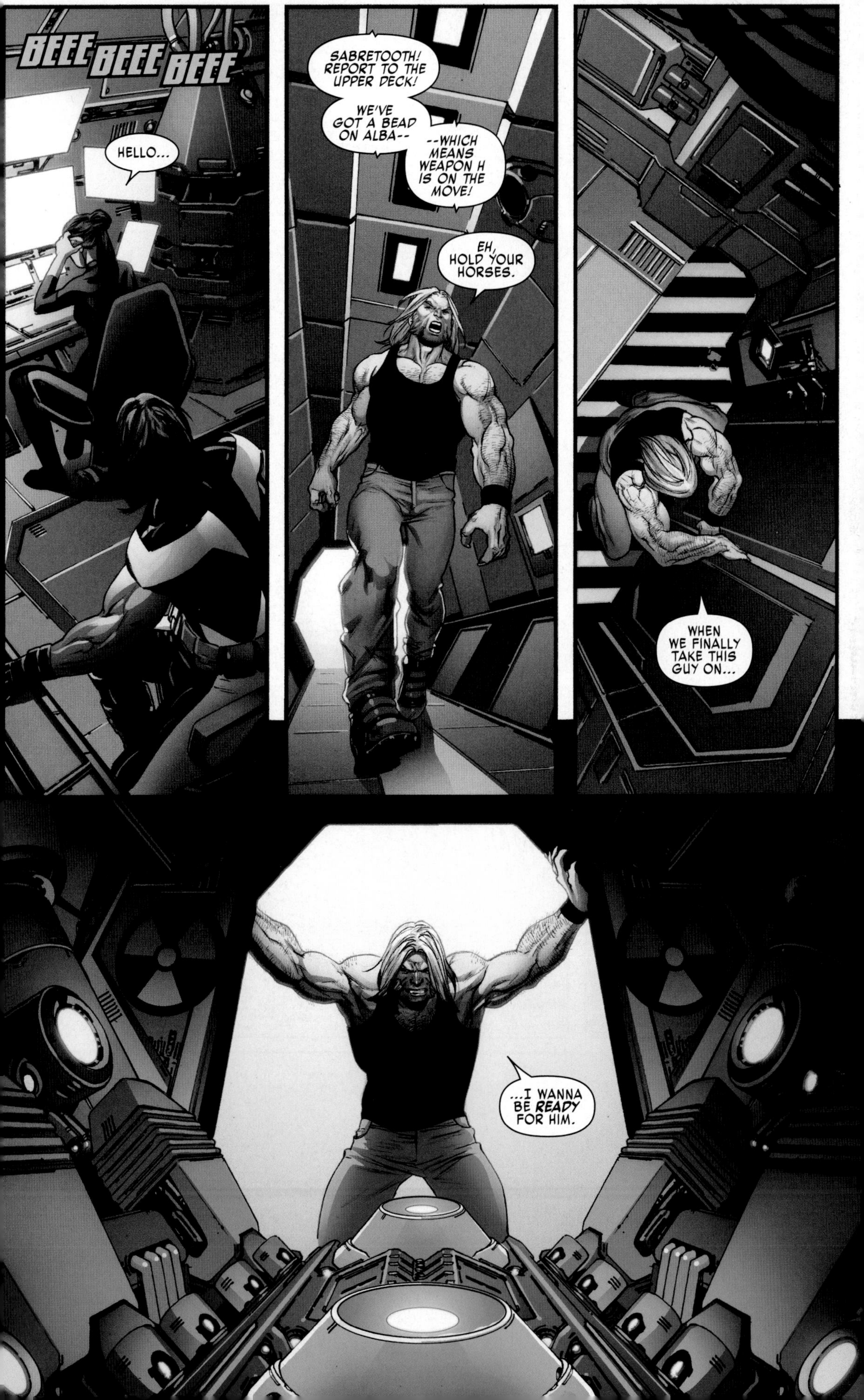
BEEE BEEE BEEE
HELLO...
SABRETOOTH! REPORT TO THE UPPER DECK!
WE'VE GOT A BEAD ON ALBA--
--WHICH MEANS WEAPON H IS ON THE MOVE!
EH, HOLD YOUR HORSES.
WHEN WE FINALLY TAKE THIS GUY ON...
...I WANNA BE *READY* FOR HIM.

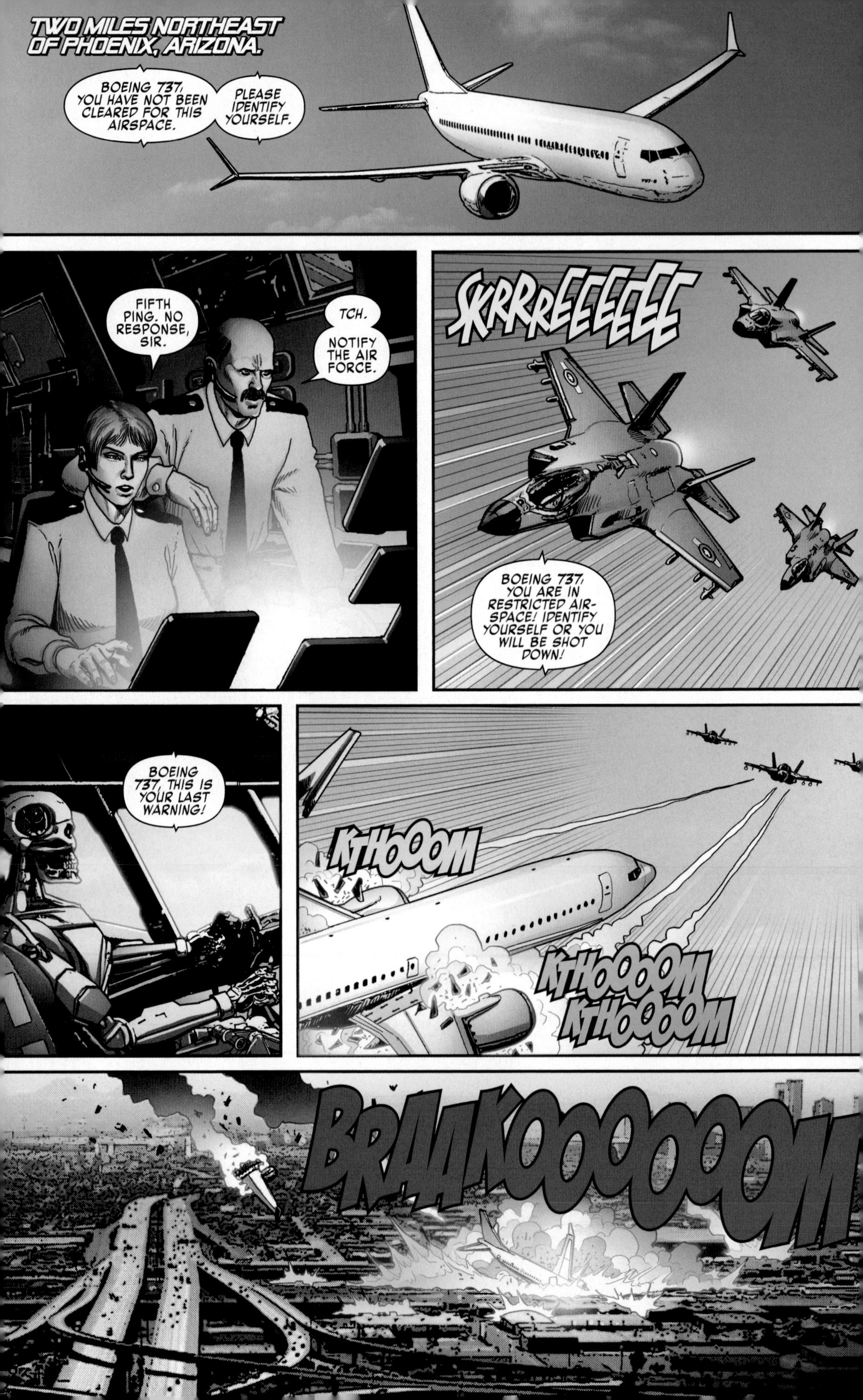
TWO MILES NORTHEAST OF PHOENIX, ARIZONA.
BOEING 737, YOU HAVE NOT BEEN CLEARED FOR THIS AIRSPACE.
PLEASE IDENTIFY YOURSELF.
FIFTH PING. NO RESPONSE, SIR.
TCH.
NOTIFY THE AIR FORCE.
SKRRREEEEEEE
BOEING 737, YOU ARE IN RESTRICTED AIR-SPACE! IDENTIFY YOURSELF OR YOU WILL BE SHOT DOWN!
BOEING 737, THIS IS YOUR LAST WARNING!
KTHOOOM
KTHOOOOM
KTHOOOOM
BRAAKOOOOOOM

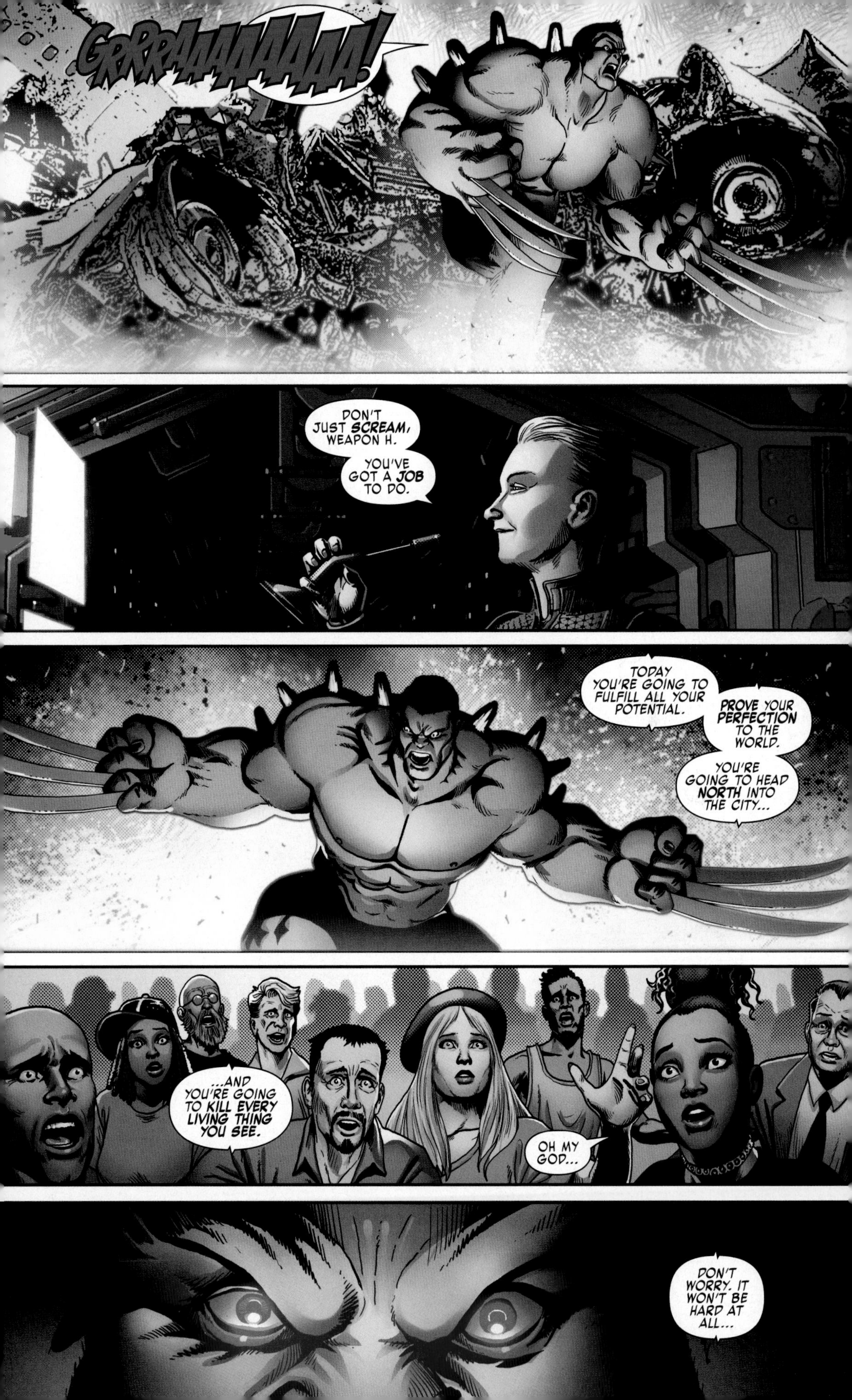
GRRRAAAAAAAAA!
DON'T JUST SCREAM, WEAPON H.
YOU'VE GOT A JOB TO DO.
TODAY YOU'RE GOING TO FULFILL ALL YOUR POTENTIAL.
PROVE YOUR PERFECTION TO THE WORLD.
YOU'RE GOING TO HEAD NORTH INTO THE CITY...
...AND YOU'RE GOING TO KILL EVERY LIVING THING YOU SEE.
OH MY GOD...
DON'T WORRY. IT WON'T BE HARD AT ALL...

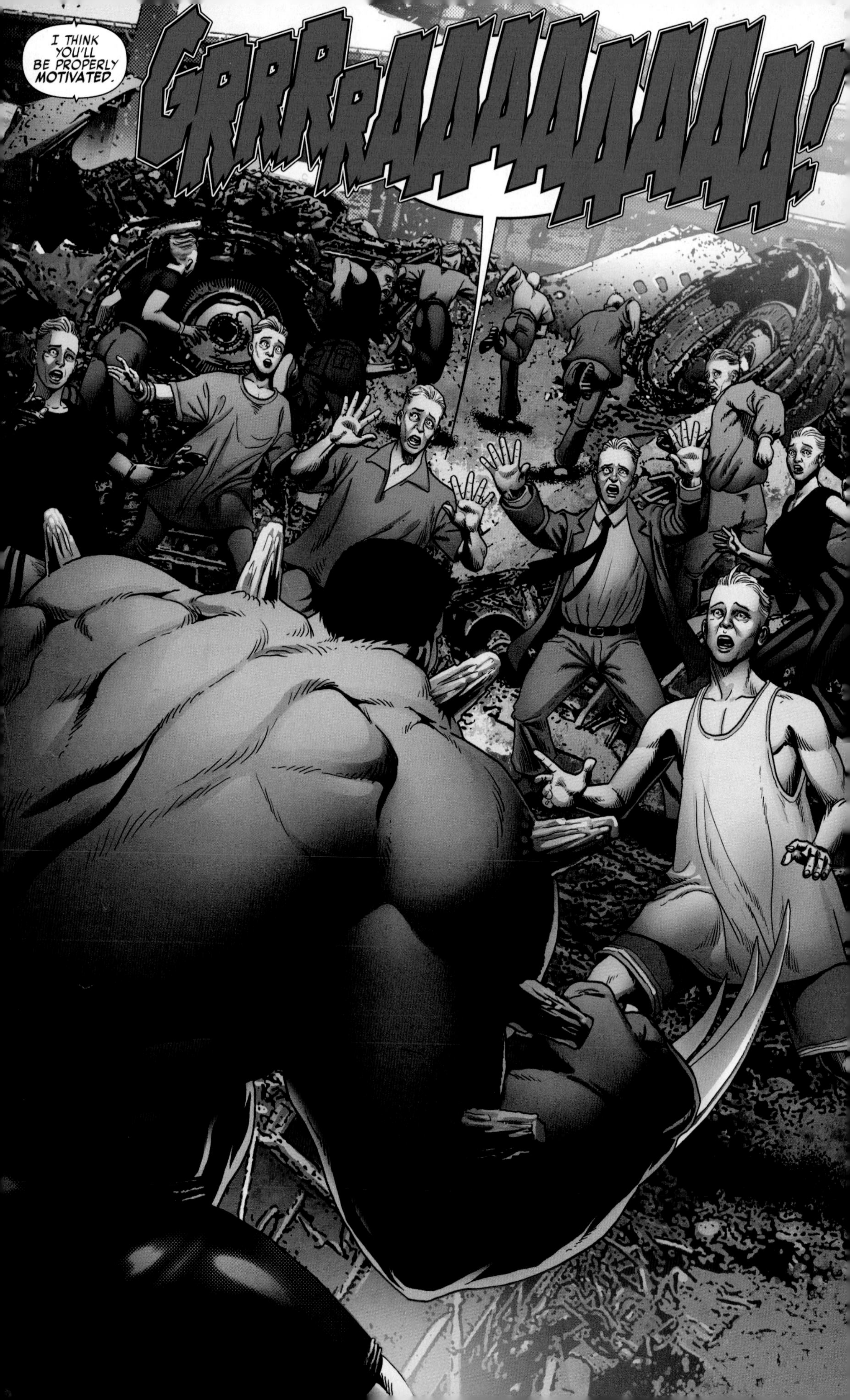
I THINK YOU'LL BE PROPERLY MOTIVATED.
GRRRRAAAAAAAAAAA!

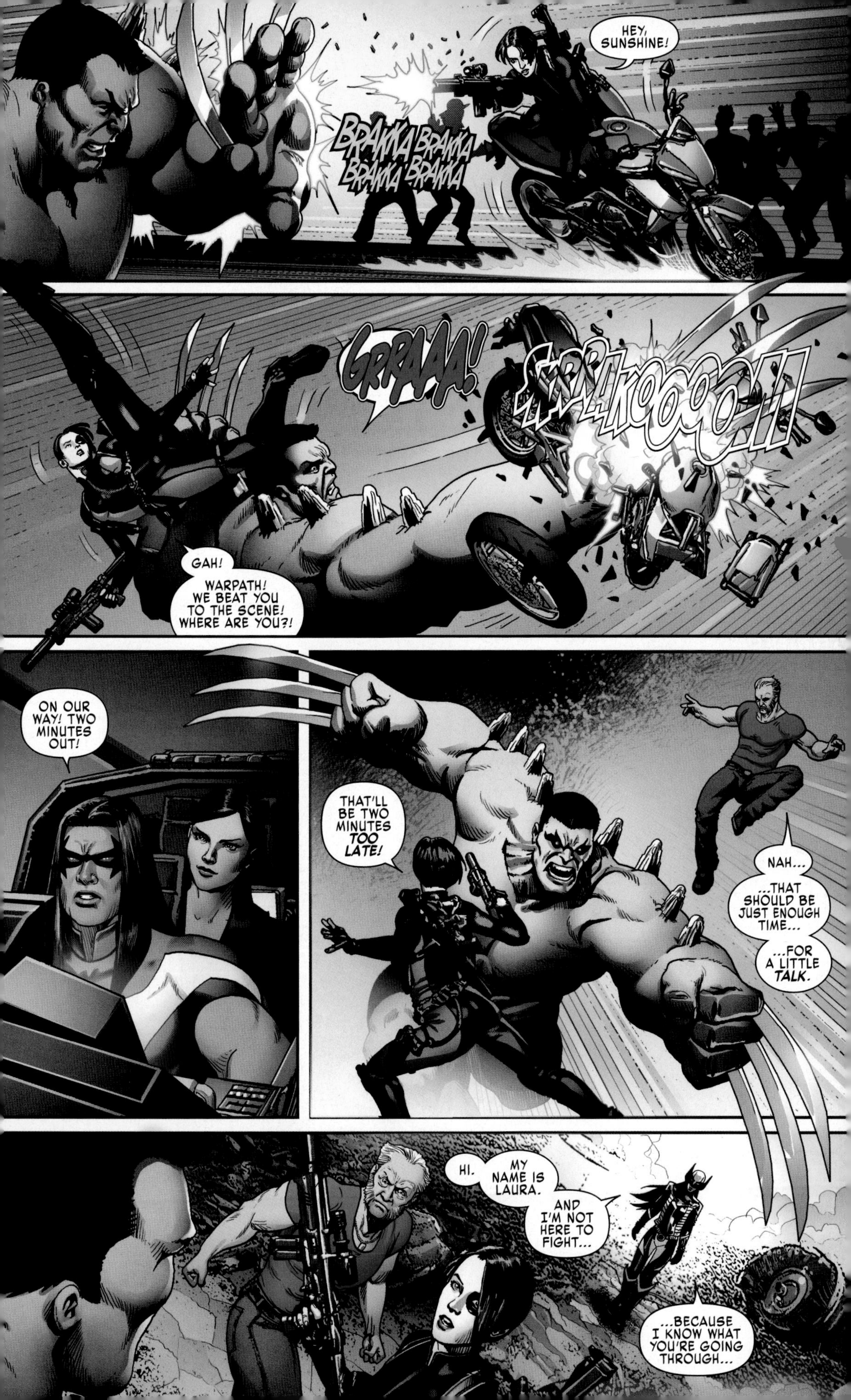
HEY, SUNSHINE!
BRAKKA BRAKKA BRAKKA BRAKKA
GRRAAA!
GAH! WARPATH! WE BEAT YOU TO THE SCENE! WHERE ARE YOU?!
ON OUR WAY! TWO MINUTES OUT!
THAT'LL BE TWO MINUTES TOO LATE!
NAH...
...THAT SHOULD BE JUST ENOUGH TIME...
...FOR A LITTLE TALK.
HI.
MY NAME IS LAURA.
AND I'M NOT HERE TO FIGHT...
...BECAUSE I KNOW WHAT YOU'RE GOING THROUGH...

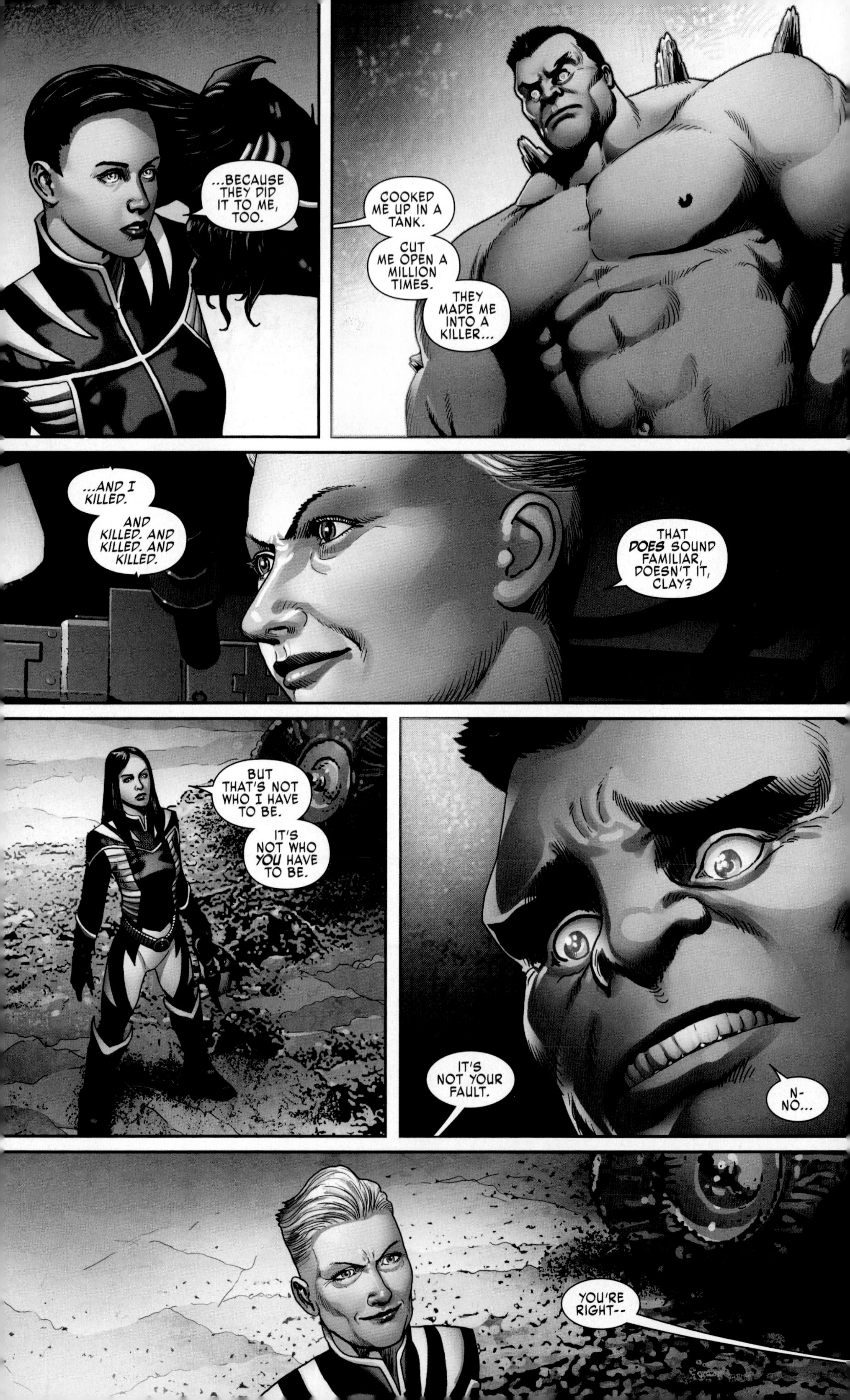
...BECAUSE THEY DID IT TO ME, TOO.
COOKED ME UP IN A TANK.
CUT ME OPEN A MILLION TIMES.
THEY MADE ME INTO A KILLER...
...AND I KILLED.
AND KILLED. AND KILLED. AND KILLED.
THAT *DOES* SOUND FAMILIAR, DOESN'T IT, CLAY?
BUT THAT'S NOT WHO I HAVE TO BE.
IT'S NOT WHO *YOU* HAVE TO BE.
IT'S NOT YOUR FAULT.
N-NO...
YOU'RE RIGHT--

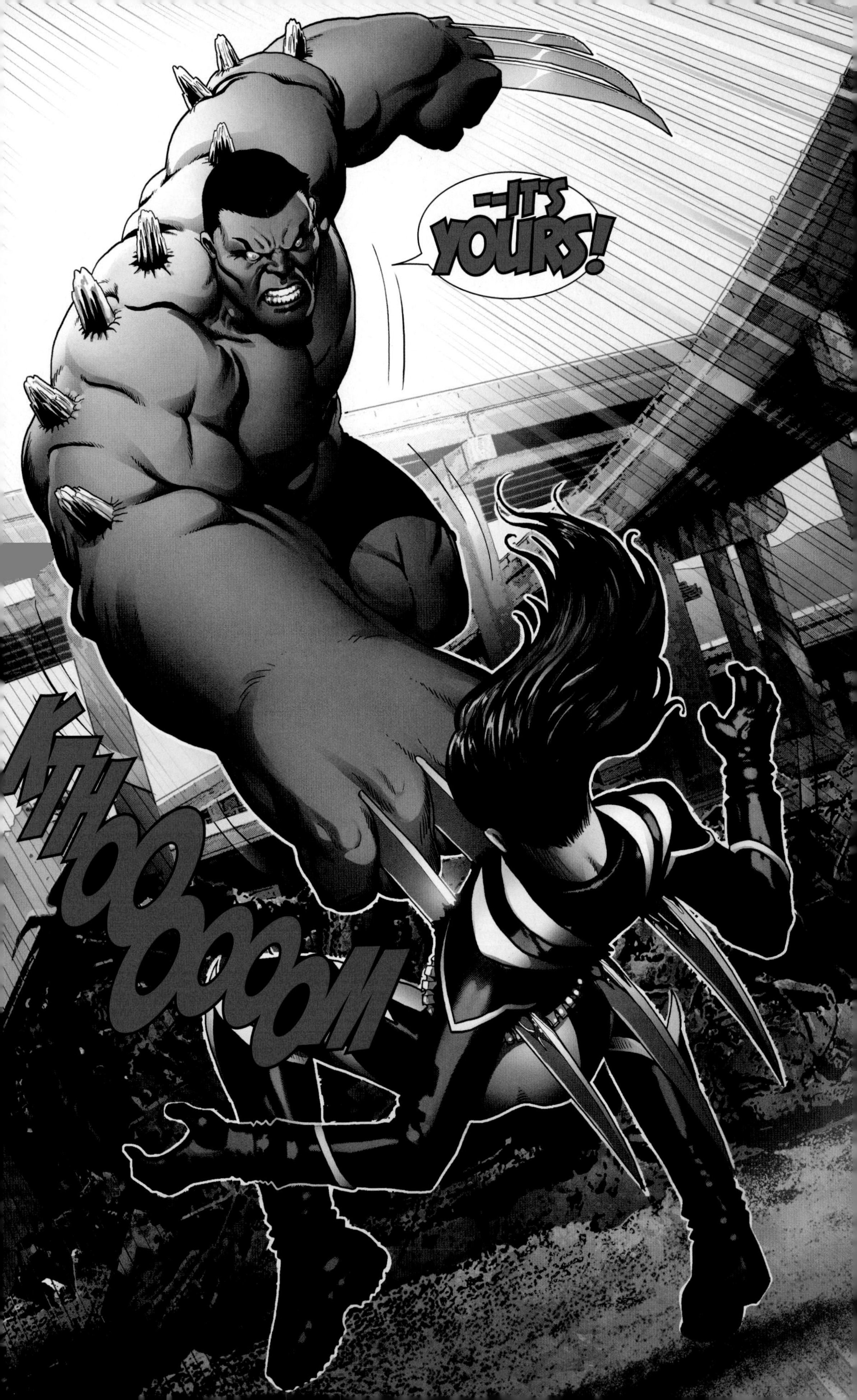
--IT'S YOURS!
KTHOOOOOOM

11

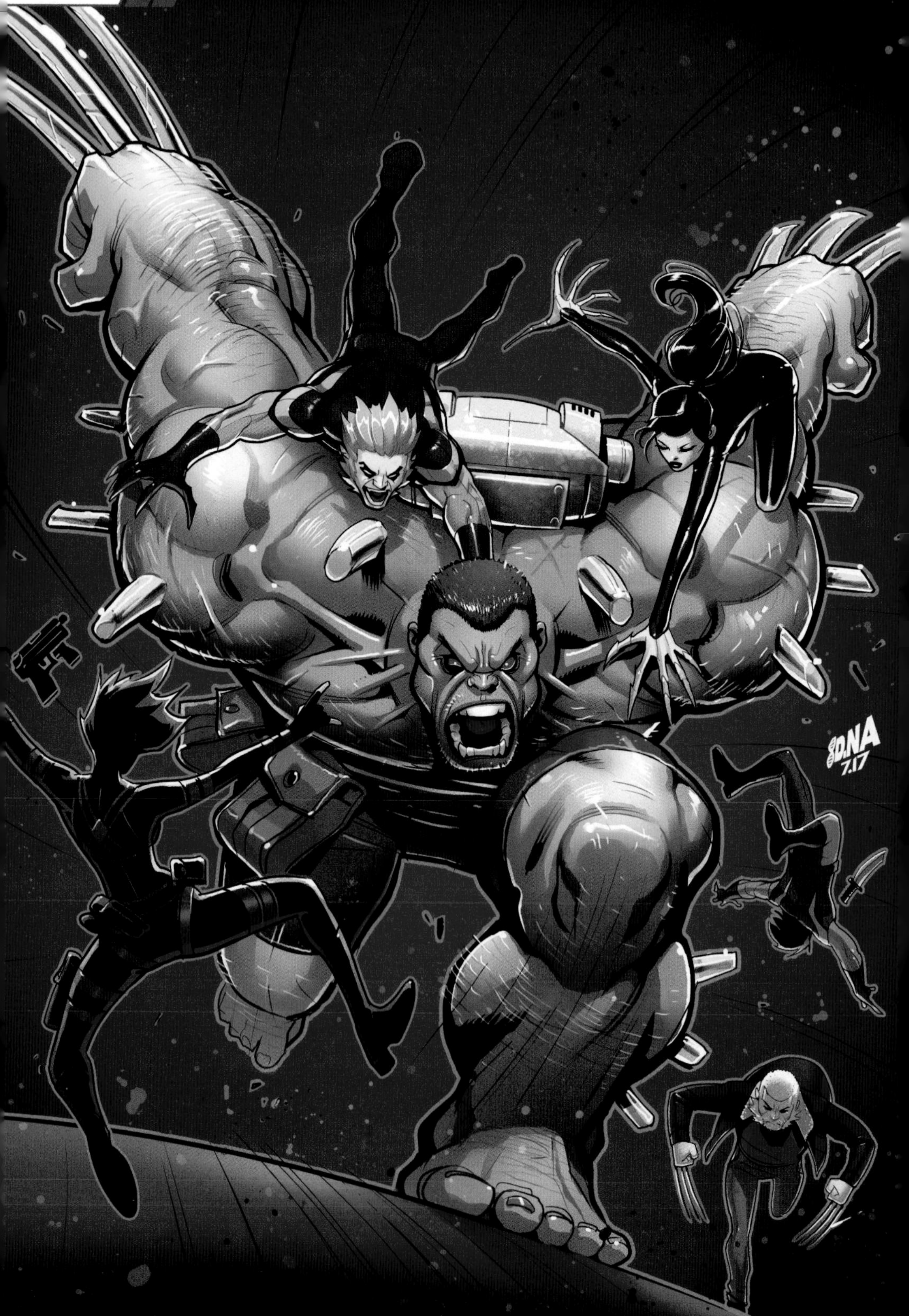
D.NA
7.17

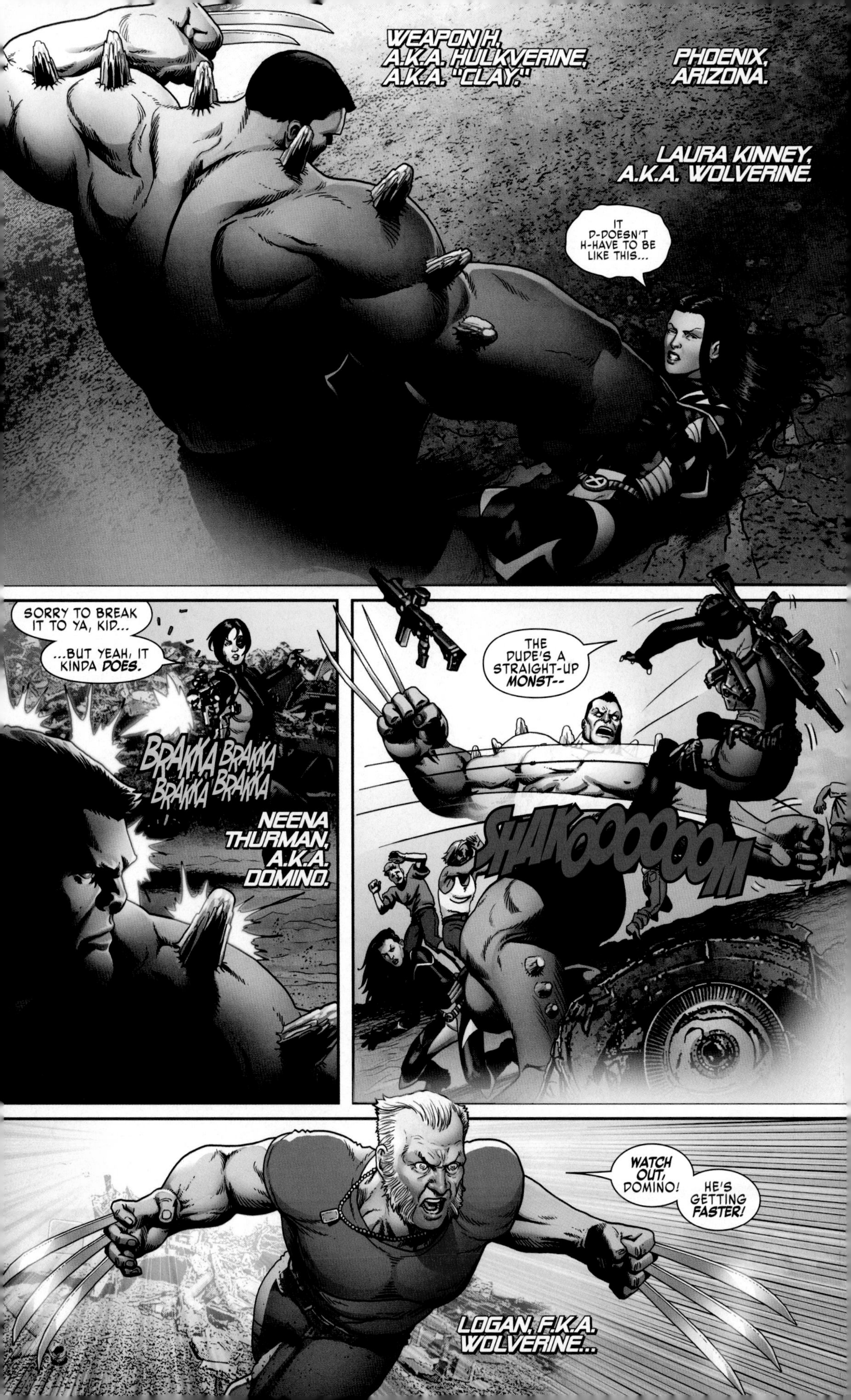
WEAPON H,
A.K.A. HULKVERINE,
A.K.A. "CLAY."
PHOENIX,
ARIZONA.
LAURA KINNEY,
A.K.A. WOLVERINE.
IT D-DOESN'T H-HAVE TO BE LIKE THIS...
SORRY TO BREAK IT TO YA, KID...
...BUT YEAH, IT KINDA DOES.
BRAKKA BRAKKA BRAKKA BRAKKA
NEENA THURMAN, A.K.A. DOMINO.
THE DUDE'S A STRAIGHT-UP MONST--
SHAKOOOOOOM
WATCH OUT, DOMINO!
HE'S GETTING FASTER!
LOGAN, F.K.A. WOLVERINE...

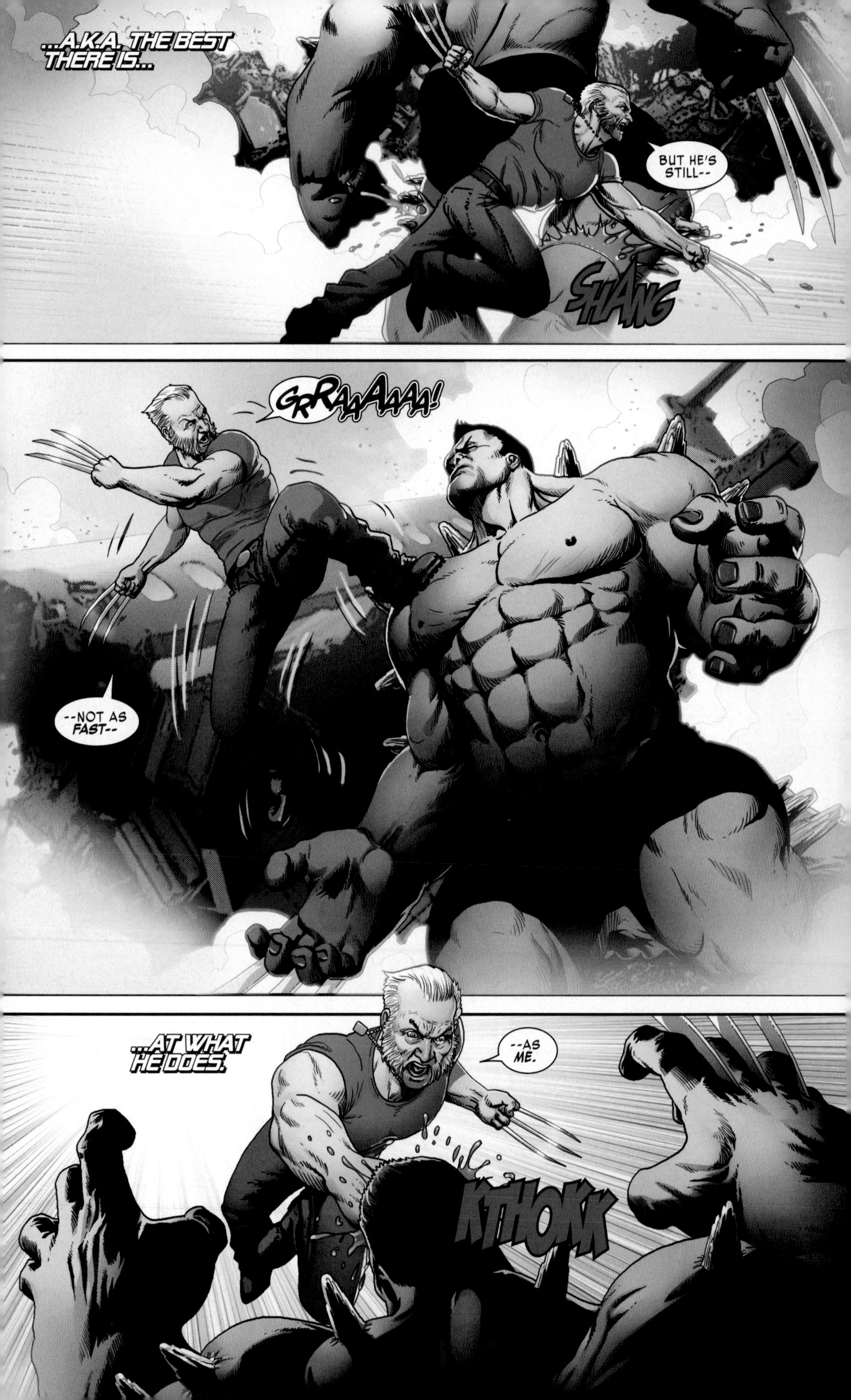
...A.K.A. THE BEST THERE IS...
BUT HE'S STILL--
SHANG
GRRAAAAAA!
--NOT AS FAST--
...AT WHAT HE DOES.
--AS ME.
KTHOKK

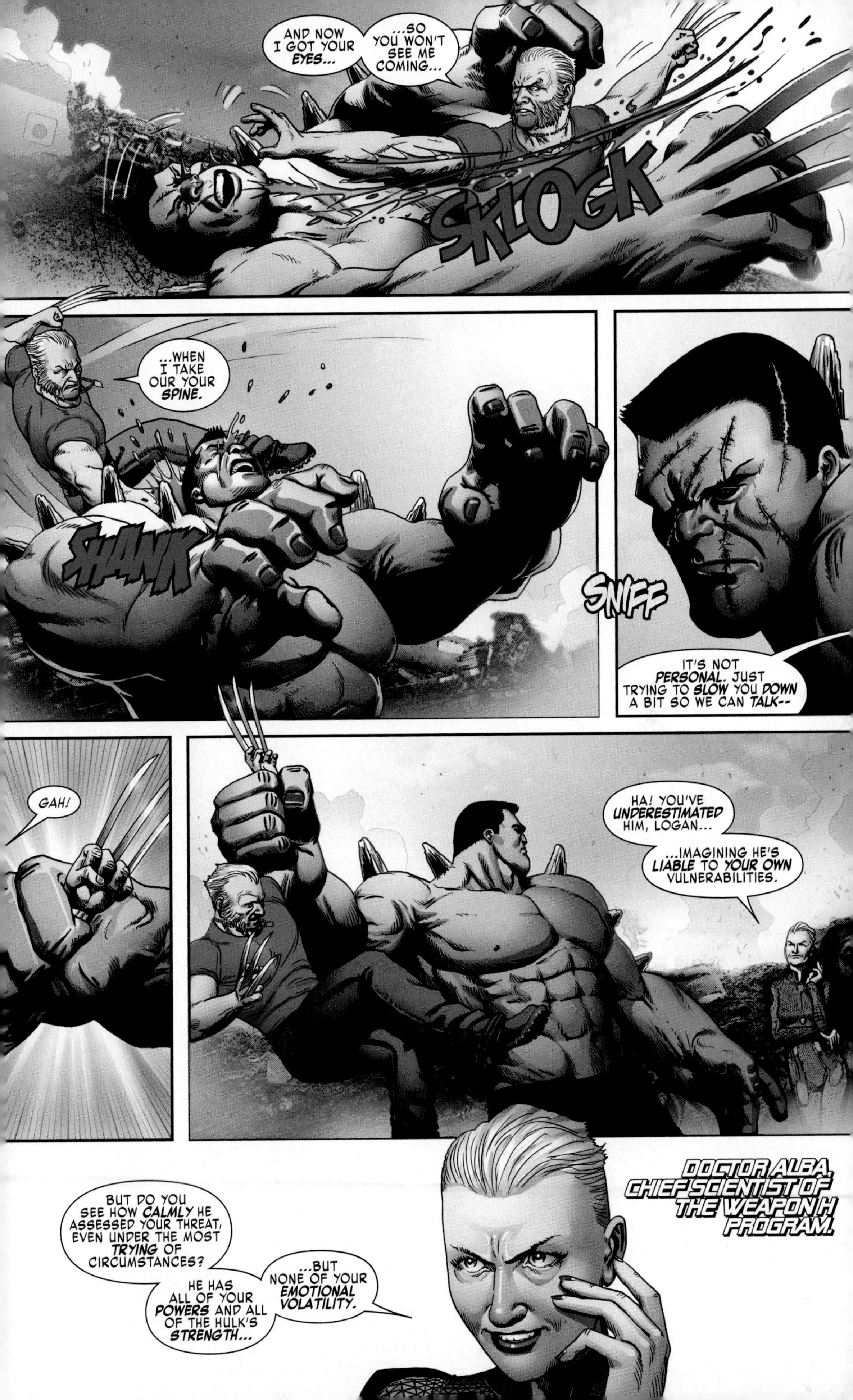

AND NOW I GOT YOUR EYES...
...SO YOU WON'T SEE ME COMING...
SKLOGK
...WHEN I TAKE OUR YOUR SPINE.
SHANK
SNIFF
IT'S NOT PERSONAL. JUST TRYING TO SLOW YOU DOWN A BIT SO WE CAN TALK--
GAH!
HA! YOU'VE UNDERESTIMATED HIM, LOGAN...
...IMAGINING HE'S LIABLE TO YOUR OWN VULNERABILITIES.
DOCTOR ALBA, CHIEF SCIENTIST OF THE WEAPON H PROGRAM.
BUT DO YOU SEE HOW CALMLY HE ASSESSED YOUR THREAT, EVEN UNDER THE MOST TRYING OF CIRCUMSTANCES?
HE HAS ALL OF YOUR POWERS AND ALL OF THE HULK'S STRENGTH...
...BUT NONE OF YOUR EMOTIONAL VOLATILITY.

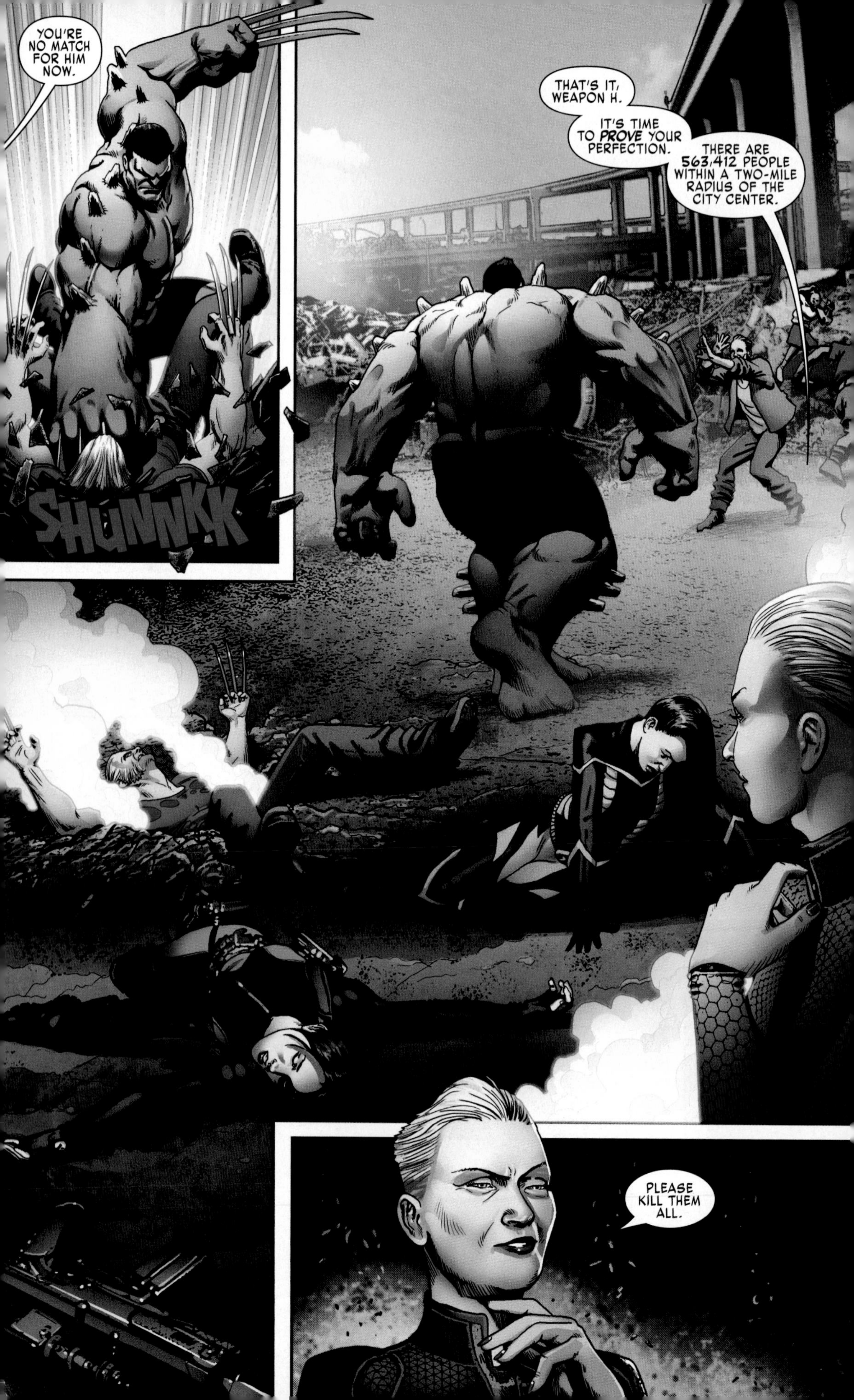

YOU'RE NO MATCH FOR HIM NOW.
SHUNNKK
THAT'S IT, WEAPON H.
IT'S TIME TO PROVE YOUR PERFECTION.
THERE ARE 563,412 PEOPLE WITHIN A TWO-MILE RADIUS OF THE CITY CENTER.
PLEASE KILL THEM ALL.

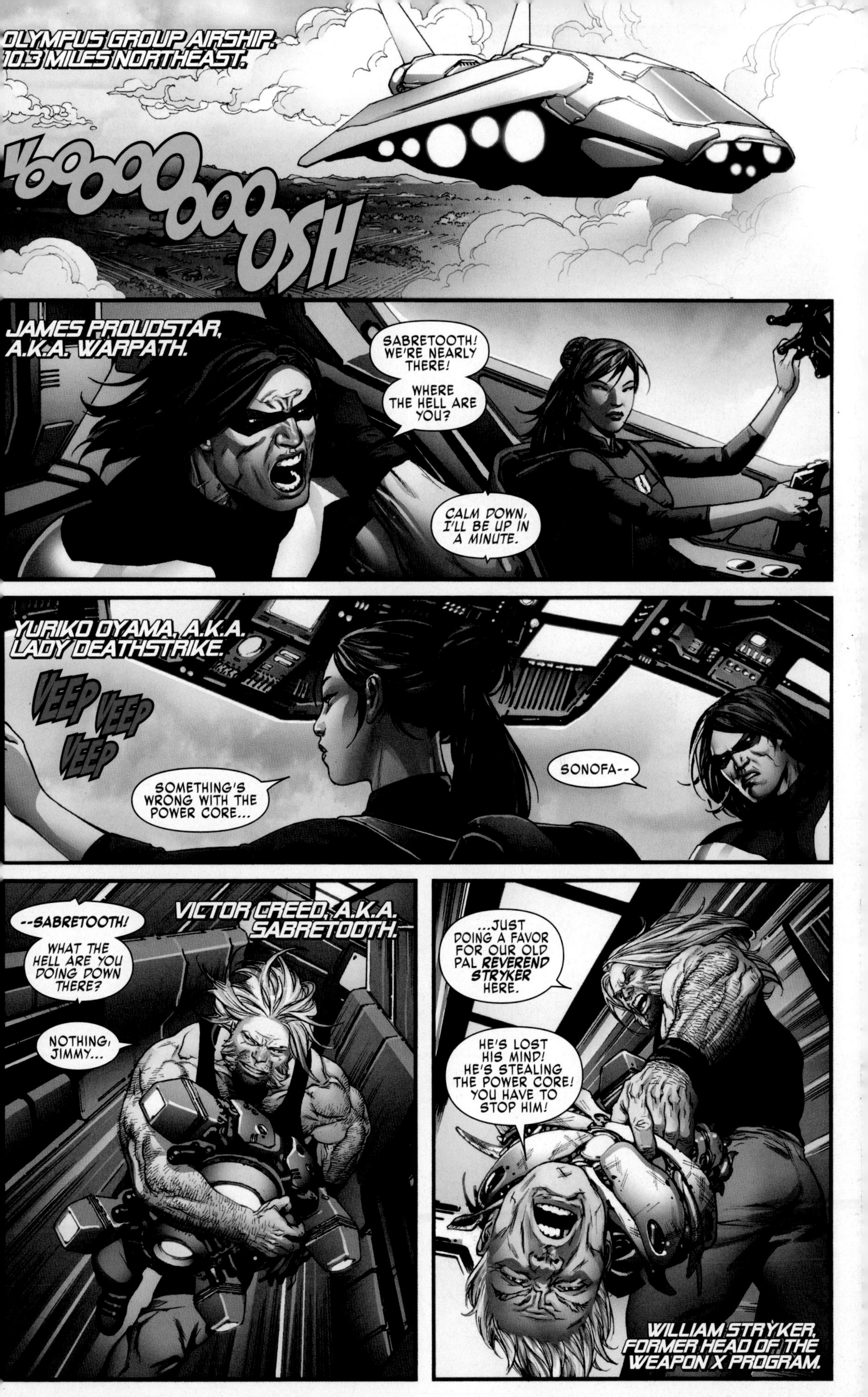
OLYMPUS GROUP AIRSHIP. 10.3 MILES NORTHEAST.
WOOOOOOOOOSH
JAMES PROUDSTAR, A.K.A. WARPATH.
SABRETOOTH! WE'RE NEARLY THERE!
WHERE THE HELL ARE YOU?
CALM DOWN, I'LL BE UP IN A MINUTE.
YURIKO OYAMA, A.K.A. LADY DEATHSTRIKE.
VEEP VEEP VEEP
SOMETHING'S WRONG WITH THE POWER CORE...
SONOFA--
--SABRETOOTH!
WHAT THE HELL ARE YOU DOING DOWN THERE?
NOTHING, JIMMY...
VICTOR CREED, A.K.A. SABRETOOTH.
...JUST DOING A FAVOR FOR OUR OLD PAL REVEREND STRYKER HERE.
HE'S LOST HIS MIND! HE'S STEALING THE POWER CORE! YOU HAVE TO STOP HIM!
WILLIAM STRYKER, FORMER HEAD OF THE WEAPON X PROGRAM.

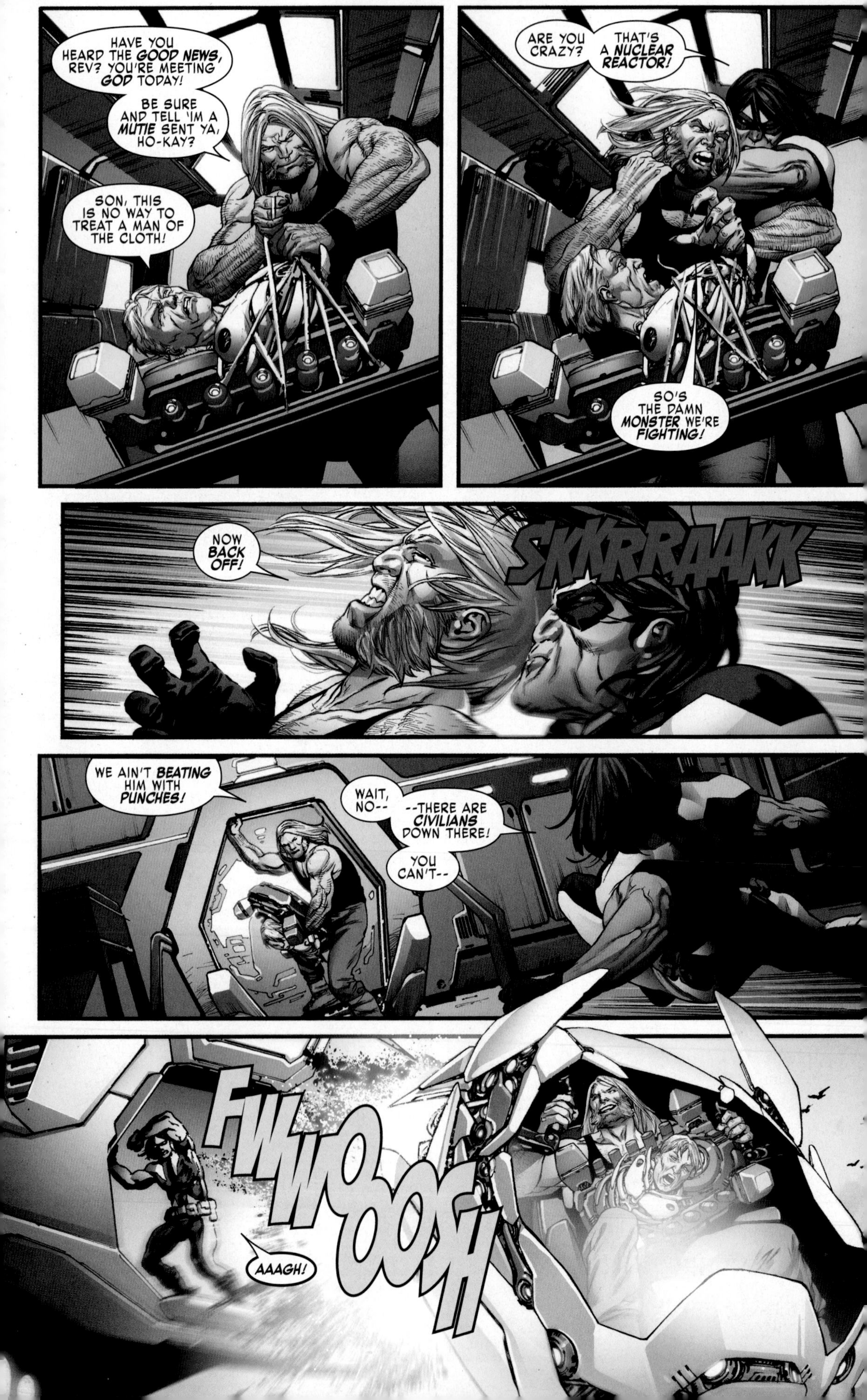
HAVE YOU HEARD THE GOOD NEWS, REV? YOU'RE MEETING GOD TODAY!
BE SURE AND TELL 'IM A MUTIE SENT YA, HO-KAY?
SON, THIS IS NO WAY TO TREAT A MAN OF THE CLOTH!
ARE YOU CRAZY?
THAT'S A NUCLEAR REACTOR!
SO'S THE DAMN MONSTER WE'RE FIGHTING!
NOW BACK OFF!
SKKRRAAKK
WE AIN'T BEATING HIM WITH PUNCHES!
WAIT, NO--
--THERE ARE CIVILIANS DOWN THERE!
YOU CAN'T--
FWWOOOSH
AAAGH!

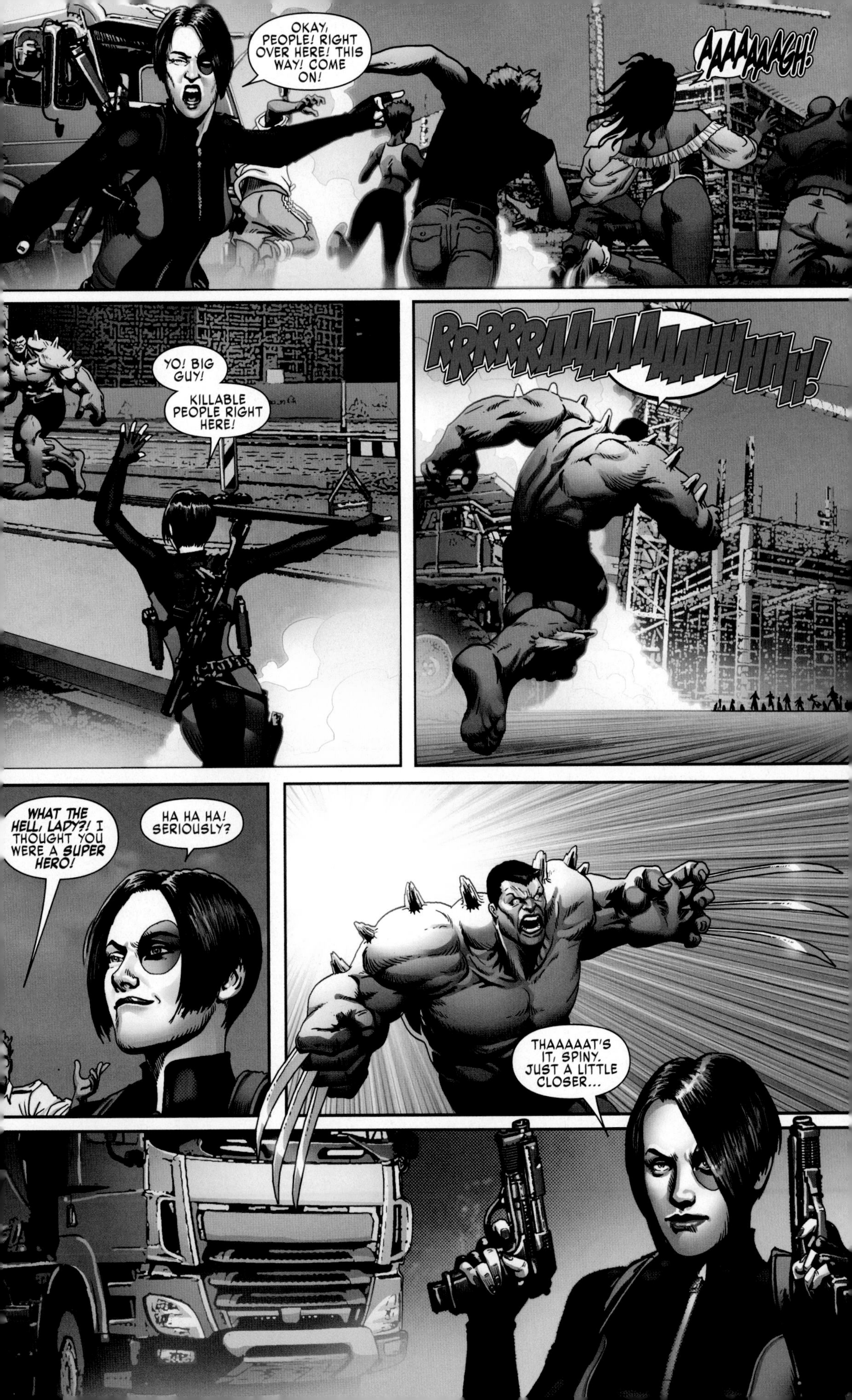
OKAY, PEOPLE! RIGHT OVER HERE! THIS WAY! COME ON!
AAAAAAAGH!
YO! BIG GUY!
KILLABLE PEOPLE RIGHT HERE!
RRRRRAAAAAAAAHHHHHH!
WHAT THE HELL, LADY?! I THOUGHT YOU WERE A SUPER HERO!
HA HA HA! SERIOUSLY?
THAAAAAT'S IT, SPINY. JUST A LITTLE CLOSER...

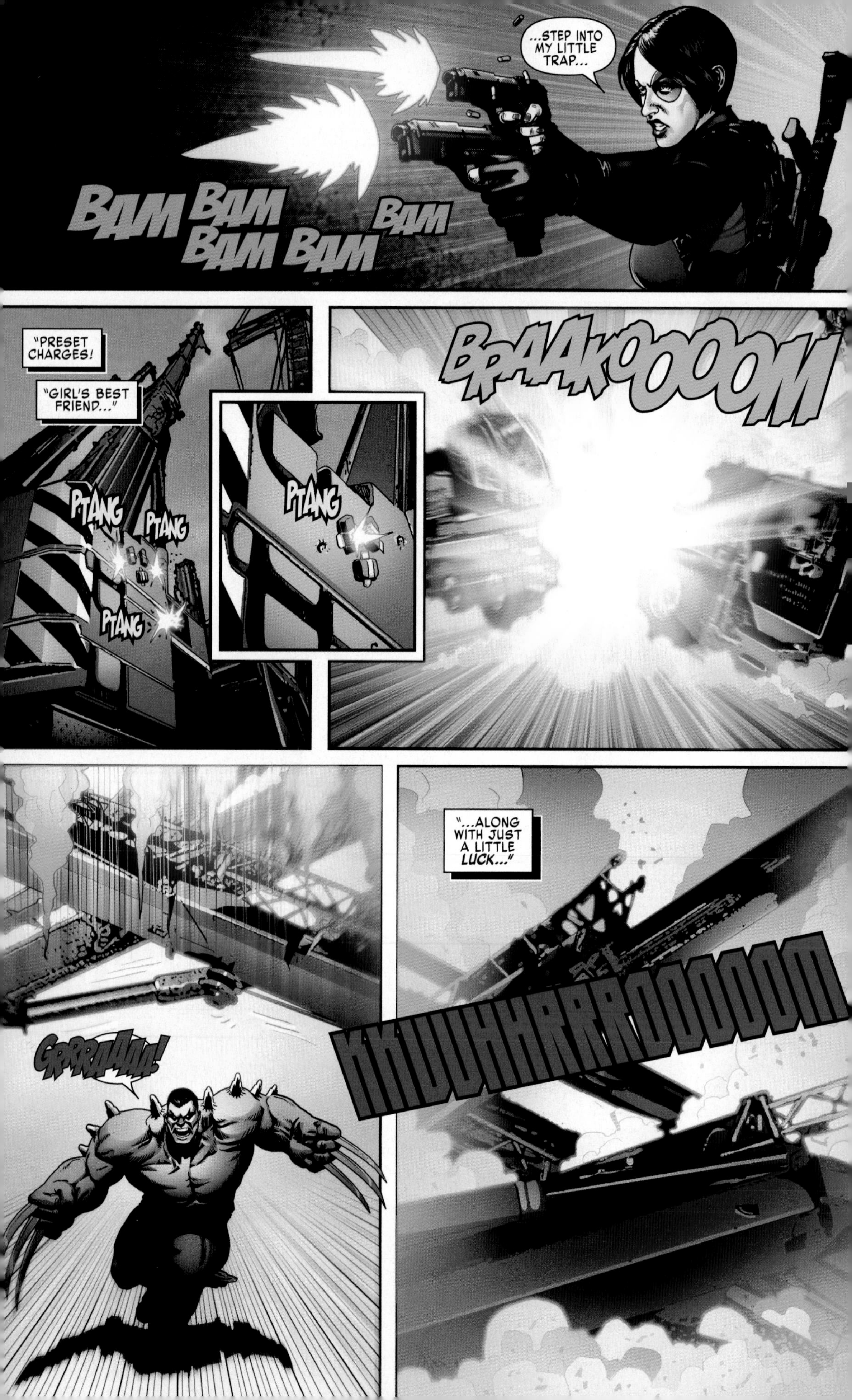
...STEP INTO MY LITTLE TRAP...
BAM BAM BAM BAM BAM
"PRESET CHARGES!
"GIRL'S BEST FRIEND..."
PTANG
PTANG
PTANG
PTANG
BRAAKOOOOOM
"...ALONG WITH JUST A LITTLE LUCK..."
GRRRAAAA!
KKUUHRRROOOOOM

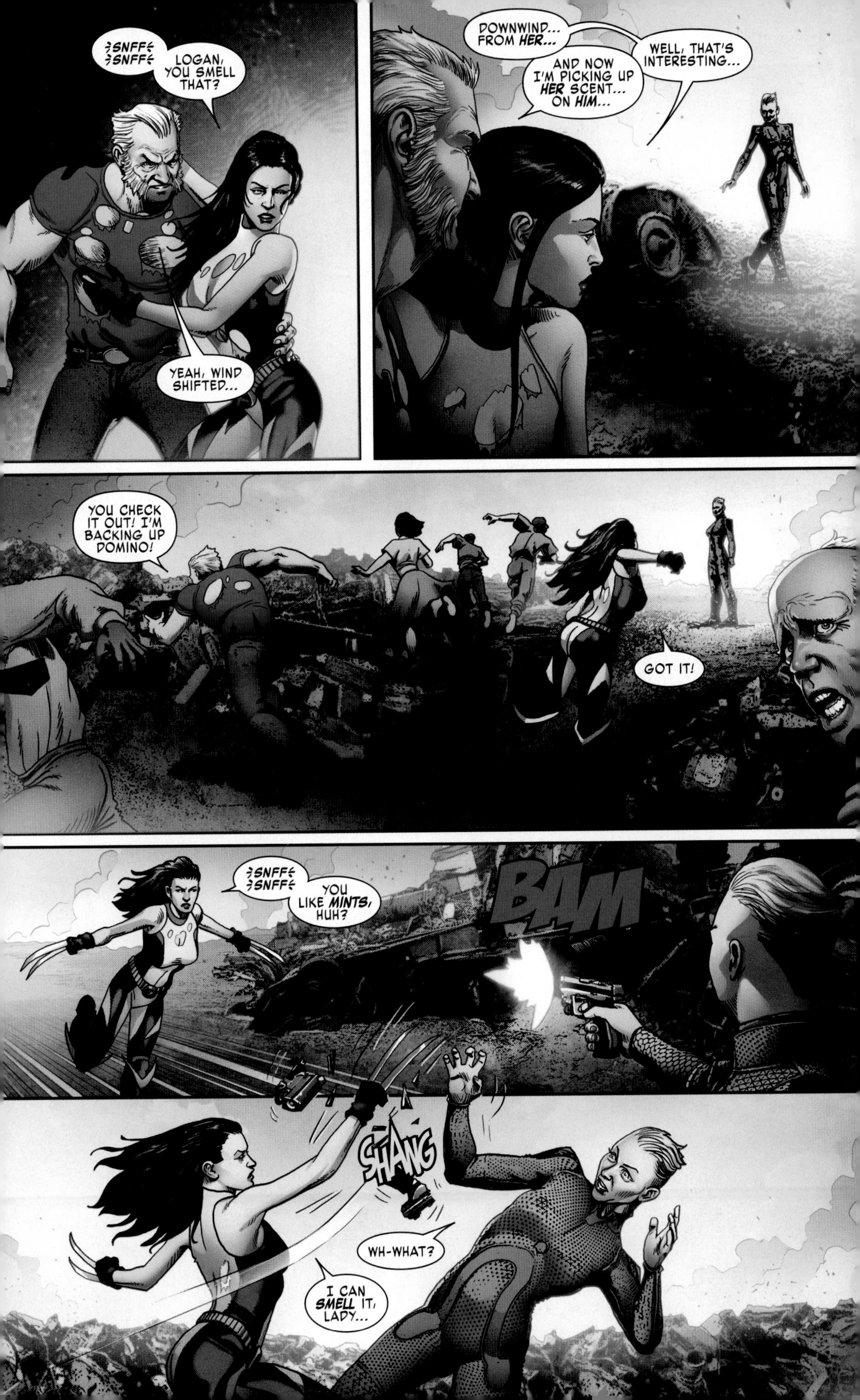
SNFF SNFF
LOGAN, YOU SMELL THAT?
YEAH, WIND SHIFTED...
DOWNWIND... FROM HER...
AND NOW I'M PICKING UP HER SCENT... ON HIM...
WELL, THAT'S INTERESTING...
YOU CHECK IT OUT! I'M BACKING UP DOMINO!
GOT IT!
SNFF SNFF
YOU LIKE MINTS, HUH?
BAM
SHANG
WH-WHAT?
I CAN SMELL IT, LADY...

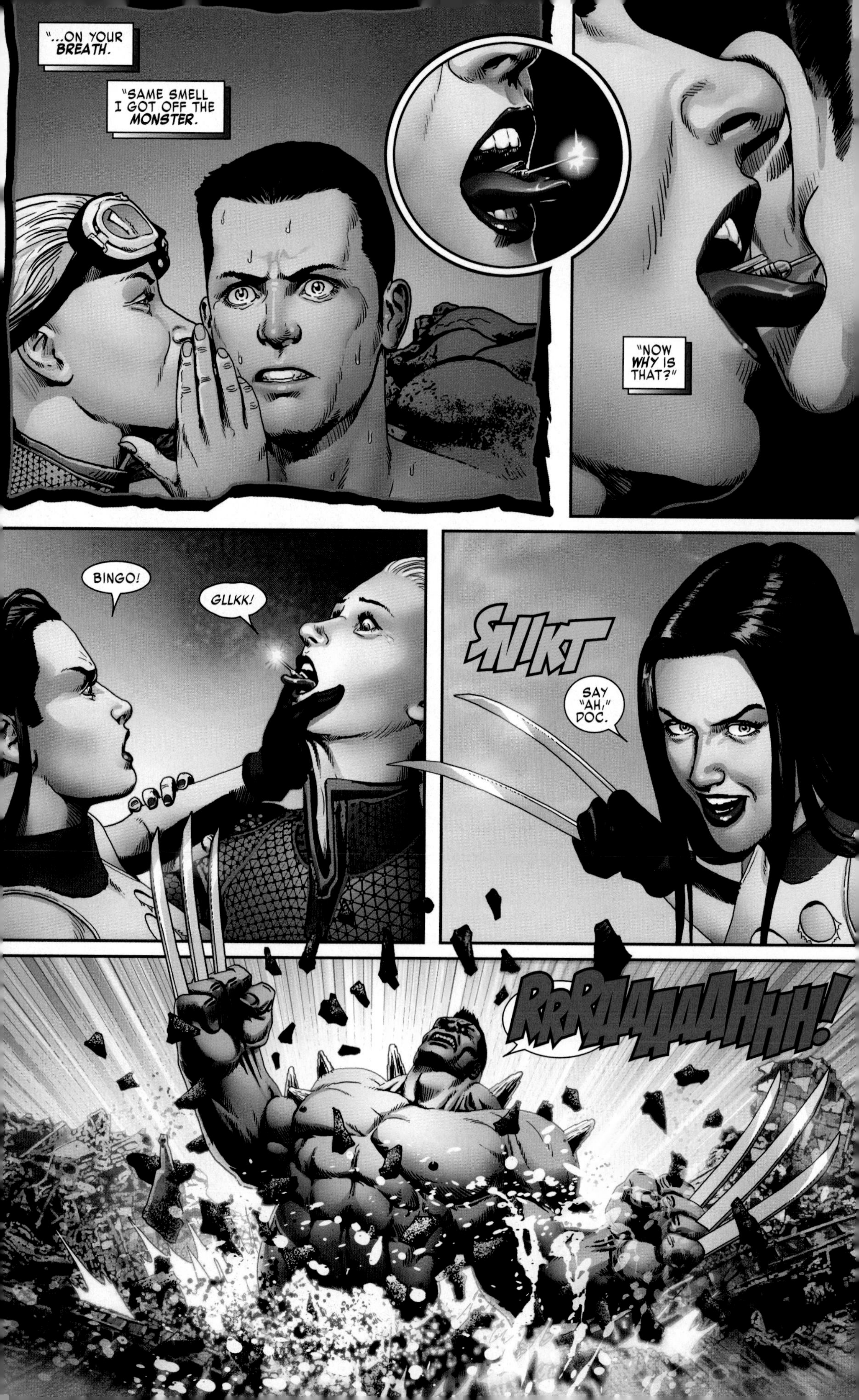
"...ON YOUR BREATH.
"SAME SMELL I GOT OFF THE MONSTER.
"NOW WHY IS THAT?"
BINGO!
GLLKK!
SNIKT
SAY "AH," DOC.
RRRAAAAAAHHH!

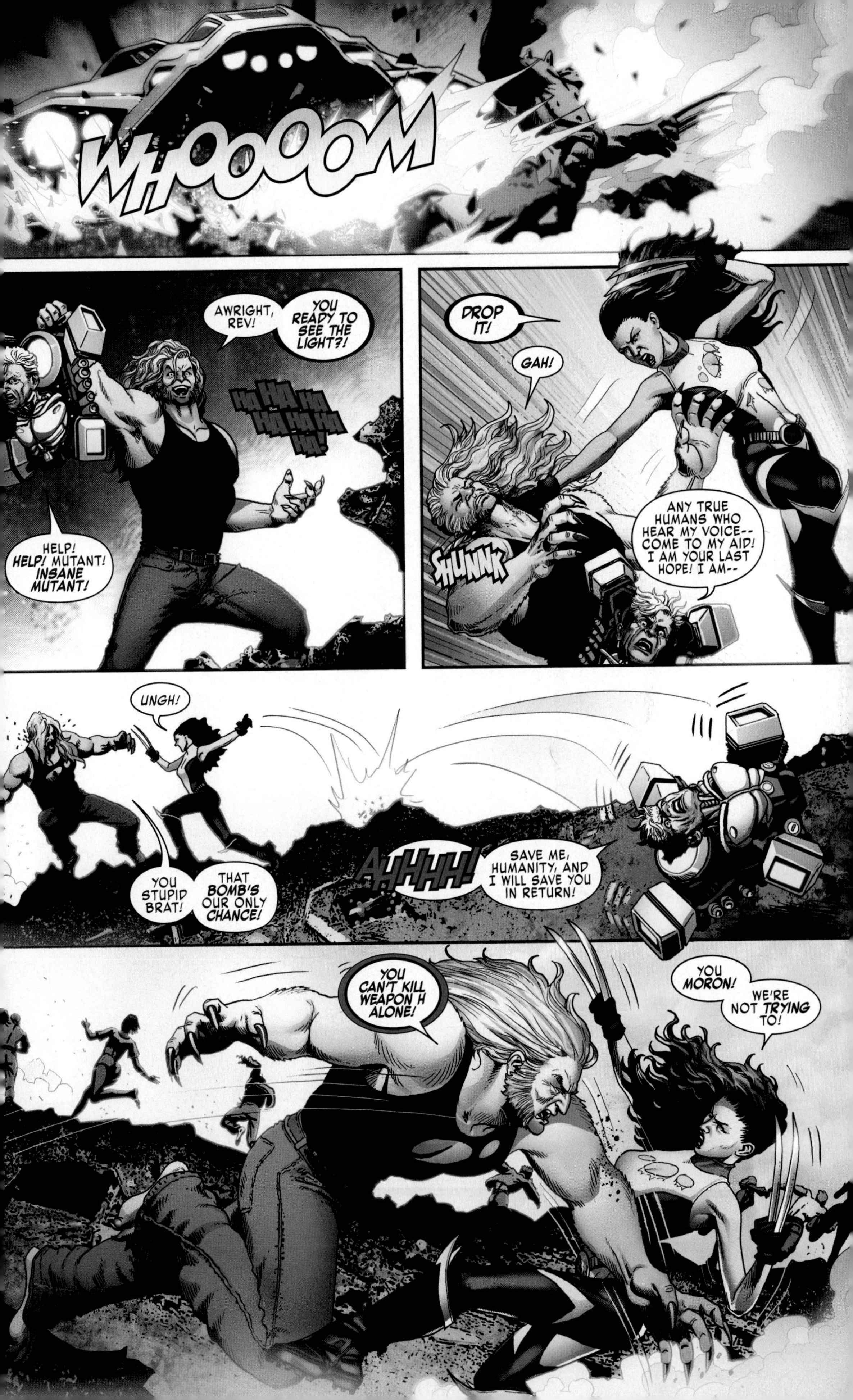
WHOOOOM
AWRIGHT, REV!
YOU READY TO SEE THE LIGHT?!
HA HA HA HA HA HA HA HA!
HELP! HELP! MUTANT! INSANE MUTANT!
DROP IT!
GAH!
SHUNNK
ANY TRUE HUMANS WHO HEAR MY VOICE-- COME TO MY AID! I AM YOUR LAST HOPE! I AM--
UNGH!
YOU STUPID BRAT!
THAT BOMB'S OUR ONLY CHANCE!
AHHHH!
SAVE ME, HUMANITY, AND I WILL SAVE YOU IN RETURN!
YOU CAN'T KILL WEAPON H ALONE!
YOU MORON!
WE'RE NOT TRYING TO!

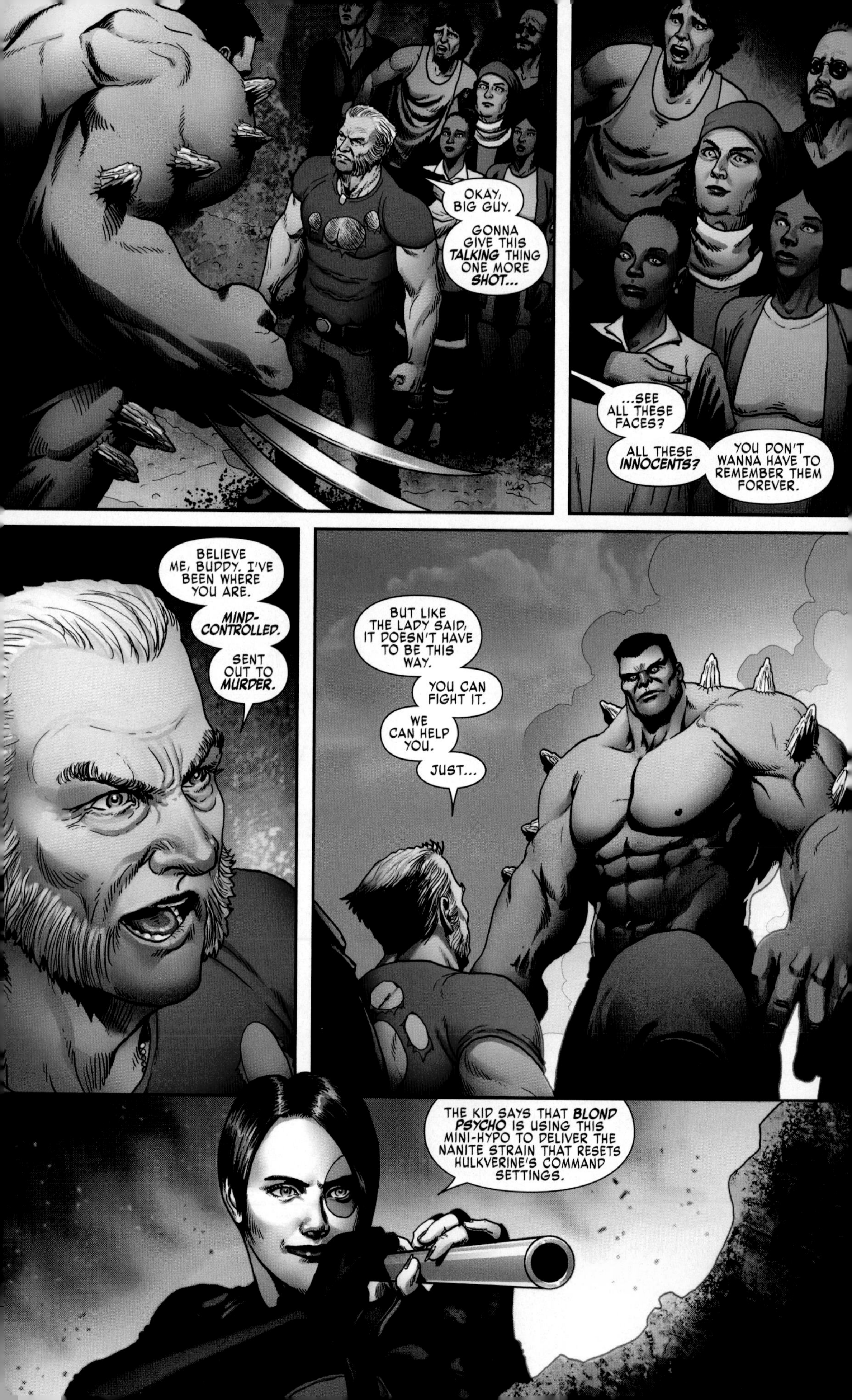
OKAY, BIG GUY.
GONNA GIVE THIS TALKING THING ONE MORE SHOT...
...SEE ALL THESE FACES?
ALL THESE INNOCENTS?
YOU DON'T WANNA HAVE TO REMEMBER THEM FOREVER.
BELIEVE ME, BUDDY. I'VE BEEN WHERE YOU ARE.
MIND-CONTROLLED.
SENT OUT TO MURDER.
BUT LIKE THE LADY SAID, IT DOESN'T HAVE TO BE THIS WAY.
YOU CAN FIGHT IT.
WE CAN HELP YOU.
JUST...
THE KID SAYS THAT BLOND PSYCHO IS USING THIS MINI-HYPO TO DELIVER THE NANITE STRAIN THAT RESETS HULKVERINE'S COMMAND SETTINGS.

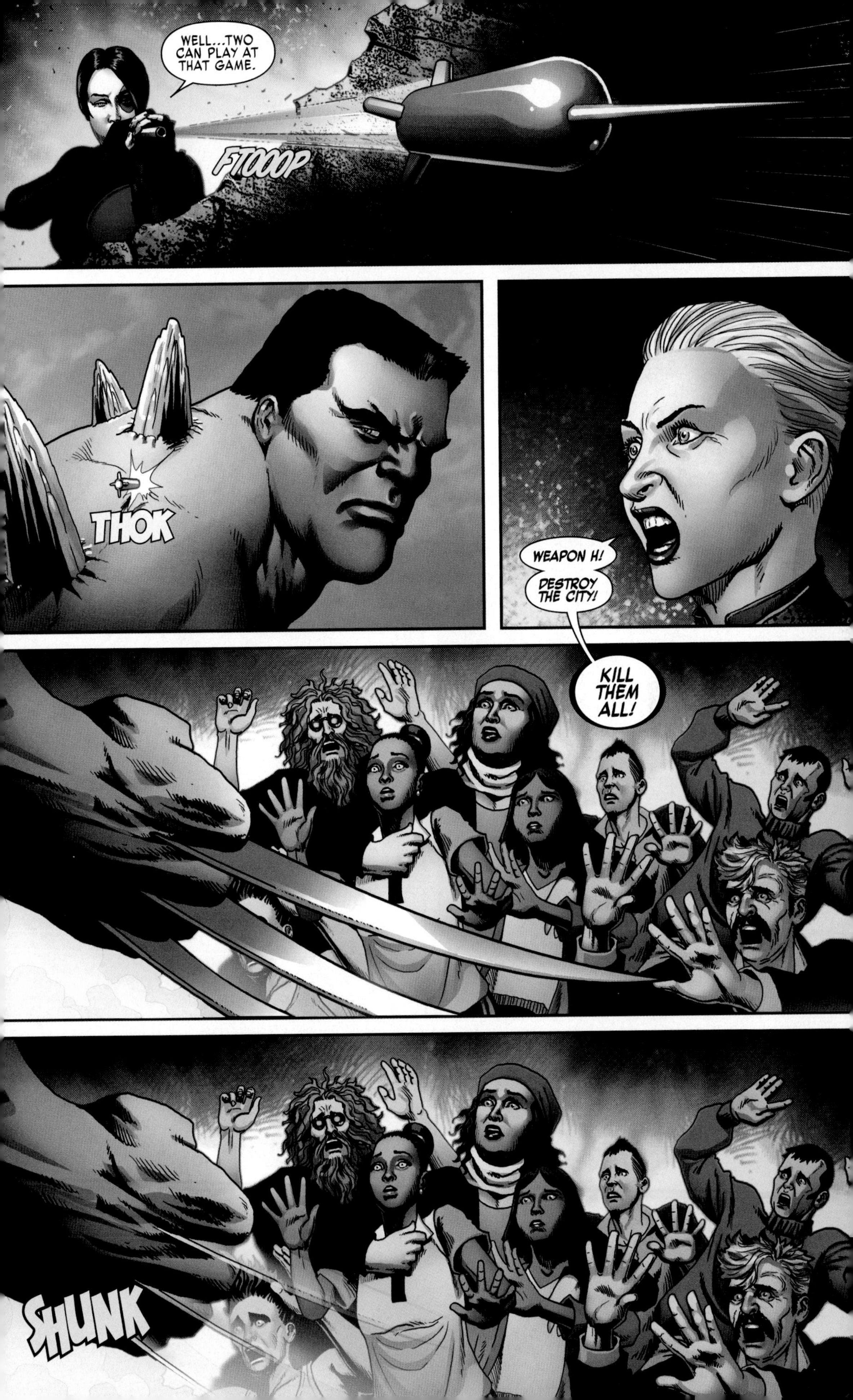
WELL...TWO CAN PLAY AT THAT GAME.
FTOOOP
THOK
WEAPON H!
DESTROY THE CITY!
KILL THEM ALL!
SHUNK

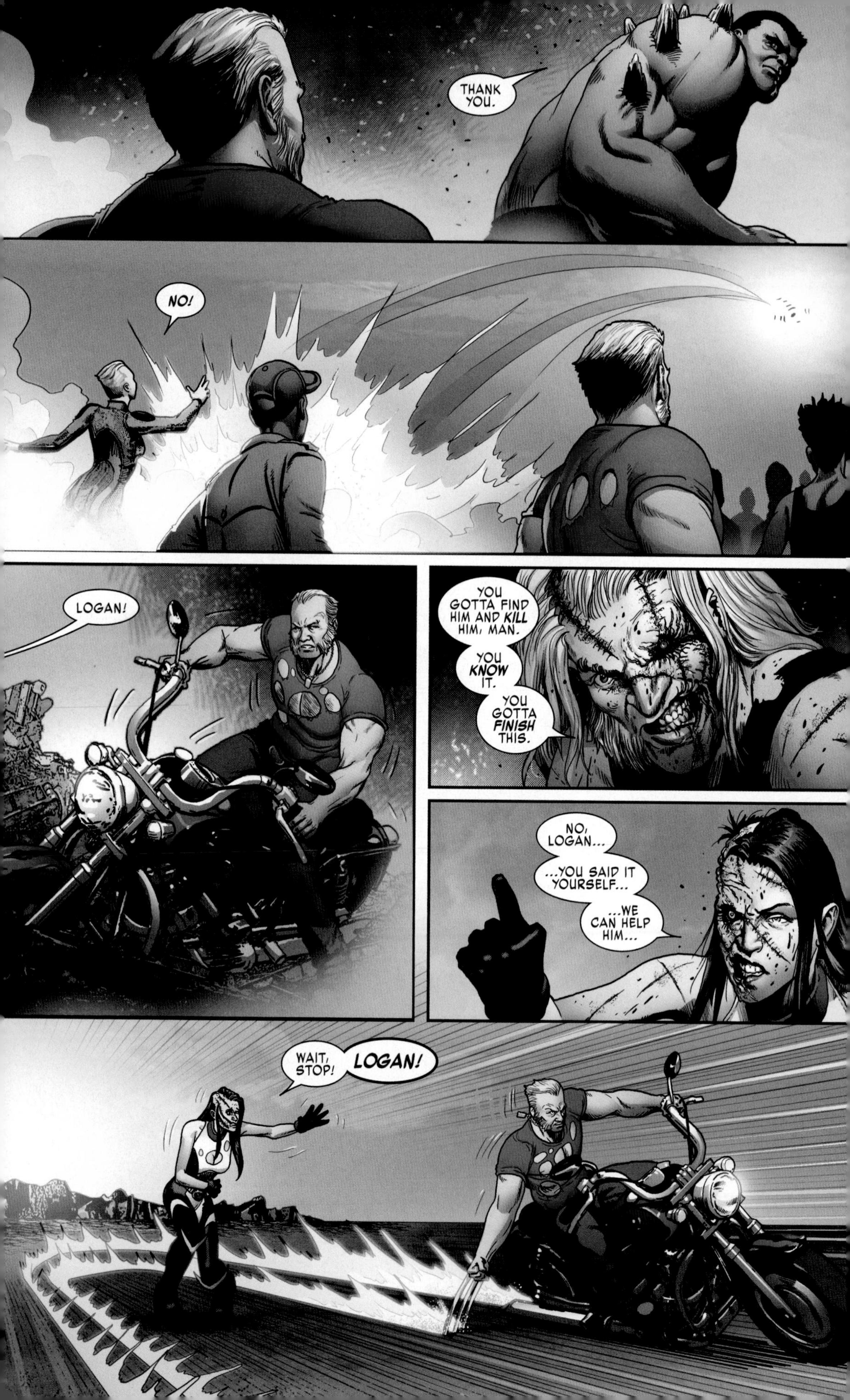
THANK YOU.
NO!
LOGAN!
YOU GOTTA FIND HIM AND KILL HIM, MAN.
YOU KNOW IT.
YOU GOTTA FINISH THIS.
NO, LOGAN...
...YOU SAID IT YOURSELF...
...WE CAN HELP HIM...
WAIT, STOP!
LOGAN!

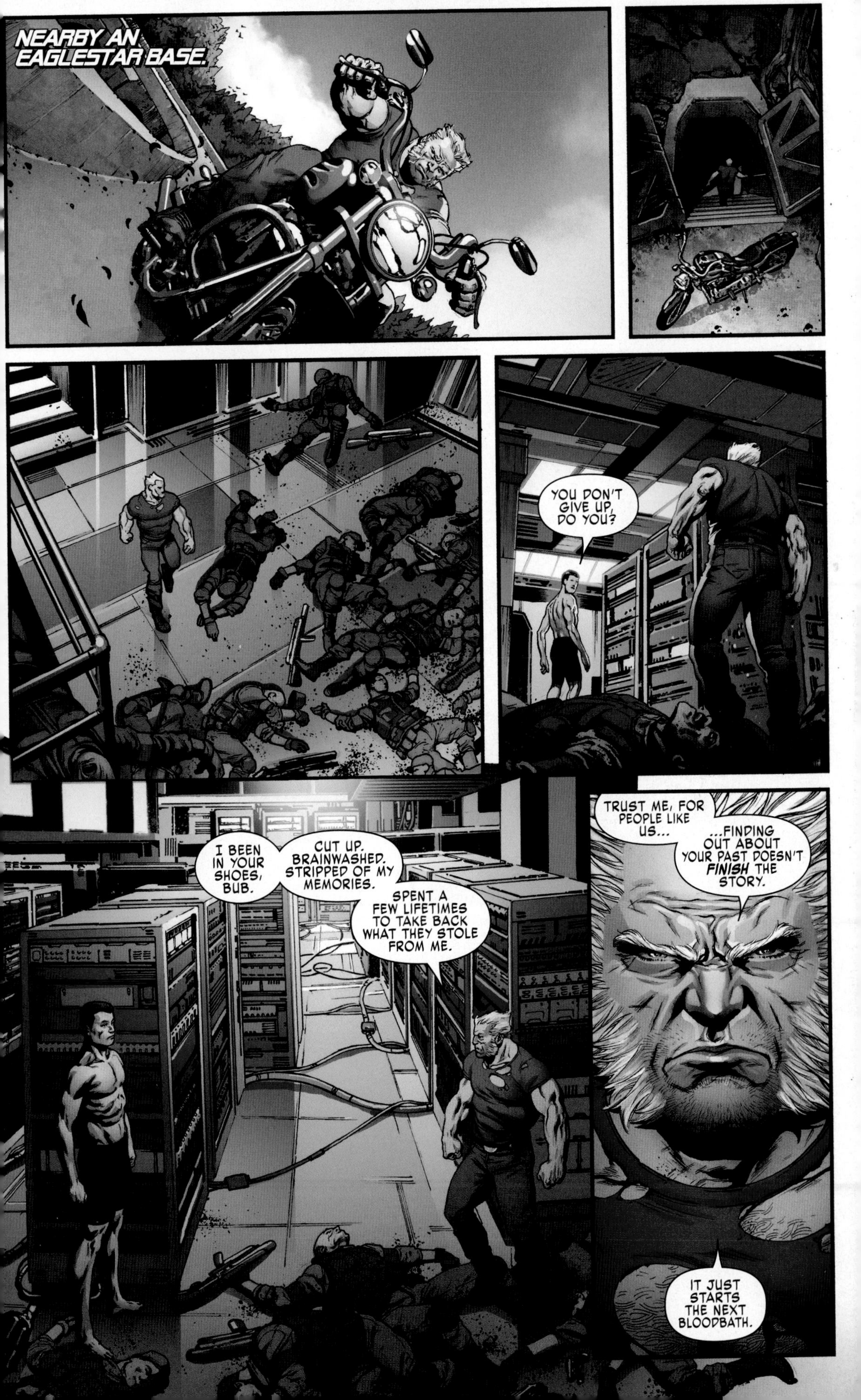
NEARBY AN EAGLESTAR BASE.
YOU DON'T GIVE UP, DO YOU?
I BEEN IN YOUR SHOES, BUB.
CUT UP. BRAINWASHED. STRIPPED OF MY MEMORIES.
SPENT A FEW LIFETIMES TO TAKE BACK WHAT THEY STOLE FROM ME.
TRUST ME, FOR PEOPLE LIKE US...
...FINDING OUT ABOUT YOUR PAST DOESN'T *FINISH* THE STORY.
IT JUST STARTS THE NEXT BLOODBATH.

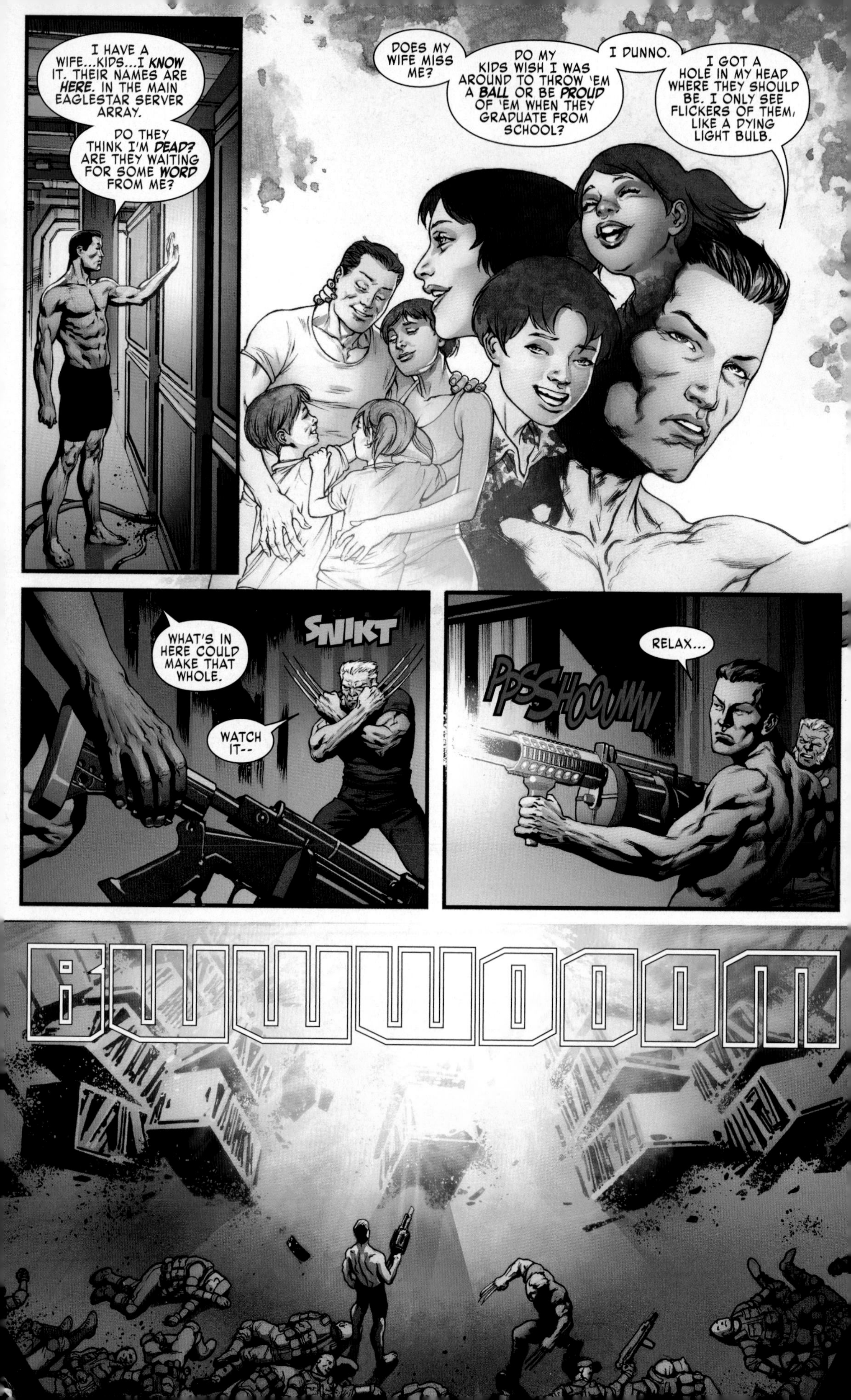

I HAVE A WIFE...KIDS...I KNOW IT. THEIR NAMES ARE HERE. IN THE MAIN EAGLESTAR SERVER ARRAY.
DO THEY THINK I'M DEAD? ARE THEY WAITING FOR SOME WORD FROM ME?
DOES MY WIFE MISS ME?
DO MY KIDS WISH I WAS AROUND TO THROW 'EM A BALL OR BE PROUD OF 'EM WHEN THEY GRADUATE FROM SCHOOL?
I DUNNO.
I GOT A HOLE IN MY HEAD WHERE THEY SHOULD BE. I ONLY SEE FLICKERS OF THEM, LIKE A DYING LIGHT BULB.
WHAT'S IN HERE COULD MAKE THAT WHOLE.
SNIKT
WATCH IT--
RELAX...
PPSSHOOUMW
BWWOOOM

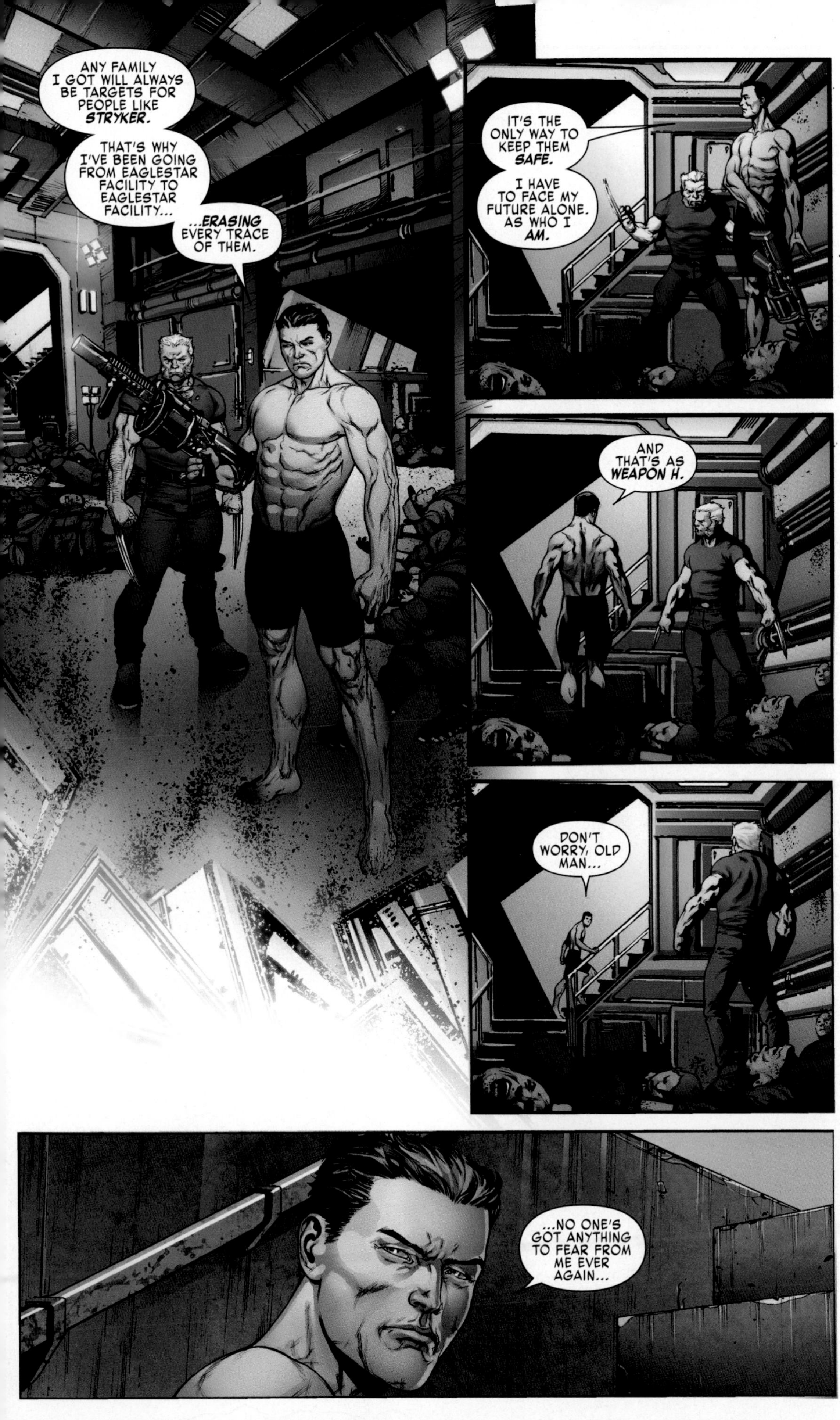
ANY FAMILY I GOT WILL ALWAYS BE TARGETS FOR PEOPLE LIKE **STRYKER.**
THAT'S WHY I'VE BEEN GOING FROM EAGLESTAR FACILITY TO EAGLESTAR FACILITY...
...**ERASING** EVERY TRACE OF THEM.
IT'S THE ONLY WAY TO KEEP THEM **SAFE.**
I HAVE TO FACE MY FUTURE ALONE. AS WHO I **AM.**
AND THAT'S AS **WEAPON H.**
DON'T WORRY, OLD MAN...
...NO ONE'S GOT ANYTHING TO FEAR FROM ME EVER AGAIN...

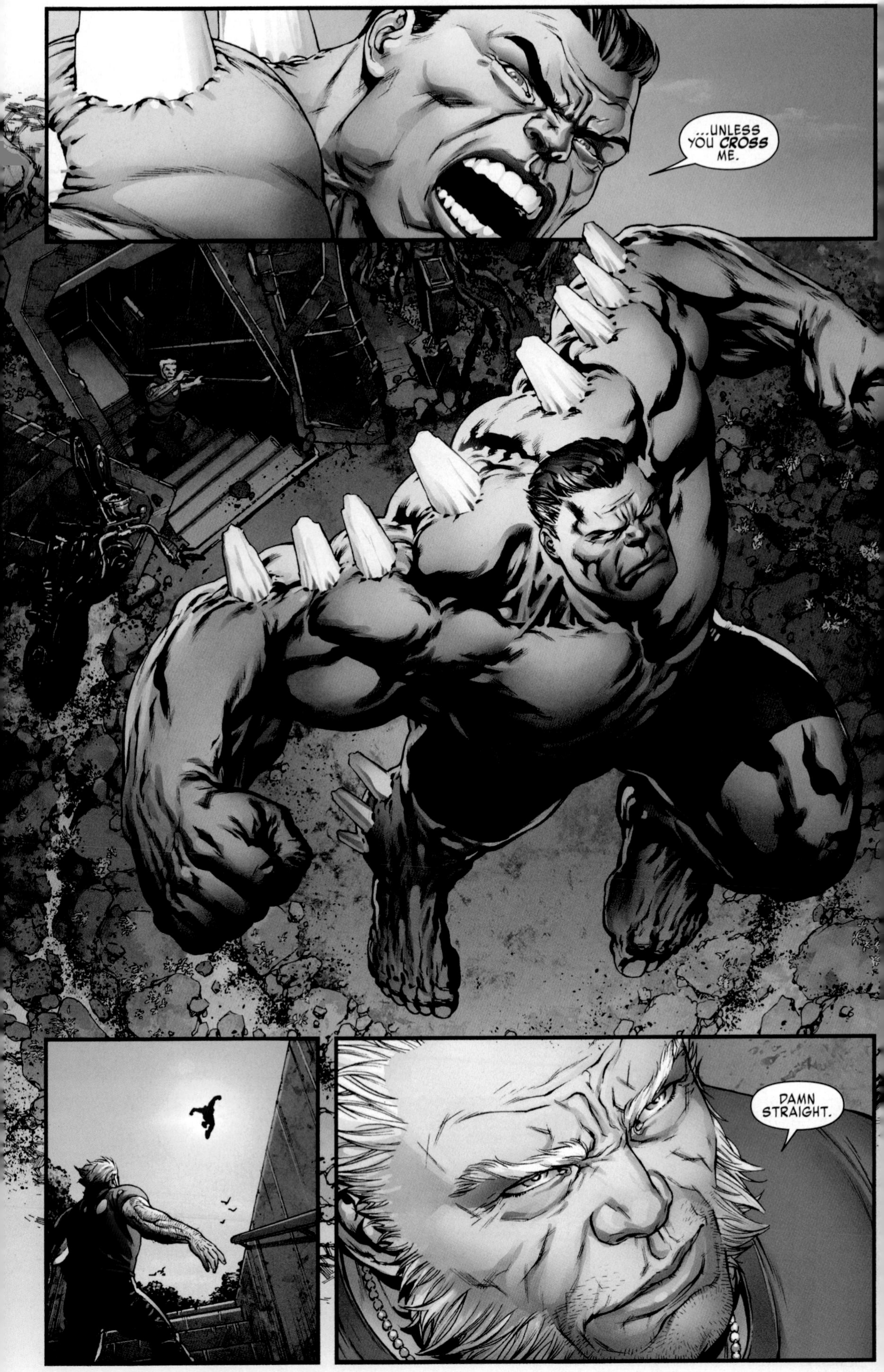
...UNLESS YOU CROSS ME.
DAMN STRAIGHT.

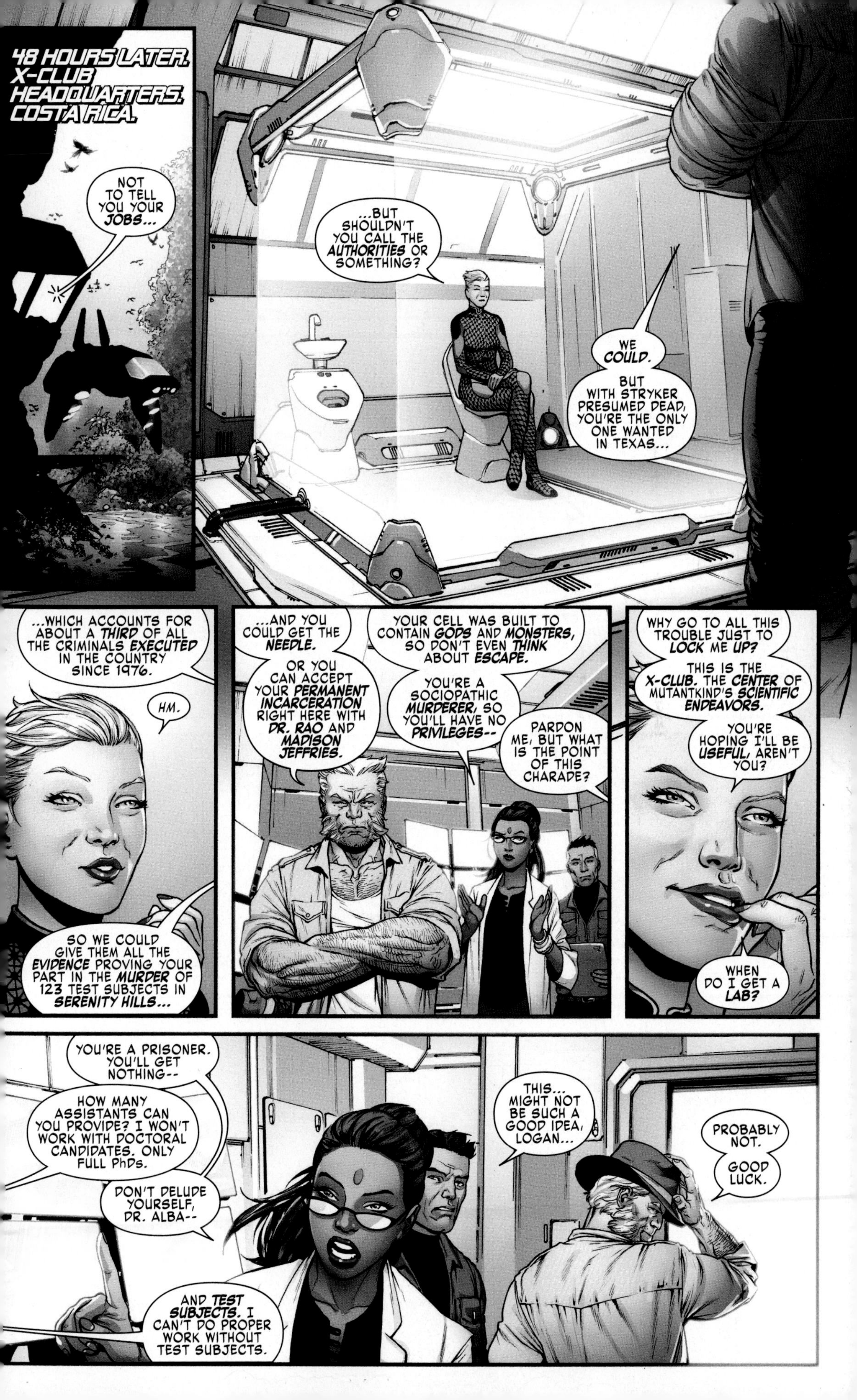
48 HOURS LATER. X-CLUB HEADQUARTERS. COSTA RICA.
NOT TO TELL YOU YOUR JOBS...
...BUT SHOULDN'T YOU CALL THE AUTHORITIES OR SOMETHING?
WE COULD.
BUT WITH STRYKER PRESUMED DEAD, YOU'RE THE ONLY ONE WANTED IN TEXAS...
...WHICH ACCOUNTS FOR ABOUT A THIRD OF ALL THE CRIMINALS EXECUTED IN THE COUNTRY SINCE 1976.
HM.
SO WE COULD GIVE THEM ALL THE EVIDENCE PROVING YOUR PART IN THE MURDER OF 123 TEST SUBJECTS IN SERENITY HILLS...
...AND YOU COULD GET THE NEEDLE.
OR YOU CAN ACCEPT YOUR PERMANENT INCARCERATION RIGHT HERE WITH DR. RAO AND MADISON JEFFRIES.
YOUR CELL WAS BUILT TO CONTAIN GODS AND MONSTERS, SO DON'T EVEN THINK ABOUT ESCAPE.
YOU'RE A SOCIOPATHIC MURDERER, SO YOU'LL HAVE NO PRIVILEGES--
PARDON ME, BUT WHAT IS THE POINT OF THIS CHARADE?
WHY GO TO ALL THIS TROUBLE JUST TO LOCK ME UP?
THIS IS THE X-CLUB. THE CENTER OF MUTANTKIND'S SCIENTIFIC ENDEAVORS.
YOU'RE HOPING I'LL BE USEFUL, AREN'T YOU?
WHEN DO I GET A LAB?
YOU'RE A PRISONER. YOU'LL GET NOTHING--
HOW MANY ASSISTANTS CAN YOU PROVIDE? I WON'T WORK WITH DOCTORAL CANDIDATES. ONLY FULL PhDs.
DON'T DELUDE YOURSELF, DR. ALBA--
AND TEST SUBJECTS. I CAN'T DO PROPER WORK WITHOUT TEST SUBJECTS.
THIS... MIGHT NOT BE SUCH A GOOD IDEA, LOGAN...
PROBABLY NOT.
GOOD LUCK.

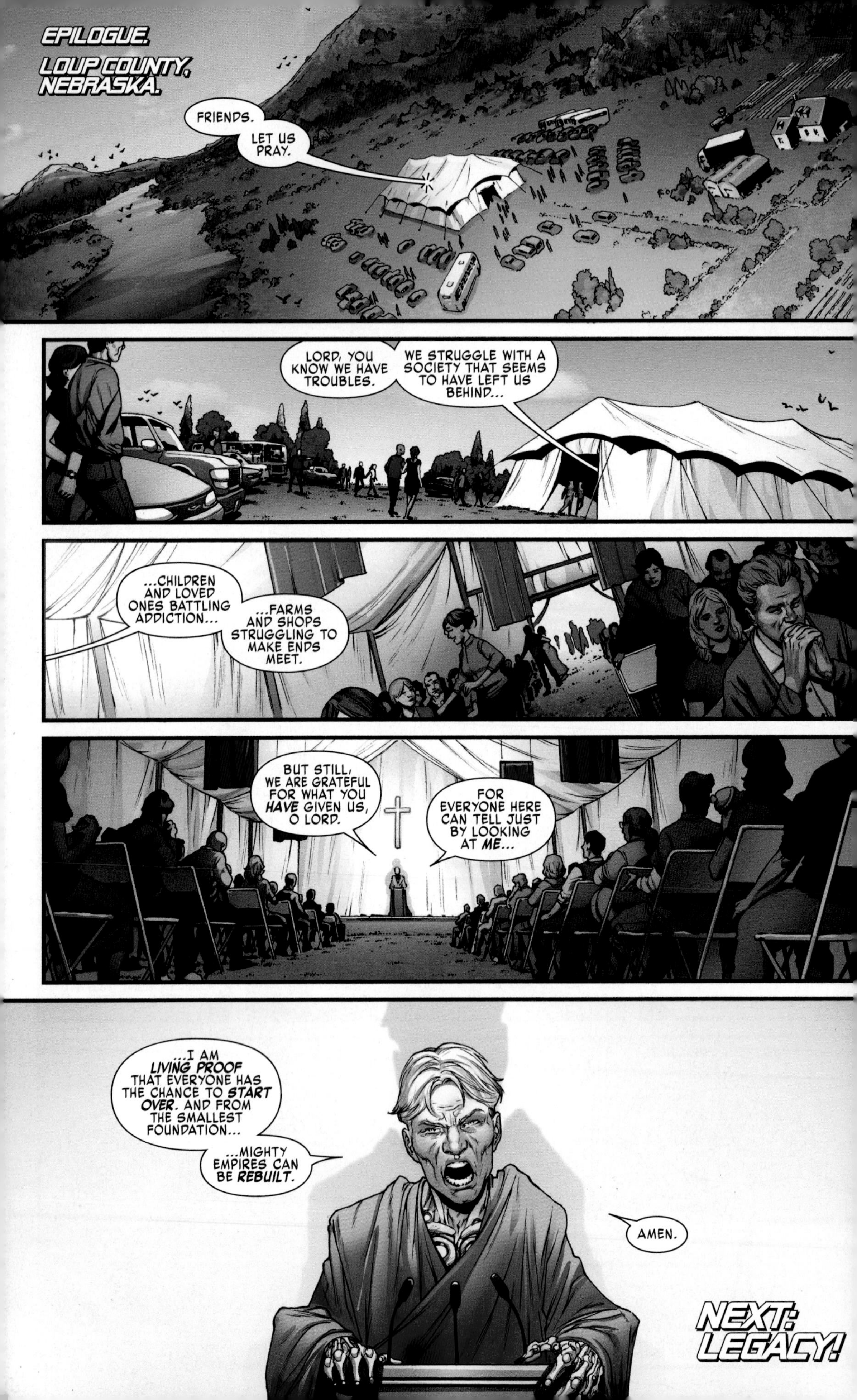
EPILOGUE.
LOUP COUNTY, NEBRASKA.
FRIENDS.
LET US PRAY.
LORD, YOU KNOW WE HAVE TROUBLES.
WE STRUGGLE WITH A SOCIETY THAT SEEMS TO HAVE LEFT US BEHIND...
...CHILDREN AND LOVED ONES BATTLING ADDICTION...
...FARMS AND SHOPS STRUGGLING TO MAKE ENDS MEET.
BUT STILL, WE ARE GRATEFUL FOR WHAT YOU HAVE GIVEN US, O LORD.
FOR EVERYONE HERE CAN TELL JUST BY LOOKING AT ME...
...I AM LIVING PROOF THAT EVERYONE HAS THE CHANCE TO START OVER. AND FROM THE SMALLEST FOUNDATION...
...MIGHTY EMPIRES CAN BE REBUILT.
AMEN.
NEXT: LEGACY!

THE SAGA OF **WEAPON H** CONTINUES IN...

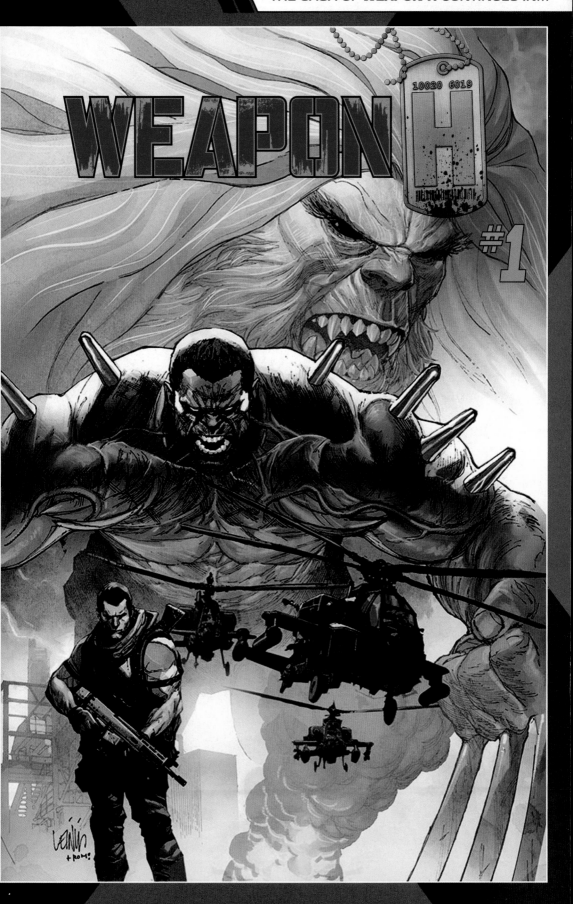

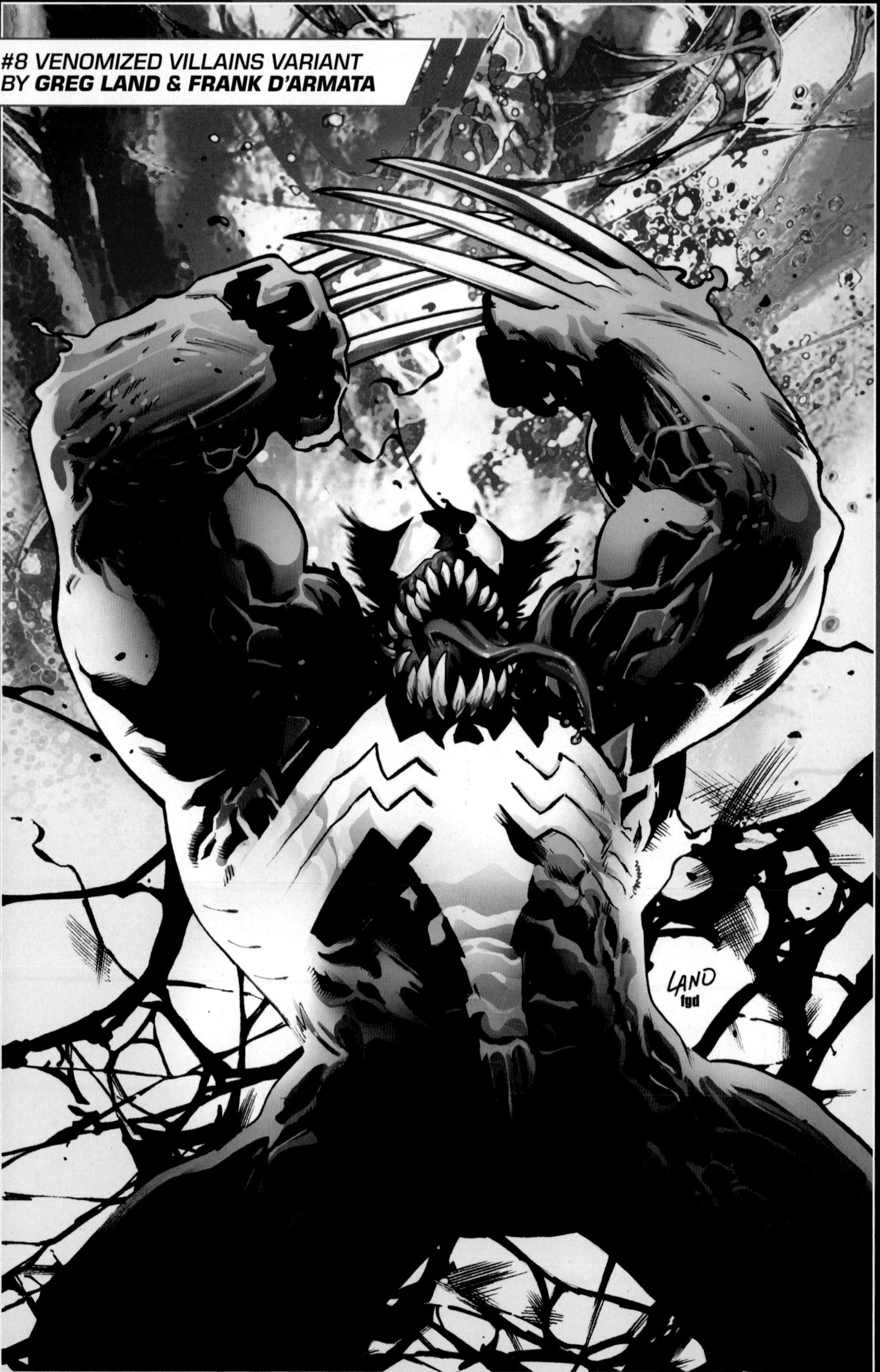
LAND
fgd

#8 VENOMIZED VILLAINS VARIANT
BY **GREG LAND & FRANK D'ARMATA**

#11 DESIGN VARIANT BY **MIKE DEODATO JR.**

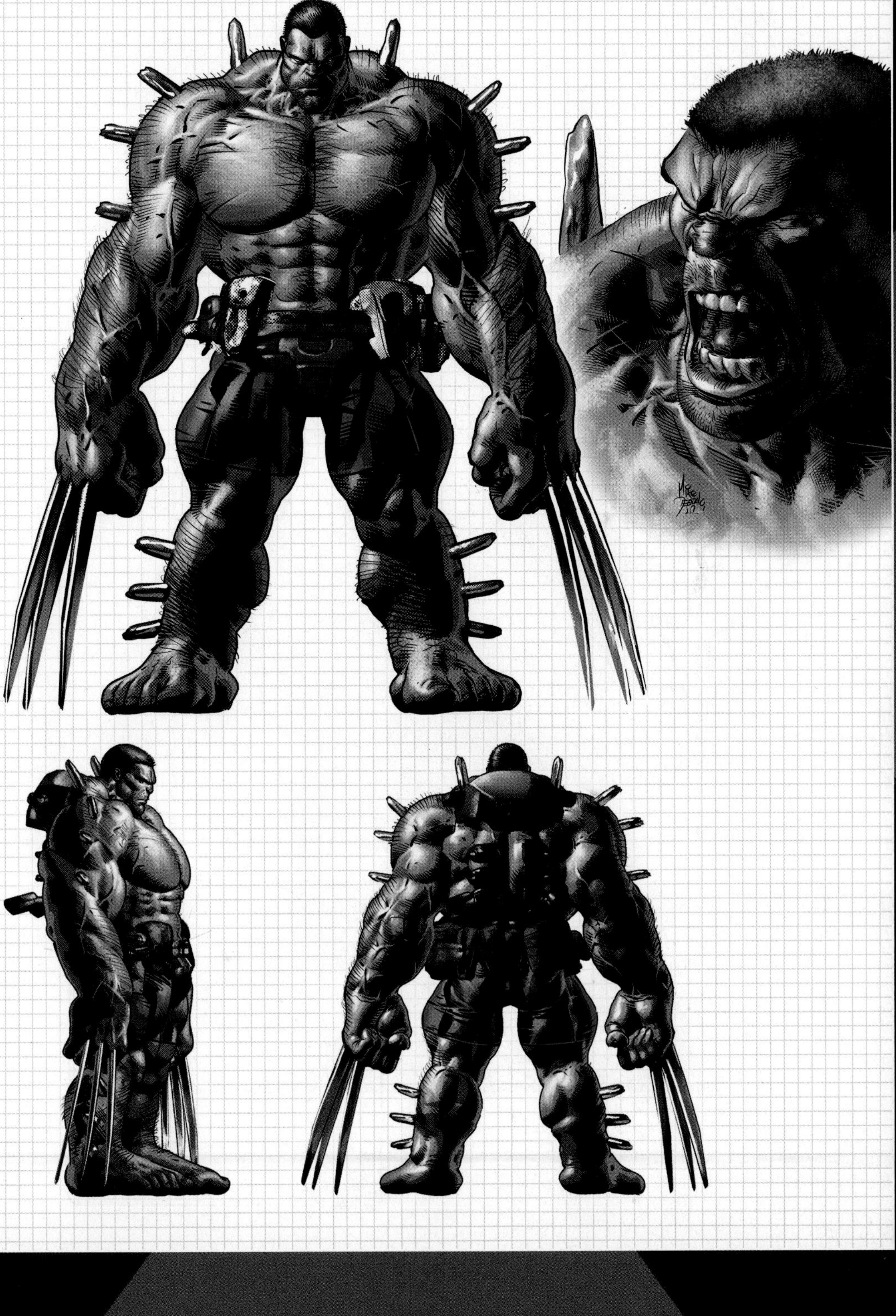

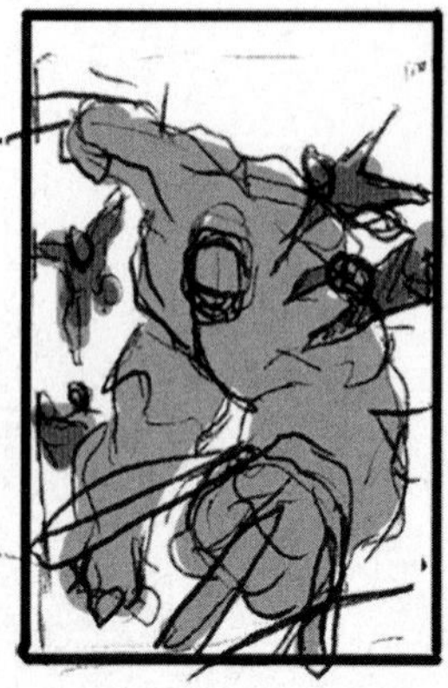

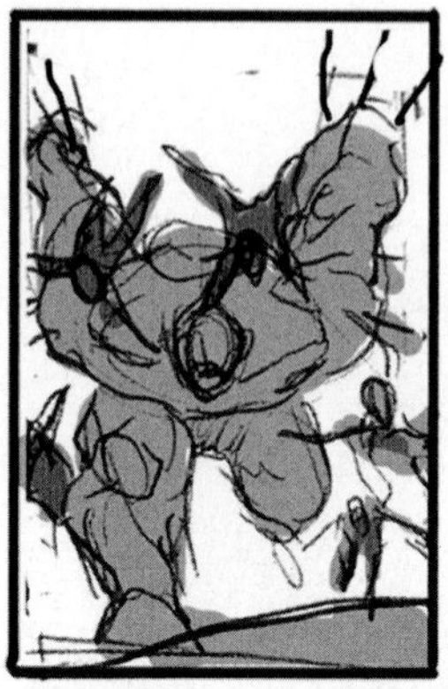

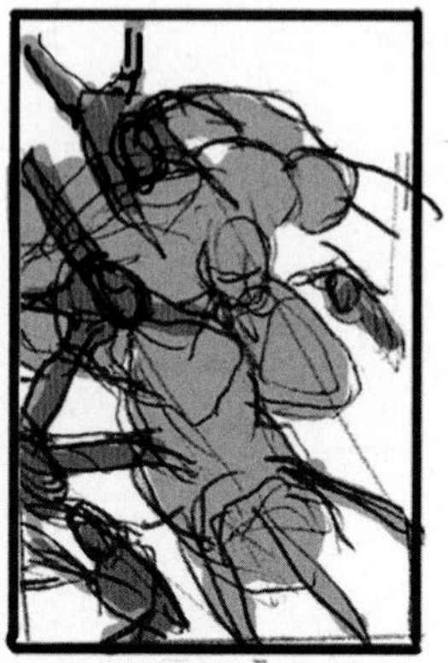

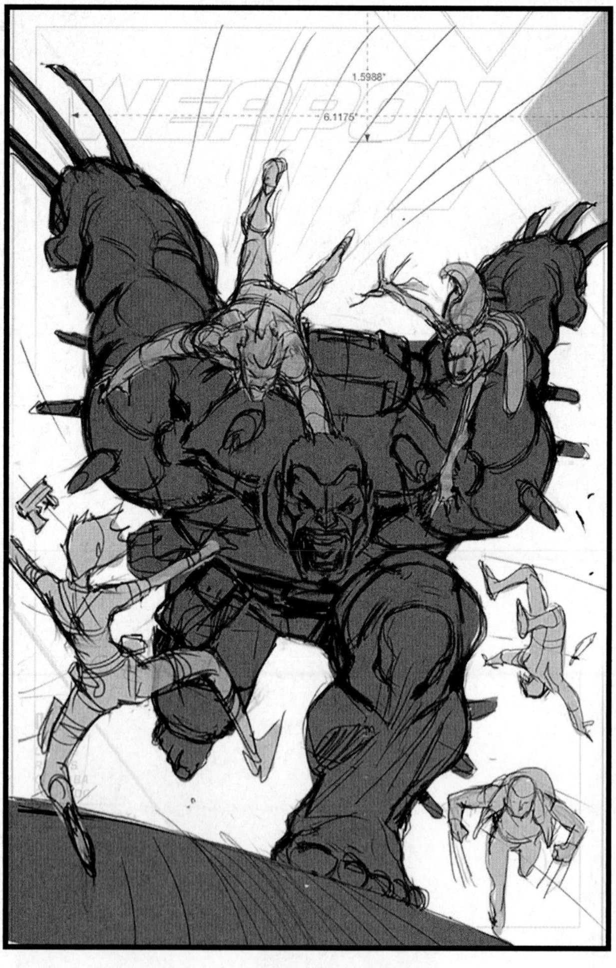
WEAPON
1.5988"
6.1175"

COVER SKETCHES BY **DAVID NAKAYAMA**